LIONHEART
LEGACY OF THE CRUSADER

PRIMA'S OFFICIAL STRATEGY GUIDE

Debra Lockridge
David Cassady

PRIMA GAMES
A Division of Random House, Inc.
3000 Lava Ridge Court
Roseville, CA 95661
1-800-733-3000
www.primagames.com

Associate Product Manager: Christy L. Curtis

Project Editor: Teli Hernandez

Acknowledgements

Thanks to all the folks at Prima for their hard work on this project. Thanks to Ion, Tom, Chris, and Eric. All of the great information they provided directly contributed to this guide being as thorough as it is. And special thanks to Paige Slaughter at Interplay for her assistance and support.

For David and Emily Lockridge.

ISBN: 0-7615-4249-3

Library of Congress Catalog Card Number: 2003106673

Printed in the United States of America

03 04 05 06 BB 10 9 8 7 6 5 4 3 2 1

CONTENTS:

CONTENTS

INTRODUCTION

uring the Third Crusades, an event occurred that would not reveal its fullest horror until 400 years later in the 16th century. This event—the Disjunction—ripped the world apart, breaching a sealed gateway to other worlds. Magic and spirits flowed in, changing the lands and the people forever.

While the Inquisition justified persecution under the banner of religion, the world sought refuge from creatures more terrifying than the monsters reigning within the dark Inquisition Chamber halls.

Now it is 1588 A.D., a critical year in a familiar, yet alien alternate history. Travel across this twisted version of reality and find your place—fighting for survival, the answers to your origin, and the identities of those who seek to destroy you.

We escort you through the bustling city of Barcelona, where your journey begins. From there, you battle your way through history, coming to the aid of characters ranging from William Shakespeare and Leonardo da Vinci to Nostradamus.

Whether you choose to follow the path of the pious Inquisitors or the way of the Warriors, all quests are revealed in the "Walkthrough" section. Before beginning your adventure, create your character using the helpful hints found in the "Character Creation" section.

Hone your knowledge of the creatures you encounter by reading up on their strengths and weaknesses in the "Bestiary." As you progress through the game, you find hundreds of items, weapons, and equipment hidden in chests scattered throughout the lands and dropped by various creatures. A detailed listing of these items is outlined for you in "Items and Equipment."

Every great adventure must begin with some basic explanation of what to expect. "Beginner's Guide to Nuevo Barcelona," provides a plethora of information to help you battle your way through the landscapes of time.

The world's fate hangs in the balance. Only those who possess the spirit of Lionheart can thwart evil—or doom humanity.

The History of Lionheart and the Disjunction

A Historical Chronology

DATE	EVENT
1095–1101	First Crusade
1119	Formation of the Knights Templar
1145–1147	Second Crusade, led by King Louis VII
1189–1192	Third Crusade, Led by King Richard the Lionhearted
1192–1220	The Disjunction. Ramifications in the kingdoms of England and France
1194–1244	Fourth Crusade, against the Storm Dragons
1204	The last known tremor settles. Ireland and Brittany are gone and England has broken into 15 separate islands.
1215	English nobles force King John to sign the Magna Carta.
1231	The Inquisition is formed.
1241	The Great Khan Ogedei cheats death and binds with the Fell Spirit Weichi, allowing Batu Kahn to continue his Eastern European campaign.
1243	After completing the Fourth Crusade, western forces engage the Mongols.
1249	The Mongols reach Italy, forcing the Holy See to move to Spain.
1250	A coalition of eastern and western forces finally forces the Mongols to retreat.
1251	Assassination of the Great Khan Ogedei. Batu Kahn is recalled from his European campaign.
1269–1275	Reconquista against rogue Wielders.
1316	Famine strikes Europe.
1347	The Black Death takes root in Italy and, by 1351, spreads throughout Europe.
1336–1389	Fifth Crusade, against the Necromancers.
1429	Emergence of Jehanne D'Arc (Joan of Arc). She reunites France.
1433	Jehanne D'Arc is killed in southern France.
1449	Lord Amonsil, the last of the Necromancers, is destroyed in Cairo, putting a definitive end to the Fifth Crusade.
1461–1464	Sixth Crusade, against the Fell Spirits.

1492–1493	Columbus's first expedition to the New World is followed by his second, which is utterly destroyed.
1521	Cortés is defeated at Tenochtitlan, ending the age of the conquistador.
1555	Nostradamus completes his "Centuries" and is branded a heretic.
1586	Assassination of King Phillip II.
1587	Galileo is imprisoned by the Inquisition for his heretical use of magic.
1588	The Spanish Armada prepares to invade England.

1192: The Third Crusade

In the year 1192, Richard the Lionhearted, King of England, ventured across Europe in the Third Crusade. At the height of this aggression, the fabric of reality was torn, allowing a short but devastating influx of magic and spiritkind to be unleashed across the Earth. Now, 400 years later, an alternate yet familiar history has evolved.

When Saladin's forces failed to pay the tribute the crusaders demanded, Richard's adviser whispered to his king that the Muslims should be punished and their threat ended. The adviser told Richard to gather several holy artifacts so that a ritual could be initiated to bless Richard's forces and curse their foes.

Trusting his counsel, Richard unwittingly brought together several creation relics possessed of such power that they began to undo reality by virtue of their congregation. Earth's material fabric tore, freeing spiritkind and magic to fill the world. Demons and strange beings of power sprang up in hordes in the streets of Acre, surrounding Richard's army.

After suffering heavy losses, Richard and Saladin joined forces to wade through the surrounding hordes. The two heroes wounded the adviser, now revealed to be a powerful mage. The adviser fled, along with a host of the evil creatures, allowing Richard and Saladin to seal the breach. The battle lasted a few hours, but the Disjunction changed history by unleashing unearthly forces across the planet.

Convinced that the ritual must never be done again, Richard and Saladin swore to divide the relics and secure them in their respective lands. The Knights Templar agreed to protect relics in the west; the Order of Saladin secured several relics in the east. These two noble orders banded together over the centuries for a series of Dark Crusades against the evil forces that escaped the Disjunction.

1192–1220 Disjunction: Ramifications in the Kingdoms of England and France

King Richard the Lionhearted was more a warrior than a politician. He assumed the throne after defeating his father in 1189 and embarked upon his crusade in 1190. He left two justiciars to control English affairs and sent his younger brother, John, south to their holdings in Brittany (what would become northwestern France).

After Richard's departure, one of the justiciars, William Longchamp, came into power as the Chancellor of England.

But William Longchamp was not to control England long. Seizing an opportunity, John wrested control from the chancellor and assumed the throne in 1191. Months later, the Disjunction changed everything.

Within hours of the Disjunction, tremors were felt in the lands surrounding the English Channel.

These earthquakes in Brittany and the English islands terrorized the common populace, but they were minor compared to the great tremor that occurred several days later. England was broken into two islands and, within a month, Scotland became a separate island.

The tremors caused great damage, but even more devastating were the floods caused by a massive rush of seawater onto newly lowered lands.

Ireland suffered little at first, experiencing no tremors or loss of land as its sister islands had. But by 1193, the Irish realized with horror that their island was sinking, slowly slipping beneath the surface of the Atlantic.

Brittany's coasts were also dissolving slowly with each quake. By the end of 1194, Brittany was all but gone. What was once the shore of the Seine River was now a beach stretching to Paris. The ocean slowly moved south, consuming acre after acre of countryside as it approached the Leone River. The lands of England, already broken into eight islands, dissolved at a steady pace.

The Irish fled their island, and Irish refugees began to populate every port city in the region. Within four years of the Disjunction, what remained of the deserted Irish landmass slipped beneath the waves.

Through all this, John ruled England even though his economic power dwindled as his holdings in both England and Brittany vanished into the ocean. With the throne shifted to London, he united the barons in the common goal of protecting their lands and holdings. Titles and lands shifted not with war but with changing geography.

Then, in late 1194, Richard contacted John and forgave him his past treacheries. Richard and John struck a deal whereby Richard would remain King in name, but John would control England as High Chancellor, as long as he continued to fund Richard's ongoing war against the tides of darkness.

It was also during this time that the devastated English first used the new magic unleashed in the world. Not only did magic find use in communication and in the repair and defense of the nation, but it also begat the re-formation of a centuries-gone power group—the Druids. Although originally few in number, Druidic orders began slowly to coalesce and gain power in remote parts of England.

The tremors plaguing the lands occurred less frequently as the century came to a close. Slowly, England emerged as a nation made of many small kingdomlike islands. To tighten his grip over the islands, John formed a pact with the emerging Druidic powers. The secretive Druids became John's greatest ally, and by 1204—the year of the last recorded tremor in England—John had an ironclad rule over his baronies.

But the Druids also demanded much from the throne, and it was rumored that John was their puppet king. Whether the rumors were valid or not, the Church indicted John in 1206 for heretical practices and excommunicated him in 1210.

Problems with the Church meant little to John at the time. His island nation had stopped splintering and now consisted of 15 primary islands. His barons were vying for independence, and he was struggling with his Druidic allies. His woes were compounded in 1208 by the Storm Dragons' invasion of northern England.

They were aware of the threat, but English forces were unprepared for the dragon invasion. In 1208, they lost control of four islands. After the initial onslaught, the English armies were able to slow the advance of the serpent armies. But by 1215, it was obvious the English were losing the fight—almost half their country lay in the hands of the Storm Dragons.

Frustrated, the remaining nobility in England forced John to sign a document called the Magna Carta. The document was intended to increase the nobles' ability to determine England's direction in the war effort, but it would have consequences even more far-reaching. It has been speculated that John signed the pact without the consent of the Druidic powers, which may have been the reason for his disappearance in 1216.

In that same year, King Henry III, a boy of 9, was crowned, and the war against the dragons stagnated into a stalemate that remained until Richard and his armies returned in 1219. United under Richard, England's armies drove the dragons from their islands in 1220.

Henry III remained on the throne for many years, although the Druids directed his actions from behind the scenes. Some suspect that the secret Druidic order controls the throne even in the 16th Century, but little evidence exists to support this.

The English in the 16th century are more open in their view of magic. In many parts of Europe, they are despised as heretics and hated by the Inquisition-controlled nations. But they are among the world's best seafarers, and London remains a center of trade and a haven for those in whose veins runs the taint of magic.

The sinking of Brittany ended in 1197. The land was devastated, but its loss had little effect on France. Continually worn down by invasion and war, France would not be re-established as a major European power until the middle of the 13th century.

1194–1244: The Fourth Crusade, Against the Storm Dragons

After the Disjunction, hordes of magical creatures scattered across Earth. The most powerful were the Storm Dragons, immense reptilian beasts capable of destruction with their claws, breath, and magic spells that could control the weather and summon natural disasters.

Storm Dragons are territorial, so they spread across the planet to carve the landmasses according to their elements. The Frost Drakes flew to northern Europe's icy reaches; the Inferno Drakes plagued the hot deserts of Africa and the Middle East. Thunder Wyrms soared to the Americas. The Kraken controlled the Pacific.

For two years after the Disjunction, King Richard remained in the Middle East to help his ally, Saladin, battle the creatures the cataclysm unleashed. Near the end of 1194, Richard was preparing to march his forces to the west when the Inferno Drakes, led by the terrible desert dragon Hassachrid, swarmed over the Middle East.

Richard stayed to help Saladin deal with the fierce attacks against the holy cities. By 1196, the crusaders had lost half of their forces fighting the dragons with antiquated methods of warfare. Conventional arrows, bolts, and ballistae were ineffective against the thick hides of the dragons.

Near the end of the 12th century, Wielders—humans who had become hosts for alien spirits—started to comprehend the extent of their new powers. They became the first human wizards, shaping a new form of energy channeled through their spirits. The Wielders were invaluable against the dragons. Their defensive magic could protect troops against the scorching dragonfires and their offensive spells could pierce tough dragon hides. By 1201, Richard and Saladin employed War Wielders to complement their forces.

As the crusaders turned the tide of the war with magic, the Frost Drakes conquered Sweden and launched a series of attacks against the Nordic territories. For several years, the Frost Drakes raided human settlements, wearing down the defenses of the depleted European armies.

In 1205, the Frost Drakes captured Norway and forced King Inge II into the first dragon-human alliance. Inge's fearsome dragonriders conquered the remaining Nordic territories, then turned their fury south.

By 1210, word reached a war-weary King Richard that Europe was in dire straits. Without the Knights Templar guarding the homeland, the Frost Drakes tore through Europe's defenses, conquering the Germanic territories and large parts of England and France.

Richard turned to the Wielders for a rapid means of transporting his army west. The Wielders, still novices, told Richard of a hazardous transportation magic involving the use of raw earth magic. Desperate to prevent the fall of European kingdoms, Richard ordered the Wielders to invoke a spell that would create a magical route through the Earth.

The Wielders combined their power and summoned magical crystals from the ground—a reckless spell that resulted in the sprouting of many such crystals randomly across the Earth. The crystals were empowered with various effects and some proved to be hazardous, but the Wielders were able to form a few stable bridges between Europe and the Middle East, saving the crusaders months of travel time.

When Richard's forces arrived through the portals, the Knights Templar and the Order of Saladin who accompanied them engaged the Frost Drakes, starting the long campaign to push the dragons out of continental Europe.

By the year 1218, Germany and France had been liberated, and in 1220, England was also free of the dragons. In 1222, the crusaders marshaled a navy to sail against the dragons in Norway and attack the heart of the dragon's empire, the glacial fortress of Icingspire.

The sea invasion proved disastrous, as the Frost Drakes summoned their water brethren, the Kraken, to aid them. Tidal waves and monsoons summoned by the sea-dwelling dragons sank the crusaders' navy. The largest of the Kraken capsized and tore apart the fleet's flagship, the vessel of King Richard the Lionhearted, and it was presumed that the crusader perished in the churning waters.

Richard's loss proved so disastrous that the crusaders could not muster another fleet for eight years, but by 1230, the crusaders landed in Denmark and slowly captured Nordic territory.

As the crusaders continued to rout the dragons, the enslaved Nordic warriors broke free and battled against their captors. In 1239, the crusaders liberated Norway with the help of King Hákon IV and drove the dragons into the sea. For the next several years, the last of the dragons gathered within their near impregnable glacial fortress, Icingspire.

The final battle of the Fourth Crusade took place in Iceland in 1244 at Húnaflói, in The Bay Battle. The crusaders brought ships from every coastal province to siege Icingspire. Armed with magical ballistae forged by the Wielders, and enchanted siegecraft designed to hunt dragons, the fleet assaulted the fortress in a siege that lasted two months and resulted in the extermination of dragonkind.

1231: The Inquisition

The Disjunction caused pervasive changes to many societies around the world. Monstrous creatures roamed the wilderness, and even in the safest streets of the western capitals some humans possessed of spirits cast dark spells against innocents. While the Knights Templar waged war against the organized forces of evil, the taint of dark magic threatened the security of the western cities.

Alarmed by the spread of magic across the world, the European people looked to their rulers and clergy and demanded protection. In 1231, the western kings and the papacy agreed to the formation of the first Inquisition, an organization of disciplined holy investigators trained to seek out and deal with the evils wrought by the Disjunction.

In the first few years of its existence, the Inquisition focused its efforts on exorcising dark spirits and tracking the monsters plaguing the outskirts of the western cities. To this end, the Inquisition worked with the Knights Templar.

Using their combined forces, the Inquisition and the Templars drove organized tribes of monsters away from the cities and into the shadows. But as the Knights Templar expanded their influence outward for greater security, the Inquisition turned its attention inward to root out evils that had infiltrated society. The Inquisition targeted not only evil beasts, but also any "inappropriate" magic-touched beings.

For the Knights Templar, the situation was delicate. The War Wielders had proved valuable in the struggle against the Templars' enemies. But they understood that not all Wielders used their power for good.

As early as the beginning of the Fourth Crusade, the magic-using Wielders had learned that their magical powers allowed them great influence among the general population. Although some Wielders could temper their magic with compassion and humility, others could not resist the urge to seize control, using their magic to subjugate and control people.

In 1249, the rampage of the Mongols devastated parts of Italy, the stronghold of the Inquisition and the Holy See. Eventually, the crusaders pushed back the overextended Mongol army, but not before it had done significant damage. Although they fought valiantly, many Inquisitors died battling the Mongol Horde. Those few who survived fled west to Spain to regroup, but the order would not recover its influence for many years.

After the Inquisitors defeated the Mongols, some of the Wielders became even more brazen, especially with the Inquisition weakened. Children of the first Wielders had already started to manifest their magical heritage's physical traits.

Those descended from magic-users with powerful fire and earth spirits became known as Sylvants, a sub-race of tainted humans with elemental features. The children of Wielders with bestial spirits became known as Feralkins, larger and more powerful physically than normal humans. Demokins, children of Wielders with fiendish spirits, walked in the streets of Europe. Many of these new races exhibited abilities beyond those of normal humans, causing a disruptive rift between the pure and "tainted" races.

By 1260, an alliance of ambitious Wielders consolidated their influence. Some of the more powerful and audacious Wielders proclaimed themselves to be dukes or governors and established minor duchies or provinces within the western kingdoms. Using their magical abilities to expand their influences, these Wielders ruled nearly a quarter of Spain and parts of France by 1263.

In 1268, the rulers of the western nations and the surviving leaders of the Inquisition convinced the Knights Templar of the need to contain the Wielders, to ensure the hegemony of the pureblood race. The Inquisition passed a series of edicts to protect citizens against magic abuses and to punish those who illegally used magic. The Inquisition used these edicts as pretense to move against Wielders entrenched in the European governments.

While some of the good War Wielders loyal to the Knights Templar accepted and understood the Inquisition's edicts, many other Wielders did not, and attacked Inquisitors attempting to reclaim their lands.

In 1269, the Spanish Inquisition formed to reclaim the lands of Spain taken by the Wielders. The Inquisitors launched the *Reconquista*, or Reconquest, a series of magical battles that engulfed Spain and France in civil war. The rogue Wielders summoned terrible elemental forces while the Inquisitors invoked Divine Magic against the rebels. The loss of life, both pureblood and tainted, was staggering.

The Reconquista lasted six years. By 1275, the Inquisition had vanquished the rogue Wielders. The War Wielders still loyal to the Templars distanced themselves from the evil wizards who had controlled parts of Europe. The Inquisition still regarded wizards with deep suspicion, however, and would never allow them to gain influence over the public again.

Many years of continuous scrutiny of Wielders followed, and more edicts restricted the movements of wizards and the tainted races. In 1343, the Spanish Inquisition decreed a union with any non-divine spirit to be a heretical offence. To escape persecution, some Wielders once loyal to the Knights Templar fled to England, where restrictions against magic use were less severe.

The Inquisition created a clear distinction between magic generated by divine spirits and other magic, and deemed only Divine Magic acceptable. Wielders who openly used magic soon found themselves in the Inquisition's dreaded chambers with little hope of escape. Other Wielders used magic to conceal themselves, yet the Inquisition tracked them down despite such sorcery.

Conditions never improved for those born with visible marks of sorcery. The tainted races were subjected to nighttime raids of their homes by the Inquisition, and to countless trials and interrogations. Many Sylvants, Feralkins, and Demokins eventually integrated into society, but those visibly tainted by magic were treated as second-class citizens.

In 1421, after the crusade against the Fell Spirits further polarized public opinion against spiritkind and the tainted races, Grand Inquisitor Tomas de Torquemada launched a campaign to purge Spain, France, and Italy of magic-users. Torquemada brought thousands of suspected wizards before the Inquisition to stand trial on using heretical magic. Some of the accused were Wielders, but many wrongfully accused innocents suffered or perished as a result of the interrogations.

Now, more than a century later, the Inquisition has driven the practice of magic underground. Few foolish wizards openly cast spells, for fear of never being seen again. Rumors abound that some clever wizards have managed to form secret havens in the larger cities where Wielders can gather safely, although the Inquisition's constant vigilance makes such shelters unlikely.

1241: Invasion of the Golden Horde

The Great Khan Ogedei cheated death by binding with the Fell Spirit Weichi. Because Ogedei did not die, Batu Khan would not be recalled from his European campaign as in conventional history. For a year, Batu's forces surged west, destroying enemy armies that were ill-equipped against the Mongol cavalry.

While continuing west, Batu gathered a vanguard force of monstrous warriors—hideous and cruel goblins formed by the union of dark spirits and humans. These creatures adapted to the Mongol style of warfare, mastering the use of crafted short bows while riding swift beast-mounts into battle.

Batu's Golden Horde swelled with goblinoid forces as he cut a swath through the Eastern European territories. Batu's progress alarmed the western nations, already weary from their war against the Storm Dragons. In 1243, the Fourth Crusade against the Storm Dragons ended, allowing the Knights Templar and the western forces to join the eastern forces against the Mongol Horde.

The coalition succeeded in slowing the Golden Horde's advances for several years, yet Batu's forces continued to gain ground. In 1249, the coalition halted Batu's advance in Italy, but not before many Italian provinces felt the savagery of the Mongol Horde. The situation appeared so desperate that the Holy See fled west to Spain, where it has remained.

In 1250, the European armies defeated the Mongol forces through attrition—both sides suffered heavy casualties. Batu dispersed his goblin tribes against the Europeans, sending the monsters through the ranks of the westerners to cover his escape. The Mongols retreated, but a few of the goblin tribes broke through the European forces to race toward the western lands.

As Batu's army retreated, he ravaged more cities, descending upon any nation that had aided the European armies. The furious march erased several powerful forces from history, including Byzantium and the Teutonic Knights.

1316: Famine in Europe

The decade after the Disjunction was a time of suffering in Europe. Cities were destroyed, continents underwent upheavals, and the swarming monsters the Disjunction released pillaged Europe's population. Agrarian communities were laid waste, which lead to food shortages and starvation. As Europe entered the 13th century, however, the use of Divine Magic and a smaller population balanced out the Disjunction's destruction. In many places, humans prospered.

In most areas, towns and cities were fewer and less densely populated. In rural areas, farmers grouped together and paid local mercenaries for protection—a farmer working his fields alone often never returned home.

Still, farmers had to work less suitable land, out of necessity. This increased the cost of food across Europe and resulted in occasional food shortages. Europeans used magic to offset these difficulties, and over the course of the 13th century, there was a population boom across Europe.

In 1316, the Inquisition declared the practice of magic to be heresy—even when it was used to offset national food shortages. This edict, combined with an increasing population, caused a famine. By the winter of 1316, almost the entire population of Europe was starving.

The price of grain fluctuated and many farmers switched to more dependable crops, worsening an already bad situation. After a poor winter in 1317, the Inquisition reversed its edict and allowed the practice of clergy-supervised magic to increase the harvest.

But the damage was done. And while some parts of Europe were sufficiently fed, the region as a whole would suffer from a food shortage for more than a hundred years.

1336: The Fifth Crusade—Rise of the Necromancers

After the Disjunction in 1192, several long-buried pharaohs returned from the afterlife to re-establish their rule over Egypt. In a brief period of civil war, the newly risen god-kings of the Nile battled each other for control of their ancient lands. Many of the pharaohs who arose were returned to the afterlife. A few retreated into Southern Africa to create new empires.

After three decades of war, Egypt came to peace and Ramses II assumed control of the Nile region. The tendrils of Egyptian rule expanded their influence over Africa. This rule would continue peacefully for more than a hundred years.

In 1390, however, a group of powerful dark wizards stole from the pharaohs a Magic Tome containing the secrets of life and death. The Book of Death detailed the art of necromancy, the magic of the afterlife, and death. After studying the book, these Necromancers twisted the ancient rituals and bound dark spirits to dead bodies, creating a powerful army of mindless undead warriors.

Beginning with an attack on the populous capital of Alexandria, the Necromancers decimated the Egyptian forces. As the city burned, the bodies of fallen warriors and citizens swelled the ranks of the undead armies. Alexandria became a city of the undead and the capital of the Necromancers' nation. Within a year, the surrounding African nations had also fallen and the Necromancers and their ever-growing army of undead controlled Northern Africa.

With the Necromancers' advance into Southern Europe and the Middle East inevitable, the Ottoman Empire and the Order of Saladin gathered their forces to wage war. The first attacks came in the winter of 1418. For several years, the Ottoman Empire and the Order of Saladin slowly lost ground to the advancing undead horde.

By early 1428, the Necromancers expanded their terror campaign by sending their bone barges across the Mediterranean and directly attacking European nations. While the undead armies attacked human forces in Asia, Africa, and Europe, the Necromancers sent their most powerful undead creatures to find the hidden artifacts guarded by the Knights Templar and Order of Saladin.

In 1431, one of the undead armies nearly succeeded in wresting one of the holy relics from a secret crypt in southern France. The Knights Templar and the Order of Saladin battled bravely, but the undead marched into the crypt's underground halls.

When all hope seemed lost, the remaining knights allowed a mystic Order of Saladin to invoke a warding-off charm. The spell sealed the crypt—with the knights inside—with a lasting magic to prevent the undead from leaving with the holy relic. Soon after, reinforcements arrived to relieve the knights, but the crypt had already been sealed.

Many years later, all but the Knights Templar forgot the crypt's location, although the valor of the trapped knights was never forgotten.

By the year 1435, the Inquisition turned the tide of the war by embracing Divine Magic's use, a power derived from the spirits of holy ancestors. The Inquisitors discovered that this divine power could drive back or destroy undead creatures, and they secretly ordered magic weapons forged—each imbued with this Divine Magic to help eradicate the undead.

The combined forces of the Inquisition and the western and eastern nations drove the Necromancers into Northern Africa and cleared the Mediterranean of the undead naval presence.

The Inquisition and the Knights Templar hunted and destroyed every Necromancer, to ensure the black arts would never be practiced. In 1449, the knights killed the last Necromancer, Lord Amonsil. Although the exiled pharaohs were innocent of the crimes perpetrated by the Necromancers, the Inquisition viewed them as abominations and dispatched them, allowing the Ottoman Empire to control Northern Africa.

Some remnants of the undead army lurk in dark forests, old graveyards, and tombs throughout the world, but few dare to practice the forbidden art of necromancy.

1347: The Black Death

The plague came to Europe from Asia via the Mongol invasion in 1346. Plague-ridden Mongol invaders laid siege to Kaffa. To make the best of a bad situation, they catapulted their disease-ridden dead over the walls. The Genoese traders panicked and fled to Sicily, taking the Black Death with them.

Famine and overcrowding in the population centers made a perfect breeding ground for the plague. It spread across the continent, killing a third of the human population.

Still, the Inquisition held fast to its 1343 decree forbidding the practice of magic. Many Wielders appealed to the courts to allow them to cure the diseased population, but were answered with imprisonment or worse. The divine Wielders within the Inquisition were too busy ferreting out rogue Wielders to assist the population. Many commoners died.

Ironically, many of the tainted were more resistant to plague. While purebloods died around them, the population of the tainted grew.

Between 1347 and the end of the 14th century, the plague struck Europe many times. Tainted births previously accounted for only a small percentage of the population, but by the beginning of the 15th century, tainted births were numerous enough that the variations in human bloodlines had taken on their vernacular names of Feralkin, Demokin, and Sylvant.

1429–1433: The Campaign of Jehanne D'Arc (Joan of Arc)

The sinking of Normandy and Brittany into the Atlantic Ocean had little effect on France. The country was a collection of feudal territories answering to the king, and much of the lost land was not in possession of the French crown. Disputes between England, Burgundy, and Spain, and encroachments by various hordes throughout the 13th and 14th centuries, shrank the royal domain.

France was able to expand its control occasionally, but by the time the Hundred Years War started in the early 1400s, much of northern France was under English control. Lower France was separated into various duchies with scant alliance to the king.

Famine and the plague had taken a greater toll on the kingdom than on its neighbors, and the continuing wars left the populace burdened. When Charles VII took the throne in 1422, France was in turmoil. The situation worsened as the threat of the Necromantic armies to the south and east began to threaten Europe.

In 1429, when it seemed as if France might lose any remaining European authority, a young woman of 17 named Jehanne D'Arc (Joan of Arc) gained audience with Charles. She persuaded the King to allow her titular command over one of his armies.

This would have been no easy task for any man or woman, but it was rumored that Jehanne was infused with an immensely powerful divine spirit. Various records state that Jehanne claimed this spirit often spoke to her, and through its power, she may have been able to enthrall others.

Jehanne soon assumed control. Sword in one hand and a banner in the other, she led her army in a sweep across France. Her abilities as a strategist and a leader were remarkable, and within a year her soldiers and most of the populace believed she was a saint. Her army grew in size as she returned area after area to the crown—although most regions were easily captured because of the extended Fifth Crusade.

By 1431, she had reclaimed lands across northern and southern France and had recaptured Paris. France's royal authority stretched from the Mediterranean to Guienne and north to Flanders.

In late 1431, the Inquisition caught Jehanne and put her on trial. The trial was notable for the fact that Jehanne proposed no defense and yet was acquitted. All members of the court of inquiry went insane within a year of the trial's completion.

Jehanne and her armies shifted focus in 1432 and joined with the Fifth Crusade against the Necromancers about the time the Necromancers' forces were plundering France in search of relics.

Jehanne and a vanguard of her men clashed with a massive undead force at a relic's resting place in a series of caverns in southern France. The amassed army and the magic-wielding undead forces caused the caves to collapse, killing her and the rest of her men.

In death, Jehanne became a martyr to the French people, and their support buoyed the French armies. The French forces played a pivotal role in the defeat of the Necromancers, and consolidated French holdings. France returned to the world theater and the French people united under their king for the first time in history.

1461–1464: The Crusade Against the Fell Spirits

Over the course of several long crusades, the European people turned to the Inquisition's leadership for stability. The kings of continental Europe maintained their titles, but discovered to their consternation that true power, the faith and influence of the people, rested with the Inquisitors. Italy, fractionalized and divided since the devastating Mongol invasion, found unity in the Inquisition and became a theocracy ruled by Inquisitors in the early 1400s.

With the threat of the Necromancers neutralized, the Knight Orders returned to their home territories to help rebuild the cities, while the Inquisition moved to establish its power. Those who spoke out against the Inquisition risked being charged with heresy.

In 1461, a respected official of the Spanish government was accused of practicing magic and was brought before the Inquisition as a prisoner. The prisoner confounded the four Inquisitors, however, by resisting their attempts at exorcism, demonstrating inhuman endurance, and speaking in ancient languages to confuse his interrogators.

After days of arduous proceedings, two of the four Inquisitors collapsed from exhaustion. The third Inquisitor fell prey to a strange malady after the prisoner asked to speak with him privately so that he could confess his sins. When other Inquisitors returned, they found the interrogator babbling about the Fell Spirits while the prisoner laughed beside him.

Learned bishops and high-ranking Inquisitors came to examine the man and were frustrated by his openly hostile and resilient attitude. Though these Inquisitors were no closer to exorcising the prisoner's demon, he spoke proudly of ages past, when the Fell Spirits were known as demons to many of the old religions. To the Hindus, they were known as the terrible Daityas, to the Persians, the Daevas. Buddhists knew them as the hungry Pretas, the Hebrews called one of the Fell Spirits Asmodeous, and the Christians feared Lucifer above all else.

Although the official record of the final interrogation with the first Fell Spirit has never been released, it is believed that the Grand Inquisitor visited the Fell Spirit and concluded the interrogation. Torquemada summoned and bound a divine spirit, one who opposed the Fell Spirit on many occasions in the past. According to these historians, Torquemada did not emerge from the Chambers for several days, but succeeded with the exorcism. Torquemada imprisoned the Fell Spirit within the Chambers of the Inquisition, so that its evil could not corrupt others.

Weeks after the Spanish incident, word of the incident with the Fell Spirit spread. It was believed that other such demonic forces had infiltrated governments of other kingdoms.

The Inquisition initiated a campaign to ferret out any other people in positions of power that could be possessed by the Fell Spirits. The resulting hysteria crippled the European capitals, as the Inquisition restricted travel and trade between the cities. Communities turned on each other, and thousands of innocents faced the harsh interrogations of the Inquisition.

In 1463, the Inquisition sent representatives to London to ensure the sanctity of English monarchy. When the Inquisitors requested an audience with Queen Elizabeth, they were allowed to meet her in the presence of her honor guard. The Inquisitors attempted to perform a perfunctory interrogation on the Queen. Offended, Elizabeth had the Inquisitors put to death. The incident damaged relations between England and the Inquisition, and the two forces nearly went to war. However, in 1464, diplomats prevailed and a truce ensued.

By this time, the Inquisition had also curtailed the search for more Fell Spirits. Though many dark creatures were found hiding in the shadows of cities, they could find no evidence of any other dreaded Fell Spirits infiltrating the European governments. This crusade's success was measured only by the hysteria it induced and the number of innocents who suffered through it.

Though the crusade against the Fell Spirits ended, the relations between England the Inquisition suffered irreparable damage. Both the English and Spanish nations built up their navies to protect their trade routes and overseas interests. Over the years, occasional skirmishes flared up, fueling the fires of discontent on both sides.

In 1587, a naval engagement between Spanish and English forces resulted in the loss of many Spanish lives, including several influential Inquisitors and Spanish nobles.

A year later, in the current time of 1588, it is known that the Inquisition has spent many months preparing for a conflict, which stems from the miserable Sixth Crusade. As the Inquisition prepares articles detailing heretical charges against England, the Spanish Armada grows, becoming one of the largest naval fleets in history.

1492: Expeditions to the New World

As the crusaders waged war against darkness, the Western kings sought to rebuild civilization. Others, ambitious rulers, even sought to expand their influence across the world. In the 15th century, Spain sent out navigators to explore the seas and search for new trade routes.

One such explorer, Christopher Columbus, set sail in August 1492 and barely survived a harrowing voyage over the Atlantic Ocean. He sailed along the north coast of Hispaniola and returned to Spain in 1493, telling the King about the wealthy and powerful New World tribes.

Impressed with his discovery, King Ferdinand funded Columbus for a second voyage in 1493, granting him a small army to establish a New World settlement. Having been knocked off course by terrible storms, Columbus's fleet landed in North America. Columbus ordered his army to clear a swath of overgrown jungle terrain and create a settlement for Spain, La Isabela. Two weeks later, the indigenous tribes, riding monstrous reptilian mounts, attacked and butchered the colonists, killing Columbus and most of his troops. The few survivors of this expedition sailed to Spain in 1494, and spoke of the horrors.

Determined to tame these savage new lands, King Phillip funded several conquistadors to explore and claim these new lands for Spain. One such conquistador was Hernán Cortés. Cortés was given a fleet of ships to conquer the New World. In his first expedition, Cortés established a foothold in southern Mexico and learned of a powerful tribe, the Aztecs, who possessed vast riches.

Cortés returned to Spain with treasures from the New World and requested more troops and resources to attack the Aztecs. In 1521, Cortés received a larger fleet and sailed to join his forces in the New World.

Joined by other tribes, enemies of the Aztecs, Cortés marched his army against Tenochtitlan, the Aztec capital. When Cortés laid siege to the city, the Aztecs unleashed a host of terrors never before seen by western eyes. Massive feathered serpents swept down from the city and destroyed the Spanish siege weapons as old Aztec gods walked among the fierce warriors, devouring the invaders. Cortés was wounded in the battle, and retreated to Spain with a single damaged vessel.

The defeat of Cortés's army was the last recorded attempt by European forces to gain a stronghold in the New World.

Today, Hernán Cortés, maimed and coinless, attempts to find funding for another expedition to the New World, but must settle his crushing debts first.

1555: The Prophet Nostradamus

In 1534, a spirit joined with Michel de Notredame, or Nostradamus, a physician from southern France. Nostradamus began to experience strange and frequent visions, dreams of past and current events, and premonitions of things to come. The dreams and visions increased over the years, and Nostradamus saw some of the near-future visions come to pass. Word spread throughout France that Nostradamus was a holy seer, a prophet who could foretell the future.

In 1550, Nostradamus moved to Salon-de-Provence and began writing a series of prophecies. Five years later, he completed the *Centuries*, a book containing more than 900 predictions. Only a few copies of the book circulated in France, but rumors spread among the populace that the prophet detailed a coming catastrophe that would threaten civilization—a catastrophe rivaling the destruction caused by the Disjunction.

Moving swiftly to prevent a panic, the Inquisition branded Nostradamus a dangerous heretic and destroyed all known copies of the *Centuries*. Inquisitors scoured France in vain for years to find the prophet.

The Inquisition believes that Nostradamus might have perished in 1587. In one of the seer's mostcryptic prophecies, Nostradamus predicted that he would fade from the mortal world and join the spirit world, which most sages have interpreted as a prediction of his death.

CHARACTER CREATION

As the game begins, you make crucial decisions that affect your adventure from beginning to end. This is the character creation process. *Lionheart* provides a limitless palette of choices for constructing an Avatar. A character need not conform to a set of classes or jobs. Your character can be anything you want it to be. This is fun, but requires thought.

You need to learn many things about characters before you start constructing one. The following gives you the basic know-how to create a character that's right for you and that will grow over time into a powerful force.

BASIC ATTRIBUTES

Each character has a basic set of attributes that are taken into account whenever an action is performed. These attributes rule the amount of damage a character can inflict, how well the character wields certain weapons, how non-playable characters (NPCs) react to him or her, and many other factors.

Before setting the attributes, you need to have an idea of what your character will be in the future, so you can select the most important attributes. It would be nice if the basic attributes could be set to 10, providing super-human abilities, but specialization is necessary. Here are the seven basic attributes and what they do.

Strength

This attribute is the character's raw physical strength. It represents the ability to lift weights, punch hard, carry equipment, and effectively use larger weapons. Stronger characters can cause more damage in melee combat. Those with aspirations of going toe-to-toe with giants and dragons want to set this attribute at 8 or higher. If you plan to focus on the thieving arts or spell-casting, Strength is secondary and should be set at 4 or lower.

Perception

Perception refers to a character's power of observation, or the ability to notice things others might miss. It is a combination of senses—touch, sight, taste, smell, and hearing. Perception affects the character's ranged-weapon distances, too. This is an important attribute for all classes, but especially for archers and thieves. Never set this attribute lower than 4, or you have a difficult time detecting hidden traps and treasure.

Endurance

Endurance influences the character's health, along with the ability to withstand punishment and physical exertion. Endurance affects the character's hit points. Endurance of 6 or above increases Poison and Disease Resistances. Those who fight with the sword and axe should set Endurance at 7 or higher, so they have plenty of hit points.

Even if you play another type of character, setting your Endurance too low—under 4—may make even the most basic of enemies a serious threat. Set it lower if you're looking for a challenge.

Charisma

The character's looks and charm add up to Charisma. High Charisma makes it easier to deal with NPCs, including the purchasing and selling of anything. More important, Charisma affects the relationship that the character has with his or her spirit, and the Mana the spirit is able to channel on their behalf.

Charisma is important for magic users, because it affects the character's Mana supply. In combination with the Speech skill, it allows casters to talk their way out of battles that might otherwise be too challenging. Those who live for a fight and rely on cold steel can get by with low Charisma. They are unlikely to care as much about their interaction with NPCs.

Intelligence

The number of skill points a character gets at each experience level is based on the character's Intelligence. This attribute also has a direct effect on a character's maximum Mana supply. Every character benefits from Intelligence, but none more so than spell casters. To explore a spell branch, large numbers of skill points are necessary. Maximizing a character's Intelligence gives access to as many skill points as possible.

Agility

Agility is a combination of the character's reflexes, balance, and coordination, and affects the character's speed. It also affects many physical skills that require dexterity, such as lockpicking. Thieves benefit from high Agility, but it's an important attribute for any character. Agility affects walking and attack speed. High Agility gives a character the ability to inflict more damage in combat, and also to run from enemies when the situation is out of control. Fighters and spell casters should have at least 4 Agility; 7 or higher is recommended for those who live by the sword.

Luck

Luck is a hard statistic to pin down. It represents a combination of fate, Karma, and good fortune. Luck of 6 or above affects Fire, Cold, and Electrical Resistances, but it is a factor in many areas even in tiny amounts. Most players skimp on Luck. It's a mystical power and its benefits aren't obvious. Fighters benefit from high Luck, however, because Luck increases a character's critical percentage. This is especially true at high levels when certain Perks provide benefits based on the character's Luck.

THE PURE AND THE TAINTED

The introduction of spirits and magic into humans created Trolls and Goblins, but some spirits developed symbiotic relationships with their human hosts. In some cases, the spirit passes from generation to generation; in other cases, only the traits of the spirit are passed on. In the 300 years since the Disjunction, humankind has settled into four broad races.

You must choose between the following four descendents of the human race when creating a character. Each race has advantages and disadvantages. They're different, but no race is preferable to another.

Demokin

Demokins are the descendents of humans imbued with fiendish or impish spirits. Taller than a pureblood human, Demokins are more adept with magic than humans and blend easily with the purebloods. Some of the traits Demokin possess are horns, small tails, or wings.

Demokins make able spell casters, thieves, and archers, as well as spell-casting fighters or battle mages. They are never the strongest warriors on the battlefield, but Demokins are a race to be feared. Because of their fearful appearance, Demokins are the most hated of the three tainted races. They're misunderstood and persecuted by the members of the Inquisition.

If you choose to be a Demokin and possess a racial trait that exposes your heritage, be ready to battle racial discrimination as much as fierce monsters. A quick wit helps Demokins through such encounters. Other Demokins are prone to empathize with their kind and are more accommodating. But don't be surprised if most Demokins you meet on your adventure are carrying large chips on their shoulders.

STARTING ATTRIBUTES

Strength	4 (min 1/max 8)	Intelligence	6 (min 3/max 10)
Perception	6 (min 3/max 10)	Agility	6 (min 3/max 10)
Endurance	4 (min 1/max 9)	Luck	5 (min 1/max 9)
Charisma	5 (min 2/max 10)	Unused Points	5 (27 flux)

RACIAL TRAITS

All Demokins must select one racial trait. Most Demokin racial traits mark you as tainted by magic and cause many untainted characters to react negatively to you. Some traits do not mark you, however, so you can keep your magical taint hidden.

Acid Blood

Your veins course with acidic blood. If you are wounded, acid splashes onto your opponent, causing 1 point of damage for every 10 inflicted on you in a strike. Crushing and Slashing Resistances are reduced by 5 percent. Your skin pallor marks you as tainted by magic and causes some people to react negatively to you.

Bloody Talons

You have fiendish razor-sharp claws that allow you to rip into your opponents. You gain a 4-point bonus to your Unarmed skill and deal +1 unarmed damage. Manipulating these talons is difficult, however. You suffer an 8-point penalty to your Ranged Weapon and Lockpick skills. Your huge talons mark you as tainted by magic and cause some people to react negatively to you.

Demonic Frenzy

Sometimes Demokins go stir-crazy because of their need to be alone and away from the rest of society. These solitary Demokins are called "crazies." You're not there yet, but you're on the edge of losing it. You suffer a 1-point penalty both to Intelligence and to Charisma, but your Strength is increased by 1, you add 15 points to your One-Handed Melee skill, and 10 points to Evasion. Because your appearance is unaltered, you can still pass as a pureblood human. This trait requires an Intelligence of 2 or higher and a Charisma of 3 or higher.

Diabolism

Your demonic background is strong and casting Thought Magic spells is easy for you. Thought Magic spells cost 10 percent less Mana to cast. But this trait makes it more difficult to cast Divine Magic spells. All Divine Magic spells cost 10 percent more to cast. Because your appearance is unaltered, you can pass as a pureblood human.

Forked Tongue

The introduction of impish blood into your family has given you a barely noticeable bifurcated tongue. The forked tongue allows you to charm your way through difficult encounters, giving you +15 to your Speech skill. Your reliance on diplomacy caused you to neglect your combat training, so you have a -5 on combat skills. The serpentlike split in your tongue marks you as tainted by magic and causes some people to react negatively to you.

Infernal Quickness

You were born with a rapid metabolism, making it difficult for you to sit still. You gain a 10 percent bonus in speed, but in your haste you often overlook things, so you suffer a 1-point penalty to Perception. Because your appearance is unaltered, you can pass as a pureblood human. This trait requires a Perception of 4 or higher.

Lucky Devil

A dark angel has always watched over your family, and things go your way. This has left you with a lack of empathy. You either never know what to say, or else succeed in saying the wrong thing. Your Luck is increased by 1, but you suffer a 15-point penalty to your Speech skill. Your appearance is unaltered, so you can pass as a pureblood human.

Scaly Hide

Your skin is covered with protective scales that add 5 to your Armor Class, increase your Piercing Resistance 5 percent, and increase your Fire Resistance 10 percent. The scales make you look sinister, so you lose 1 Charisma. Your scaly skin marks you as tainted by magic and causes some people to react negatively to you. This trait requires a Charisma of 3 or higher.

Shroud of Darkness

Your demonic heritage causes shadows to gather around you. This trait grants you a 20-point bonus to your Sneak skill and increases your Armor Class by 5, but the shadowy shroud lowers your Perception by 1. The unnatural shadows mark you as tainted by magic and causes some people to react negatively to you. This trait requires a Perception of 4 or higher.

Vampiric Fury

You draw strength from the blood of others. Every time you strike an opponent with a melee attack, you gain at least 1 HP. In addition to your base of 1, for every 10 points of melee damage you inflict, you heal one additional HP. Healing spells and potions, however, are half as effective for you. Because your appearance is unaltered, you can pass as a pureblood human.

Feralkin

Feralkins are the descendents of humans imbued with the magic of a beast or a bestial spirit. Stronger and more skillful than their pureblood counterparts, Feralkin are also easily spotted and often persecuted. Feralkin may have more feral traits, which can include excessive body hair or pronounced jawbones.

Feralkin make the best fighters and thieves, but they also suffer from racial persecution. They are not known for their ability to interact with others, and often suffer when trying to talk their way out of a sticky situation. Because Feralkin traits are easy to identify, they always suffer when dealing with racist pureblood humans, and can expect to be shunned in many shops. But if you choose the path of the warrior or rogue, interaction with others is not a priority. Feralkins are good to their own kind, so expect certain favors from other Feralkins throughout your adventure.

STARTING ATTRIBUTES

Strength	7 (min 3/max 10)	Intelligence	3 (min 3/max 9)
Perception	6 (min 2/max 10)	Agility	6 (min 2/max 9)
Endurance	7 (min 3/max 10)	Luck	5 (min 2/max 10)
Charisma	3 (min 1/max 9)	Unused Points	4 (25 flux)

RACIAL TRAITS

All Feralkins must select one racial trait. All Feralkin racial traits mark you as tainted by magic, so you can never pass as a pureblood and can expect a cold reception from many people you meet.

Beast of Burden

Because of your massive hands and strong back, you have a greatly increased ability to carry things, which has fed your neurotic compulsion to hoard useless gear. Your carry weight is increased by 20 pounds, but the random equipment you've stuffed in your pockets and tied to your pack make noise, so you suffer a 10-point penalty to your Sneak skill. This trait, like all Feralkin traits, marks you as tainted by magic and causes some people to react negatively to you.

Chameleon

You have the ability to adjust your skin color and blend in with your surroundings. Because of this, you get a 20-point bonus to your Sneak skill. Unfortunately, your skin is frail and more susceptible to damage. Your Armor Class is reduced by 5 and your Crushing Resistance suffers a 5 percent penalty. This trait marks you as tainted by magic and causes some people to react negatively to you.

Eagle Eye

You have the eyes of an eagle, but the lightweight bones of a bird as well. You receive a 15-point bonus to your Ranged Weapon skill, but your carrying capacity is reduced by 30 pounds. This trait marks you as tainted by magic and causes some people to react negatively to you.

Elephant Hide

Your skin is calloused. Your pain threshold is higher (+1 to Slashing and Crushing damage thresholds), and you get a 5 percent bonus to your Slashing and Crushing Resistances, but you suffer a -1 penalty to Agility and your Lockpick skill is reduced by 10 points. This trait marks you as tainted by magic and causes some people to react negatively to you. This trait requires an Agility of 3 or higher.

Monkey Brains

A whimsical monkey spirit passed on an uncanny cleverness to your family. Add 5 points to your Speech, Find Traps/Secret Doors, and Lockpick skills. But your inability to control your primate mannerisms lowers your Thieving/Barter skill by 10 points and your Ranged Weapons skill by 5 points. This trait marks you as tainted by magic and causes some people to react negatively to you.

Rabid Fervor

In combat, you rely on your bestial instincts. You gain 15 points in One-Handed, Two-Handed Melee, and Unarmed combat skills and a +5 percent chance to land a critical blow; but suffer a -1 penalty to Intelligence and Perception. This trait marks you as tainted by magic and causes some people to react negatively to you. This trait requires an Intelligence of 4 or higher and a Perception of 3 or higher.

Regeneration

Your bestial heritage allows you to quickly heal wounds. Add +1 to your healing rate. However, your metabolism cannot heal Poison and Disease well, so you receive 15 percent penalty to your Disease and Poison Resistances. This trait marks you as tainted by magic and causes some people to react negatively to you.

Serpent's Tongue

Snake spirits have coiled into your family line, entrenching themselves in your mannerisms and bodily defenses. Their cunning grants a 15-point bonus to your Speech skill, but your Acid, Fire, and Electrical Resistances are decreased by 8 percent because of your skin's odd spiritual makeup. This trait marks you as tainted by magic and causes some people to react negatively to you.

Tusks

A pair of eight-inch tusks mar your otherwise human face, making it difficult for others to understand you. This reduces your Speech skill by 15 points. But when Speech fails, you deal +1 damage in unarmed combat. This trait marks you as tainted by magic and causes some people to react negatively to you.

Wolf Hide

You have a thick coat of fur covering your body. Your Armor Class is increased by 7 and you gain a 5 percent bonus to your Piercing and Slashing Resistance. Your lupine features are noticeable, however, and lower your Charisma by 1. Your fur is also a haven for ticks and fleas, decreasing your Disease Resistance by 7 percent and your Fire Resistance by 5 percent. This trait marks you as tainted by magic and causes some people to react negatively to you. This trait requires a Charisma of 2 or higher.

Pureblood Human

The purebloods are untainted humans, their bloodlines unaffected by the magic pervading from the Disjunction. Although it is hard to find a human that is untouched, purebloods exist and exhibit no signs of magic ancestry.

Purebloods are average at everything, they possess no racial traits, they are treated fairly by most people, and they can excel at any skill. Pureblood humans are a good starting race for those unfamiliar with the Lionheart engine or role-playing games. Playing such a character results in few surprises, which allows a player to get his or her feet wet without difficulty. This is also the race of choice if you wish to avoid racial confrontation during your adventures. Some racial discrimination is inevitable when dealing with Feralkins, Demokins, or Sylvants, but less than would be experienced otherwise.

STARTING ATTRIBUTES

Strength	5 (min 1/max 10)	Intelligence	5 (min 3/max 10)
Perception	5 (min 1/max 10)	Agility	5 (min 1/max 10)
Endurance	5 (min 1/max 10)	Luck	5 (min 1/max 10)
Charisma	5 (min 1/max 10)	Unused Points	6 (32 flux)

RACIAL TRAITS

Humans have no racial traits. This is both an advantage and a disadvantage. Purebloods are unmarked by magic, but are not eligible for potential bonuses that might come in handy during the adventure.

Sylvant

Sylvants have been touched by the magic unleashed by the Disjunction. They are shorter than normal humans, and often display pointed ears, metallic gold or silver hair, and tanned to dark-brown skin. Sylvants trace their ancestry to humans bound with powerful elemental spirits and possess a superior magical potential.

Sylvants have a gift for using magic and are the best choices for those wishing to live the wizard's life. Their racial traits give them advantages over other races when it comes to wielding the powers of fire, ice, and electricity. They also make strong spell-casting fighters, but are not the best choice for those wishing to don the largest sword and heaviest armor. Sylvants are easy to spot, so they're persecuted for their magical heritage and many consider them heretics.

STARTING ATTRIBUTES

Strength	3 (min 1/max 9)	Intelligence	7 (min 3/max 10)
Perception	5 (min 1/max 10)	Agility	5 (min 1/max 10)
Endurance	4 (min 1/max 10)	Luck	5 (min 2/max 10)
Charisma	7 (min 2/max 10)	Unused Points	5 (30 flux)

RACIAL TRAITS

Every Sylvant must select one racial trait. Sylvant racial traits mark the bearer as tainted by magic, causing many people to react negatively toward that person. Sylvants cannot pass themselves off as purebloods.

Bond of Nature

Your magical connection to the Earth is strong, so casting Tribal Magic spells is easier. Tribal Magic spells cost 10 percent less Mana to cast. This connection makes it more difficult to cast Divine Spells, which cost 10 percent more to cast. This trait marks you as tainted by magic and causes some people to react negatively to you.

Dark Gift

Your family line has been touched by the Dark Beyond. This closeness to the dark side gives you a deeper understanding of others. You receive a 15-point bonus to your Speech skill. However, your dark affinity has separated you from some magical presence. All Thought Magic spells cost 10 percent more Mana to cast. This trait marks you as tainted by magic and causes some people to react negatively to you.

Earth Ancestry

Your skin is crusted over with stone and your hands are as hard as rock. You gain +1 to unarmed damage, but your movement rate decreases by 10 percent. This trait marks you as tainted by magic and causes some people to react negatively to you.

Fiery Ancestry

One of your parents had a strong affinity for fire. Elemental magic exudes from you. You get a 10 percent bonus in the ability to inflict Fire damage, and your Fire Resistance is increased by 20 percent. You also suffer a 20 percent penalty to Cold Resistance and all Cold damage you do is reduced by 10 percent. This trait marks you as tainted by magic and causes some people to react negatively to you.

Frost Ancestry

A frost spirit entered your family many years ago. Elemental magic exudes from you. You get a 10 percent bonus in the ability to inflict Cold damage, and your Cold Resistance is increased by 20 percent. You also suffer a 20 percent penalty to Fire Resistance and all Fire damage you do is reduced by 10 percent. This trait marks you as tainted by magic and causes some people to react negatively to you.

Gossamer Skin

Your skin is fair, almost translucent. This allows you to sneak well, granting a bonus of +15 to your Sneak skill. Your delicate skin is more vulnerable to attack, however, so you take more damage from Slashing weapons. Slashing Resistance is reduced by 10 percent. This trait marks you as tainted by magic and causes some people to react negatively to you.

Polyelemental

Your family has been tainted by multiple elemental spirits throughout the years, mixing powers and passing down various abilities. Add 10 percent to your Acid, Cold, Disease, Fire, and Poison Resistances, but suffer a 5 percent penalty to your Crushing, Piercing, and Slashing Resistances. This trait marks you as tainted by magic and causes some people to react negatively to you.

Skin of Thorns

Thorny growths erupt from your body at odd angles and in uncomfortable places. Luckily, these thorns break off and grow back easily. Anyone who attacks you gets a face full of pain. Even archers take damage from this thorny strike. You give back to your attacker 10 percent of physical damage given to you. You also receive a 10 percent bonus to your Crushing, Piercing and Slashing Resistances. The downside is that your Charisma reduces by 1 and your Acid, Cold, Disease, Electrical, Fire, and Poison Resistances decrease by 10 percent. This trait marks you as tainted by magic and causes some people to react negatively to you. This trait requires a Charisma of 3 or higher.

Storm of Arrows

The introduction of a storm spirit into your family line has given you lightning reflexes and incredible hand-eye coordination. You deal +2 damage with bows and crossbows. You are so focused on fighting at a distance, however, that you have a predisposition not to fight well in close quarters. You receive a 10 percent penalty to Crushing and Slashing Resistances. This trait marks you as tainted by magic and causes some people to react negatively to you.

Wind Ancestry

The taint of a wind elemental in your bloodline grants you swiftness. You gain +1 to your Agility and +10 to AC. But you are less substantial than other Sylvants, so you suffer a 1-point penalty to Strength and your carrying capacity reduces by 20 pounds. This trait marks you as tainted by magic and causes some people to react negatively to you. This trait requires a Strength of 2 or higher.

SPECIAL TRAITS

Special traits are those that your character has acquired because of a lifestyle or life-altering event that occurred before this adventure began. Unlike racial traits, you're never required to select any of these traits, but you may choose as many as two of them if you wish. Be careful what you choose. Special traits provide excellent bonuses, but also have negative side effects. For instance, increasing your ability with one weapon type may reduce your effectiveness with another.

Special traits are invaluable if you have a well-developed idea of what your character is to become, because you can sacrifice skills you don't plan on using and enhance the ones you intend to focus on.

Arrows for Words

Pick 'em off first, and when they're wounded and dying in the dirt, put the hard questions to them. Add 15 points to your Ranged Weapons skill, but you suffer a 10-point penalty to your Speech skill and a 10-point penalty to your Thieving/Barter skill.

Ascetic

Living several years with an austere monastic order taught you focus and patience—the monks "encouraged" you to study for long hours. This arduous training grants you +10 skill points, reflecting the broad range of studies you pursued at the monastery. You never forgot the hard lifestyle of the monks, however, so you don't feel right about accumulating too much gold. Over the course of your adventure, you find 10 percent less wealth.

Fast Metabolism

Your metabolic rate is faster than normal. You are more susceptible to Disease and Poison damage, but your body heals faster. Your Disease and Poison Resistances start at -10 percent. Feralkins cannot take this trait.

Finesse

Your attacks show a lot of finesse. You don't do as much damage, but you cause more critical hits. Your physical attacks do -20 percent damage. Your critical chance is +10 percent. Cannot be combined with Heavy-Handed.

Gifted

You have more innate abilities than most, so you have not spent as much time honing your skills. Your statistics are better than the average person's, but non-magic skills are lacking. Attributes have a +1 modifier, and no attribute is allowed to exceed 10. Non-magic skills are reduced by 10 points. You receive 4 fewer skill points per level.

Good-Natured

Your natural charm allowed you to get along with everyone while growing up. You rarely got into fights and spent more time hitting the books instead. Your combat skills start at a lower level, but your Thieving/Barter skill improves, with a 35-point bonus. You also get a 5-point penalty to starting melee combat skills (One-Handed, Two-Handed, and Unarmed). Cannot be selected with Nasty Disposition.

Heavy-Handed

You swing harder, not better. Your attacks are brutal, but lack finesse. You rarely cause a good critical hit, but you always do more melee damage. You do +2 points of damage in melee combat (hand-to-hand or non-ranged weapons). Your critical hit chance receives a 30 percent penalty. Cannot be combined with Finesse.

Nasty Disposition

Your quick temper got you into fights while growing up. You suffer a 15-point penalty to your Speech and Thieving/Barter skills, but your Unarmed, One-Handed, and Two-Handed Melee skills each get a 10-point bonus. You cannot have both Nasty Disposition and Good-Natured traits.

One-Handed

One of your hands is dominant. You excel with one-handed weapons, but two-handed weapons cause a problem. You suffer a 10-point penalty to your Two-Handed Weapon and Ranged Weapon skills but get a 10-point bonus to your One-Handed Weapon skill.

Renaissance Man

You're a connoisseur of the arts, a deep thinker, and willing to give new ideas a go, but your highbrow intellectualism doesn't mean much when you get punched in the face. You gain +1 to Intelligence, but suffer a 10-point penalty to One-Handed and Two-Handed Melee, Ranged Weapon, and Unarmed skills. Your Armor Class (AC) also decreases by 3. Feralkins may not take this trait.

Skilled

You spend more time improving your existing skills than anyone else would. The tradeoff is that you do not gain as many extra abilities. Every time you level up, you get 3 additional skill points, but you gain a new Perk every four levels instead of every three.

Small Frame

You are not as big as others of your race, but that never hampered you. You may not be able to carry as much, but you are more agile. You get a +1 bonus to your Agility, but your carrying capacity is 50 pounds less than normal. This trait requires that your Strength be 3 or higher. Feralkins may not take this trait.

Studious Tinkerer

You spent your formative years hunched over a workbench, tinkering with random bits of magical things that nobody else would touch. Trouble is, you've ruined your eyes! You get a 15-point bonus to your Lockpick skill, and spell branches that you spend skill points in start out at skill level 4 instead of skill level 1. You suffer a -1 penalty to Perception, and your Ranged Weapons skill is reduced by 10 points. This addition does not apply to items that add skill points to magical skills.

Thick-Skinned

Your skin is calloused, more so than your peers'. Add 5 percent to damage resistances and 4 to your AC. But you have a thick head as well and suffer a -1 penalty to Intelligence and a 10-point penalty to your Lockpick skill.

GUARDIAN SPIRITS

As the scion of *Lionheart*, you have a powerful spirit within you. This spirit manifests itself from time to time in one of three forms: elemental, bestial, or demonic. Which of the three spirits you choose is up to you. The only benefit of picking one over another is that each spirit has a propensity for a particular type of magic. Elemental favors Divine Magic, bestial favors Tribal Magic, and demonic favors Thought Magic. A 1-point bonus is attributed to the spell branches under the type of magic your spirit prefers. If you choose the elemental spirit, for example, you automatically begin the game with at least 1 point in every Divine Magic branch.

This isn't a huge bonus, so if you prefer the voice and attitude of one spirit rather than another, but prefer to use a different magic, the loss of one point isn't devastating.

SKILLS

You define your character's role by assigning skill points to one of many skills as you gain levels. The more points you put into one skill, the better you become at it. The skills are broken into five groups: Fighting, Thieving/Barter, Divine Magic, Thought Magic, and Tribal Magic. Each type of magic has several branches under which you can learn four or five spells. As you pump skill points into a spell branch, you increase the power of spells you already know and learn new spells along the way.

No character is able to master every skill, so specialization in a few select skills with a basic knowledge of a few others is normal. Which skills you should choose can only be determined by knowing what sort of character you wish to create.

Fighting Skills

If magic isn't your thing, you may want to become a fighting machine. If the way of the warrior is for you, check out these physical combat skills.

> **NOTE** *Even spell casters need to be skilled with at least one type of weapon. You never know when Mana will run low in the middle of a battle and steel will be your only option. A skill of 105 is sufficient for most spell casters.*

UNARMED

This represents your ability to fight without a weapon. A skilled Unarmed combatant is a deadly foe. Specializing in unarmed combat allows you to avoid carrying heavy weaponry, but you lack the versatility of someone skilled with One- or Two-Handed Melee weapons. All damage caused is Crushing damage, where as other warriors can switch between Slashing and Crushing weapons as easily as changing socks. Unarmed fighters also lack the benefit of magical enhancements placed on weaponry. Still, a strong pugilist is one of the fiercest and fastest combatants available, and fists are as devastating as the largest enchanted hammer.

ONE-HANDED MELEE

This represents your ability to use and fight with any weapon that needs one hand to wield, such as a sword or a mace. Those who specialize in one-handed weapons may not be as strong as Unarmed or Two-Handed Melee fighters, but they have the advantage of being able to carry a shield. When one chooses between One-Handed and Two-Handed Melee, the choice is between higher AC verses higher attack power. You rely on your ability to prevent damage, rather than eliminating enemies to minimize damage. One-handed weapons also are faster and lighter than their larger cousins. A major advantage to One-Handed Melee versus Unarmed combat is that the fighter can switch between Slashing and Crushing weapons to take advantage of enemy weaknesses.

TWO-HANDED MELEE

This represents your ability to use and fight with any weapon that requires two hands to wield, such as a Two-Handed Sword or Battle Axe. Two-handed weapons cause a great deal of damage, but they're slow and cumbersome. They also prevent the user from carrying a shield, so the user must sacrifice some AC for a high attack power. Two-handed prowess is best chosen by strong fighters who can handle the extra weight and have the endurance to go toe-to-toe with fierce beasts and mighty warriors. A wise warrior carries both a hammer and an axe, to be able to switch between Crushing and Slashing damage and take advantage of various enemy weaknesses.

RANGED WEAPONS

This represents your ability to use and fight with ranged weapons such as bows and crossbows. There is no penalty for using a ranged weapon at point-blank range. Ranged weapons are slower and less powerful than other weapons. They cause Piercing damage, which is ineffective against strong undead creatures. Though ranged weapons require arrows or bolts, Arrows or Bolts of Infinity are provided, so ammunition is always available.

To take full advantage of a Ranged Weapon skill, magically enchanted arrows and bolts are required. These are expensive, but they are necessary only for very tough creatures and bosses, not for the most basic creatures encountered during your adventures. Ranged weapons shine in areas with ledges or divides where the user can stand in safety and pick off enemies from a distance. Fast archers can run from enemies, take a few shots from a safe distance, and run again before the enemy can get into attack range.

EVASION

This represents your ability to evade blows during combat, and increases your Armor Class at high levels. Evasion allows characters to dodge enemy attacks rather than block them. This is important for characters who choose to wear lighter armor, such as thieves who sneak through the shadows unnoticed, or combatants who wish to remain speedy. Though it does nothing to protect against magic, at high levels it allows a character to dodge shots from even the most skilled warriors.

Thieving and Diplomacy

Stick to the shadows, or talk your way out of a tight spot. Try out these roguish skills, which represent your ability to manipulate verbal and environmentally related encounters.

FIND TRAPS/SECRET DOORS

This represents your ability to detect hidden treasure, traps, and secret doors. Don't overlook this skill. While important for rogues, all characters benefit from this skill. There are many treasures hidden throughout the game. Not only do they provide some fantastic armor, weaponry, and accessories, but you get experience each time you discover a hidden item or trap. Even the most grizzled warrior should be searching the area when not involved in a battle.

> **TIP** *Finding traps, treasures, and secret doors is fun and rewarding. Even if you don't aspire to play a rogue, boost your Find Traps/Secret Doors skill and Lockpick skill to 100. If you don't want to use the skill points in this fashion, find items you can equip when you need a quick boost to these skills and keep them on hand. It's also possible to buy potions that temporarily increase your Thieving Barter skill. Secret treasures, doors, and traps are noted throughout the guide. An exceptionally high skill isn't necessary in most cases, because you already know where to look.*

LOCKPICK

This represents your ability to pick locks. Increasing this skill allows you to pick any lock previously marked as too complex. An increase can come in any form. Spending skill points, equipping a piece of armor that enhances the skill, or drinking a potion can change the level sufficiently to allow another attempt at a lock. Locks vary in difficulty from very easy to nearly impossible. The tougher the lock, the more experience you earn when you pick it.

SNEAK

This represents your ability to sneak around without being detected. By sneaking past an enemy, you can earn up to 75 percent of the experience points available from it. The remainder must be earned by slaying it. Use Sneak to slip through dangerous areas without being detected, or to reach an advantageous position before engaging in combat. It's useful in areas where archers are protected from attacks, but can still target anyone walking past. It's also used to steal from chests without drawing the attention of those nearby. This is useful when robbing merchants or anyone else you wish to clean out without causing them to attack. Save your game before attempting to steal from anyone, especially while in Barcelona where one false move could cause every guard to turn against you.

SPEECH

This represents your ability to convince others that your way is the right way. This skill falls under the Diplomacy group and increases with the Thieving/Barter skill. Speech is important for those who wish to fully experience the game. A high Speech skill gives you a wider variety of options when dealing with NPCs, and you often can outwit opponents rather than fighting them. A high Speech skill affects the end of the game.

THIEVING/BARTER

This represents your ability to get cheaper prices when buying items and strike deals with people you encounter. Thieving/Barter is an easy skill to overlook, because it affects one's coin purse. However, bartering is a powerful tool, especially when working with a group. One player with a high Thieving/Barter skill can ensure the team gets as much gold as possible for its bounty and can equip the entire team for less. Even when you play alone, the difference is notable.

Divine Magic

This Magic Discipline gains its power from a spiritual source. This is the most physical of the spell types, and complements fighter characters the most.

DIVINE FAVOR BRANCH

Reciting these spells grants the caster spiritual favor, strengthening the sword, steadying the hand, or summoning a goodly knight to come to the caster's assistance. This line is helpful to One-Handed Melee and Ranged Weapons specialists.

- Divine Might
- Blessed Aim
- Greater Sight
- Divine Power
- Spiritual Knight

FORTITUDE BRANCH

These spells enable the caster to call upon divine power to fortify constitution, to heal, or to grant resistance to physical harm. This line is clerical in nature and essential for a group. A high healing ability allows a character to maintain the health of comrades in battle.

- Healing
- Purify Body
- Resist Elements
- Divine Assistance
- Greater Resistance

SMITE BRANCH

Calling upon the power of the celestial host, the caster can bring down the wrath of the heavens upon foes. Use this set in group settings, in which someone else can focus on the attack. While these spells are helpful to solo warriors, a warrior's limited Mana supply prevents their frequent use.

- Weaken Enemies
- Cripple Enemies
- Celestial Smite
- Exorcism
- Righteous Fury

PROTECTIVE BRANCH

Spells from this branch wrap the caster in a divine cloak, protecting the caster from enemies and harming those foolish enough to attempt to do harm. Any warrior worried about AC will find this a favorable branch. It's a great way for thieves and other warriors who choose to wear light armor to bolster their defenses without overburdening themselves.

- Aid
- Physical Aura
- Holy Fire
- Mana Shield

Tribal Magic

This Magic Discipline is powered by the Earth's awakening. Rocks, trees, and other parts of the environment release energy absorbed during the Disjunction.

DOMINATION BRANCH

This spell branch grants the power to control the minds of others. This is a great support branch that works best in group settings. One person can focus on weakening monsters while others go on the attack.

- Slow
- Discord
- Sleep
- Dominate

NECROMANCY

The dark arts of Necromancy beckon to the intrepid wizard who dares to unlock them. These spells give casters the power to call forth frightful creatures from beyond the grave. Pure Necromancers are weak at the start, because the Raise Enemy and Corpse Bomb spells aren't powerful until boosted. Well-developed Necromancers are fierce opponents on the battlefield. Should you choose this path, develop your Ranged Weapon skill to aid your creatures in battle without having to stand on the frontline.

- Raise Enemy
- Corpse Bomb
- Raise Undead
- Undead Energy
- Vampire

NATURE'S FURY BRANCH

Nature is red in tooth and claw, a maxim reflected by this branch of spells. This is a great branch for fighters of all types in that it allows the warrior to increase damage, scout areas before entering, and call on a companion when necessary.

- Feral Lash
- Shamans Eye
- Balance of Nature
- Monster Summoning
- Insect Plague

PROTECTIVE BRANCH

These spells allow the caster to be as quick and cagey as a fox, or tough and resilient as a rhino. This is a good branch for thieves. It allows for a large Sneak bonus and improves Agility. Absorb Spirit is also a unique way to heal battle damage, although not as effective as other healing spells.

- Absorb Spirit
- Shroud of Darkness
- Armor of Bones
- Animal Grace
- Mana Shield

Thought Magic

This Magic Discipline gains power by channeling the arcane magical spells and abilities that leaked through from the Disjunction. This magical type is the most aggressive.

ELECTRICAL BRANCH

These spells channel the wild energies of electrical storms into explosive torrents of magical power. Electricity is powerful on the battlefield and can stun and paralyze opponents.

- Static Charge
- Electrical Burst
- Lightning Bolt
- Lightning Storm
- Thunder Clap

FIRE BRANCH

The disciplines of fire char the caster's foes, reducing them to ash and smoke. Fire is the most damaging of spells. It allows the caster to cause direct damage to a target and secondary damage a few moments later. Any would-be wizard should consider this line of spells.

- Fire Orb
- Dragon's Breath
- Fire Circle
- Fireball

ICE BRANCH

The caster can focus the terrible power of deepest winter into physical projectiles that chill and rend foes. Ice not only causes extensive damage, but also has the added effect of sometimes slowing opponents. This is a great line of spells for those casters working with warriors.

- Frost Spike
- Ice Javelin
- Ice Ring
- Ice Missile
- Ice Storm

PROTECTIVE BRANCH

The clever Thought mage is careful to protect the physical form with these spells while engaged in burning or freezing enemies. This protective branch is best suited for those who can be described as battle mages, skilled in magic and with weaponry. It allows for a fighter to cause indirect damage to multiple creatures while focusing on a single enemy.

- Magical Shield
- Poison Ring
- Halo of Frost
- Halo of Fire
- Mana Shield

> **TIP** *For detailed information on spells, check the spells appendix in the back of the guide.*

PERKS

As a character progresses in level, he or she earns special Perks every few levels. Perks are similar to traits except that Perks have no downside—other than trying to choose between them. They are the primary attributes that can turn an ordinary character into an unstoppable force.

Each character has different Perks available, based on the character's level and the level of individual skills. For instance, if you choose to focus on Unarmed combat, Perks that only provide benefits to Unarmed fighters are available as your prowess improves. These can include bonus damage, improved Chance to Hit, faster attacks, and more critical hits. Each skill has Perks that are specifically related to it. The back of the guide has detailed information on Perks. Pay close attention to the requirements when plotting your character's growth.

BASIC CHARACTER TYPES

Now let's consider some basic character types and what skill sets and attributes are best suited to each.

The Barbarian

The mightiest of the mighty, the toughest of the tough, the muscle-bound hero with the bloodstained axe. Barbarians are the steamrollers of the fantasy world, able to carve through hordes of monsters and brush off wounds that would disable a lesser combatant.

Race: Feralkin
Racial Trait: Wolf Hide or Regeneration
Strength: 10
Perception: 5
Endurance: 9
Charisma: 2
Intelligence: 4
Agility: 6
Luck: 5
Special Traits: Nasty Disposition, Thick-Skinned, or Heavy-Handed
Tag Skills: Tribal Magic (Nature's Fury), Fighting (Two-Handed Melee and Evasion)

This character's focus is to cause as much damage as possible with two-handed weapons. This warrior beast relies on power rather than intellect and social skills, and never flees from a battle. This is an excellent choice when playing in a group.

The Paladin

Pious to a fault, righter of wrongs, the ultimate do-gooder with a head full of high ideals. Paladins are strong fighters, but also possess basic magic abilities that allow them to assist others and themselves.

Race: Human
Racial Trait: None
Strength: 8
Perception: 5
Endurance: 8
Charisma: 4
Intelligence: 5
Agility: 6
Luck: 5
Special Traits: One-Handed Melee and Finesse
Tag Skills: Fighting (One-Handed Melee and Evasion), Divine Magic (Fortitude)

This combatant relies on a higher AC and critical chance in exchange for less damage. This also requires specialization in a line of spells that can heal and bolster defenses when facing strong enemies.

The Martial Artist

Deceptively powerful and hard to hit, martial artists are among the strongest fighters and quickly develop. They are excellent solo fighters, and make good use of Thieving/Barter skill and magic.

Race: Feralkin
Racial Trait: Tusks
Strength: 10
Perception: 6
Endurance: 8
Charisma: 1
Intelligence: 3

Agility: 8
Luck: 5
Special Traits: Heavy-Handed and Nasty Disposition
Tag Skills: Fighting (Unarmed and Evasion), Tribal Magic (Nature's Fury)

Martial artists are powerful fighters. When properly developed, they can cause unbelievable amounts of damage. They suffer in that they exclusively deal in Crushing damage. It's important to develop the Ranged Weapons skill enough so that the martial artist has something to fall back on when facing enemies resistant to Crushing damage.

The Necromancer

Dark and creepy, shunned by society, surrounded by an evil stench. Though Necromancers aren't well-liked in the world of *Lionheart*, they're among the fiercest of magic users. They are normally regarded as evil, but you aren't required to sell your soul to study the dark arts.

Race: Sylvant
Racial Trait: Bond of Nature
Strength: 3
Perception: 7
Endurance: 4
Charisma: 9
Intelligence: 8

Agility: 5
Luck: 5
Special Traits: Gifted and Renaissance Man
Tag Skills: Tribal Magic (Necromancy), Fighting (Ranged Weapons), Thieving/Barter (Diplomacy)

This character focuses on the ability to create minions to do close-range fighting, and builds a fair Ranged Weapons skill for support. Because Necromancers aren't as effective in combat, the ability to persuade others comes in handy for avoiding battles and taking advantage of the weak-minded.

The Wizard

Harnessing the power of the elements, the wizard lays waste to the enemy's evil minions. The wizard is the most powerful of spell casters, but frailer than most adventurers. While such characters excel in groups, being a young wizard on your own can be a trying experience.

Race: Sylvant
Racial Trait: Fiery Ancestry
Strength: 3
Perception: 7
Endurance: 3
Charisma: 9

Intelligence: 8
Agility: 6
Luck: 5
Special Traits: Gifted and Renaissance Man
Tag Skills: Thought Magic (Fire and Protective), Thievery/Barter (Diplomacy)

Because of the wizard's low number of hit points, specializing in the Protective Branch of the Thought Magic Discipline is important. It helps keep the caster alive when fighting alone. If working with a group, you can trade this out for a weapon skill such as Ranged Weapons or One-Handed Melee. Though casters grow to be powerful, they're initially difficult to play. Develop your main attack magic skill first and other skills second, or develop weapon skill first, then work on developing a magical offense.

The Rogue

Slipping through the shadows, the nimble thief sneaks past enemies and relieves the wealthy of the burden of their fortunes. Though not as skilled in combat, a rogue often talks through tough situations or avoids them. Still, not all situations can be resolved with a silver tongue and fast hands.

Race: Demokin
Racial Trait: Shroud of Darkness
Strength: 3
Perception: 8
Endurance: 4
Charisma: 8

Intelligence: 4
Agility: 9
Luck: 5
Special Traits: Small Frame and Finesse
Tag Skills: Thievery (Sneak), Find Traps/Secret Doors, and Lockpick

Because a rogue sticks to the shadows, combat skills are often neglected and confrontation is avoided when possible. Rogues should master the thieving arts, focusing on the ability to Sneak. Pick one weapon skill to develop. Ranged or one-handed weapons work best. This is a fun, but challenging path to take.

TAKE CONTROL OF YOUR DESTINY

These are a few suggestions on how to develop a character. Be anything you want to be. If you're playing with friends online, talk to each other and define your roles ahead of time. You can avoid overlapping without reason and ensure a well-rounded party. When playing alone, you must provide for all of your basic needs. A well-rounded character is essential to your survival, and makes the game more entertaining in the long run.

Beginner's Guide to Nuevo Barcelona

FROM HUMBLE BEGINNINGS

Your entry into the world of *Lionheart* is anything but glamorous. Held in a dank pit within a stony cell, you await the moment when your captors hand you over to the Inquisition. There you'll undoubtedly be tortured until death takes you or your mind is broken. Then fate intervenes and you're suddenly whisked away, penniless and wounded, but alive and free.

As you take those first few steps from slave to hero, Barcelona may seem like an enormous city. Walking into such an unfamiliar land alone and nearly naked can be frightening. But your worries are over. In this section, we provide everything you need to know about adventuring in *Lionheart* so you can step into an unknown universe with confidence.

EXPLORATION AND INTERACTION

Nuevo Barcelona and the surrounding world are huge areas of untamed wilds and budding cities. The adventure begins in Barcelona. There's no need to wander immediately into the wilderness and into the waiting arms of bloodthirsty Goblins or savage beasts. Take time to explore the city.

Merchants have a variety of equipment and potions to sell, interesting people have tales of woe and daring escapades, and these will become long-term allies as you battle the forces of evil.

Crossing Borders and Entering/Exiting Buildings

Not all buildings can be entered, but many are open to you. If the doors are locked, you can pick the locks to gain entry. To identify doors that can be entered, move the cursor over the opening. If the building can be entered, the icon changes to an opening door. Left-click, and if the door is unlocked, you enter the structure. If it's locked, a message appears. If your Lockpick skill is high enough, you can then attempt to pick the lock.

NOTE *Be careful when breaking into areas when you're at a low level. Some buildings house unfriendly NPCs who object to being disturbed.*

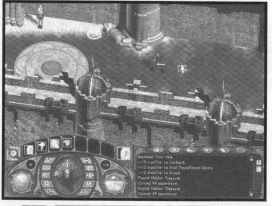

The game has many different areas. Barcelona is divided into three parts: Gate District, Temple District, and Port. Alleys lead between each area. When you near the map's edge, a circling green arrow is added to the cursor. Left-click in this area to leave the current area and enter the next. In most cases, you can cross from one area to another at any time.

NOTE *Enemies cannot cross between areas. If you're outmatched in a battle, flee to a different area. Summoned creatures also cannot cross between areas. If you cross while a summoned creature is under your command, the creature is destroyed. Other companions, such as NPCs met during your adventure, can follow you between areas.*

Conversing with NPCs

To converse with someone, place the cursor over the NPC and a turning bubble with an exclamation point is added to the cursor. Left-click on the NPC, and the person either makes a short statement or begins a conversation.

Once a conversation has begun, you may be presented with a selection of replies based upon your character's Speech and Thieving/Barter skills, Charisma, and knowledge of events that may pertain to the NPC, such as a quest. You'll notice small icons next to some of the responses.

- **Exclamation Point (Blue):** This indicates a response that came up in dialogue because of the player's Speech skill.

- **Open Book (Yellow):** This indicates a quest-related response. This response either leads to the conclusion of a quest, is an important part of a quest, or is the offering of a quest.

- **Sword (Red):** Hostile response. This response won't necessarily lead to a fight, but it indicates an aggressive tone.

- **3 Gold Bars:** This indicates a response that came up because of a player attribute, such as high Strength or high Endurance.

- **Two Arrows (Light Blue):** This indicates a response that came up in dialogue because of the player's Thieving/Barter skill.

- **Circular Arrow (Green):** Attempt to end the conversation. This indicates the player's intent; some characters could continue conversation even if the player wanted to say goodbye.

> **NOTE** *How you interact with characters impacts the game. Think about this before choosing the rudest response. What do you want your character to become?*

Chests

Chests containing treasure are in nearly every part of the world. To open a chest, place the cursor over the container. The outer ring spins as the box flashes. Left-click and your character attempts to open it. If successful, any items inside the chest fall onto the ground. If the chest is locked, a message appears. You can then attempt to pick the lock.

Many chests have owners. Look to see if anyone is standing nearby. If so, chances are good that they'll be upset if you steal their belongings, and a fight will ensue. Remember this when working with merchants. Skilled thieves can steal from such chests without being noticed by using their Sneak skill in combination with Lockpick skill, but there are always risks involved.

EQUIPMENT

Adventurers have a natural tendency to become packrats throughout their adventures. There are so many powerful swords, axes, bows, and pieces of armor that choosing what to keep isn't always easy.

What to Wear

With a few exceptions, every adventurer can equip the same gear, no matter which course of development they choose. One can wear a breastplate, gauntlets or bracers, belt, boots, helmet, necklace, two rings, shield, and a weapon. Within each of these categories are thousands of choices. Knowing which is best can be determined by considering your character's skills.

Items are either non-magical or enchanted. Enchanted items provide bonuses to a character's attack, defense, skills, and in rare cases even attributes. Even basic armor has bonuses and penalties that can affect AC, movement speed, and skills.

The main things to consider when choosing gear are your weight limit, the bonuses granted by the items, and any penalties. Thieves can wear plate armor, but suffer from the weight. One-handed weapons specialists can carry huge shields that grant a substantial AC bonus, but they may dislike the added encumbrance. Archers can wear helmets, but it reduces their sight range, making it difficult to target enemies from a distance. When choosing your gear, consider what you want your character to become and which factors are most important to you.

COMBAT

No matter what type of character you choose to play, eventually you have to battle. When that time comes, you want to be well prepared.

Friend or Foe

Place the cursor over an NPC, and one of two things happens. Either the cursor changes to the conversation icon (a spinning bubble with an exclamation point inside) or it splits into four pieces with a red cross in the center. The split cursor lets you know that the NPC you're targeting is hostile and can be attacked without having to force the attack. If a creature is hostile, it attacks as soon as it sees you, so attack when you are within its sight range and not behind an obstacle.

Targeting

To target and attack an NPC, place the cursor over the hostile NPC so that the cursor splits into the attack cursor, then left-click on the NPC. If you're using a melee weapon and have a clear path to the NPC, your character automatically moves into striking distance and attacks. If your character has no clear path, you do not attempt to reach the target. Once an NPC has been selected as a target, your character attacks the target until it is defeated or your character dies.

If you cast a spell during combat, be it a support or attack spell, you must retarget your enemy to continue the attack. Moving also breaks the attack. It isn't necessary to continually click the mouse to attack or to hold the button. This is done automatically.

TIP *If you hold* shift *down when left-clicking on an enemy, the character will not move if the left-click is accidentally on the ground instead of the enemy.*

Damage Types and Resistances

There are three basic types of damage, not counting damage caused by magic. These are Slashing, Crushing, and Piercing. Slashing Damage is related to weapons with blades, such as swords or axes. Blunt weapons like hammers, maces, and morning stars cause Crushing Damage, as do the fists of an Unarmed warrior. Bows and crossbows use arrows and bolts that cause Piercing Damage. No melee weapons cause Piercing Damage.

No one type of damage is superior to any other, but some creatures are more susceptible to one type of damage than another. For instance, the undead are resistant to Piercing Damage. Ogres and Rock Titans are resistant to Crushing Damage. When fighting such creatures, switch to the most effective weapon.

For archers and martial artists this isn't always easy. They tend to specialize in either Unarmed or ranged combat, ignoring one and two-handed weaponry. Those who choose to study One-Handed and Two-Handed Melee can easily switch between weapons that cause Crushing and Slashing Damage. Keep one weapon of each type on hand at all times, so you can make adjustments if an enemy is resisting your attacks.

> **TIP** *One-Handed and Two-Handed Melee specialists should keep a Crushing and a Slashing Damage weapon on their hotkeys, so they can switch between them in the middle of combat.*

Health and Mana

Two of the most important factors are your character's Hit Points and Mana. Hit Points indicate the amount of damage your character can suffer before dying. Mana is used to cast spells. Each spell has a specific casting cost. If your Mana is too low, the spell is unusable until you have enough Mana to cover the casting cost.

Restoring your Hit Points by healing after battles is important. Do this by casting spells, drinking healing potions, resting and allowing your health to regenerate, or by collecting life energies (red orbs) dropped by slain opponents. Having a stock of healing potions is important, especially toward the end of the game when rapid healing is often necessary. Purchase these potions often and stockpile them until they're necessary.

It's good to have at least one healing spell at your disposal so you can take advantage of an abundance of Mana and spirit orbs (blue orbs). Increasing the rate at which your health regenerates can also conserve healing potions and Mana during a journey. This can be done through traits, Perks, and by equipping certain enchanted items.

Mana is usually in abundance, but those who rely heavily on magic inevitably run out. Mana regenerates more slowly than health, so waiting for your Mana to refill isn't an option. The easiest way to restore Mana is to collect spirit orbs dropped by slain enemies. These provide a varying supply of Mana. The size of the spirit orb suggests the amount of Mana it restores when collected.

Companions and Summoned Creatures

Though you fight alone throughout most of your single-player adventure, there are times when a companion joins you. Though they're never as tough as your Avatar, they can help draw attention away from the hero and make it easier to battle through difficult areas. Companions can't be revived once they're killed. You quickly learn which situations your companions can handle and which they can't. Summoned creatures work in a similar way, except they're expendable and they slowly drain the caster's Mana while they remain on the field.

Two keys are important when working with companions. The first is the "Companion Follow/Stop Following" key, which is found in the commands at the bottom of the screen. When you enter an area where you know your companion cannot survive for long, use this key to order him or her to stay put until you're ready to move on. This is important when escorting a defenseless person out of a dangerous area. The last thing you want them to do is wander into danger. If companions need to heal, leave them in a cleared area and pick them up later.

> **TIP** *You can have multiple companions if you can keep them alive. Use Mass Healing potions to heal your Avatar and your companions at the same time.*

If you leave your companions near where you're fighting, you can draw the enemy back to them. They join in the battle as soon as they see the enemy approach. This is safer than having them walk with you into battle. Companions are aggressive and rush headlong into situations they can't survive, and once they're on the warpath it's difficult to coax them into retreating. Once the fighting has ceased, they return to the safety of the positions in which you left them.

The second important key is the "Quick Status," also found at the bottom of the screen. When this option is on, a visual representation of every companion's health is displayed below his or her feet. You also can see how much health your enemies have remaining. This makes it easier to know when to heal and when to run.

THIEVERY

Being a rogue or dabbling in the art of thievery can be a rewarding decision. You find lots of great items, extra gold, and well-hidden secrets, and earn experience while doing it all. Even if you choose to be the noblest of characters, you should have a basic amount of skill in the Find Traps/Secret Doors and Lockpick.

Searching for Traps, Treasures, and Secret Doors

Traps and hidden treasures are nearly everywhere. When located, hidden treasures appear as green circles on the ground. Traps appear as a variety of red shapes. Secret Doors appear as glowing spots in walls. To search for treasures, traps, and doors, select the "Search for Traps and Secret Doors" button at the bottom of the screen. Speaking or fighting disables this option, but it can be reactivated when the conversation or battle is over.

Not all hidden objects are as easy to find as others. The higher your skill, the more likely you are to find things, and the faster you can locate them.

If a trap is located, it can still be triggered if you walk over it or activate the object to which it is attached. To disarm a trap, place the cursor over it and left-click. Your character walks to the trap and automatically disables it.

Lockpicking

Many doors and chests are locked and block your access to some interesting areas. When you encounter a locked object and attempt to open it, the word "locked" appears. To attempt to pick the lock, select the "Lockpick" button from the bottom of the screen and the cursor transforms into a pair of lockpicks. Left-click on the locked object. It either opens or you receive a failed message. You may fail three times before the lock jams and the "too complex" message appears.

When you receive this message, you can't try to pick the lock again until you've increased your Lockpick skill. Do this by spending skill points on the Lockpick skill, equipping armor that provides a bonus, or using a potion that temporarily increases your skill.

THE QUEST BEGINS

THE SLAVE PITS

The slavers lock you in a rusty cage in the Slave Pits, awaiting an opportunity to sell you to the Inquisition for a handsome fee. Before they can make an exchange, a mysterious demon attacks in search of the one possessing the spirit of Lionheart—which you've recently learned is you. You need a quick escape plan.

This is an excellent opportunity to explore how you can solve one situation in several ways. For every quest, there are multiple solutions—in this case, five.

The door to the cell is locked; pick the lock, or persuade the guard outside to unlock it for you. Those who practice the art of thievery may enjoy picking the lock, but it's old and rusty, so anyone can pick it with little difficulty. Sneak from the cell to the grate in the east wall and make a quick escape, or kill both of the guards.

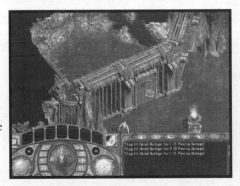

Challenging the guards is dangerous, but if you eliminate them, you find a sword and a small amount of gold, and earn a larger amount of experience.

NOTE *When you sneak past or eliminate an enemy, you earn experience. You can get up to 75 percent of a creature's experience value by sneaking past it. If the player moves quickly around an enemy, they will probably not get the entire 75 percent. To get 100 percent, defeat the creature in combat.*

By sneaking past an enemy, you can get up to 75 percent of the experience points available from it. The remainder must be earned by slaying it. If defeating a creature is worth 100 experience points, for example, you earn 75 experience points by sneaking around it. If you decide to eliminate the creature later, you only receive 25 experience points for the defeat.

If you choose to speak with the guard outside the cell, you have three speech options:

1. *I heard it friend—Let me out and I will fight alongside of you. Uhh…two shipmates like us need to stick together.*

2. *Could be Templars, coming to arrest us. We should leave before they sell us to the Inquisition.*

3. *My boot—your ass. No more noise.*

In most cases, the number of speech options available is directly related to your character's Speech skill, but in this case everyone gets the same options. Each option brings a different result.

If you persuade the guard to fight alongside you, he opens the cell door and gives you a sword before running away. A suggestion that the Templars are near causes the guard to flee, leaving you locked inside the cell. You can then pick the lock and escape. Threatening the guard prompts him to enter the cell and attack. This is risky, because the guard has a weapon and you don't.

The choice is yours, so weigh the rewards and risks. Picking the lock, then killing both guards gets you the most gold, but is the riskiest option. Suggesting that the guard fight by your side gets you the most experience with minimal risk. Other options—including picking the lock and sneaking out, or baiting the guard into a fight—work, but they offer less reward.

Throughout the game, you encounter situations in which you choose ways to perform a task. In some cases, the choice is a simple one between good and evil, right and wrong. In other cases, options allow you to earn extra gold, items, or experience. We will describe as many options as possible, but because the options are based on a character's skills, not every option may be available.

As you leave the Slave Pits, Signor Leo Da Vinci appears and uses magic to transport you to the safety of Barcelona.

BARCELONA

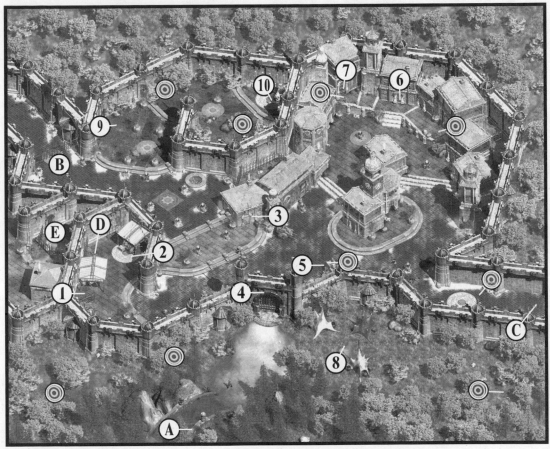

The Gate District

Ⓐ The Crossroads

Ⓑ The Temple District

Ⓒ The Port District

Ⓓ The Hidden Wall

Ⓔ La Calle Perdida

① Tainted Merchant

② Merchant (Ranged Weapons)

③ Eduardo the Blacksmith

④ Signor Leonardo Da Vinci

⑤ Lope the Merchant

⑥ Weng Choi

⑦ Quinn the Herbalist

⑧ The Saracens

⑨ Squire Santiago

⑩ Acolyte Garcia

◎ Hidden Item

The Temple District

Ⓐ The Gate District		④ The Observatory	
Ⓑ The Sewers		⑤ Machiavelli	
① The Inquisition Chambers		⑥ Noble Park Guard/Cervantes	
② The Armory (Sir Auric)		⑦ Shylock the Moneylender	
③ The Cathedral (Lord Javier Fernandez)		⑧ Inquisitor Dominguez	
		◎ Hidden Item	

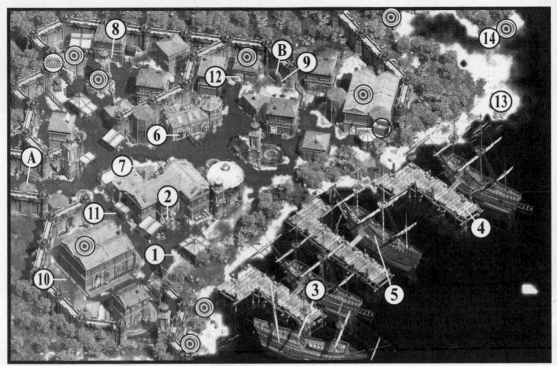

The Port District

(A) The Gate District	(9) Marisol
(B) The Sewers	(10) Benito the Thug
(1) Inquisitor Ramon de Alvarez	(11) Bartolome
(2) The Serpent's Bile	(12) Thug Selling Gem
(3) Captain Isabella	(13) Fernand Desoto
(4) Mute Sailor	(14) Fernand's Brother
(5) Duke of Medina Sidonia	Chest
(6) Signor Leo Da Vinci	Hidden Item
(7) Carlos Desoto (Fish Monger)	Trap
(8) William Shakespeare	

There are many merchants to buy from in Barcelona, but most of the items they're selling are too expensive for you. Complete some easy quests to earn some gold.

You can travel around the Gate District or go to the Port District. To enter the Temple District, however, you must speak to the Knight Squire or Inquisitor Acolyte near the Temple gates about joining their factions. Then approach one of the guards at the gates and do some name-dropping to gain entrance. You can also bribe the guards to gain entry or, if your Speech skill is very high, outwit them by pretending to be a noble.

CHOOSING A FACTION

Signor Leo Da Vinci has told you to join a faction. You have three choices—the Knights Templar, the Inquisition, or the Wielders. Align yourself with one of these factions to learn about the mysterious power within you and the forces trying to capture you. You take one of three separate paths at the beginning of the game, but when you become a full initiate, all paths merge.

KNIGHTS TEMPLAR

Within the Knights Templar, the Order of the Lion is a special sect dedicated to protecting the holy relics of the west. Members of the order are descendents of the original knights who served King Richard the Lionhearted. Very rarely, they invite outsiders who demonstrate tremendous faith and ability to join their cause.

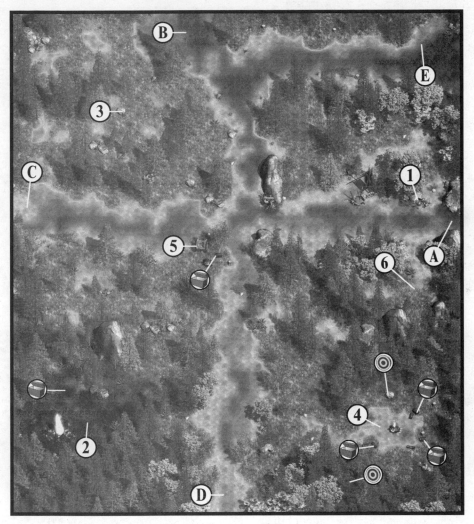

Crossroads

Ⓐ Barcelona   ③ Wasp Nest

Ⓑ Scar Ravine   ④ Thieves Camp

Ⓒ El Bosque   ⑤ Merchant

Ⓓ Rio Ebro   ⑥ Pet Bear

Ⓔ Inquisition Exterior   ⬭ Chest

① Guard Esteban   ◎ Hidden Item

② Goblin Camp

AREA ENEMIES

Black Wolf   Ramon

Brown Wolf   Tainted Wasp

Goblin   Thug Archer

Grey Wolf   Giant Wasp

Mongol Goblin

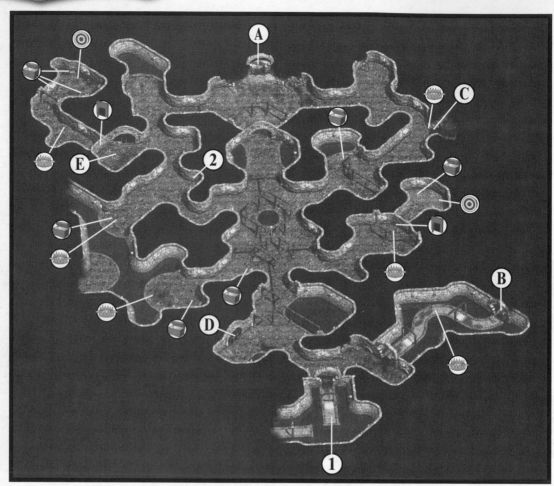

Sewers' Main Entrance

Ⓐ Temple District

Ⓑ Port District

Ⓒ Hall of Beggars

Ⓓ Dungeon

Ⓔ Thieves Congregation

① Skulker (Merchant)

② Skulker (Merchant)

🗑 Chest

◎ Hidden Item

▣ Secret Wall

⬮ Trap

AREA ENEMIES

Brittle Skeleton
Decayed Zombie
Guard Dogs
Thief
Vodyanoi
Vodyanoi Feral
Wererat

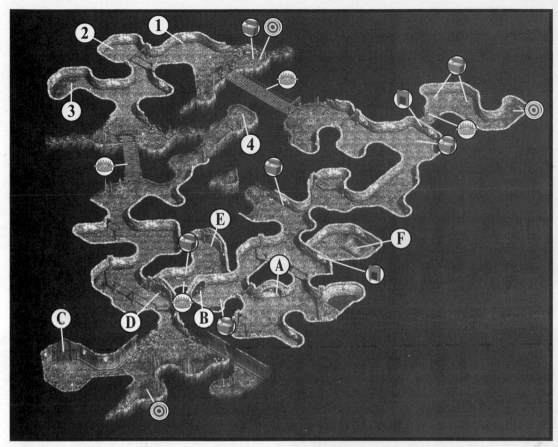

Thieves Congregation

Ⓐ Sewers' Main Entrance

Ⓑ Locked Door (Access from Other Side)

Ⓒ Unholy Oubliette

Ⓓ Doorway to Hall

Ⓔ Dungeon

Ⓕ Thieves Den

① Skulker (Merchant)

② Thief Captain Juanita Suarez

③ Thief Holding Enrique's Short Sword

④ The Lost Knight Templar

🛡 Chest

◎ Hidden Item

▣ Secret Wall

✦ Trap

AREA ENEMIES

Decayed Zombie

Guard Dogs

Thief

Thief Archer

Vodyanoi

Vodyanoi Feral

Vodyanoi Spawn

Weak Terror

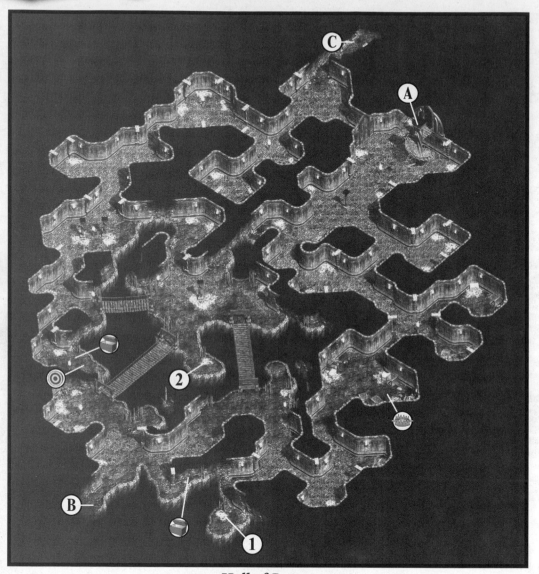

Hall of Beggars

Ⓐ Sewers Main Entrance

Ⓑ Dungeon

Ⓒ Troll Pit

① Enrique Garcia, the Beggar Leader

② Felgnash

🪙 Chest

◎ Hidden Items

AREA ENEMIES

Brittle Skeleton	Vodyanoi Feral
Decayed Zombie	Vodyanoi Spawn
Huge Brittle	Weak Terror
Skeleton	Wererat
Vodyanoi	

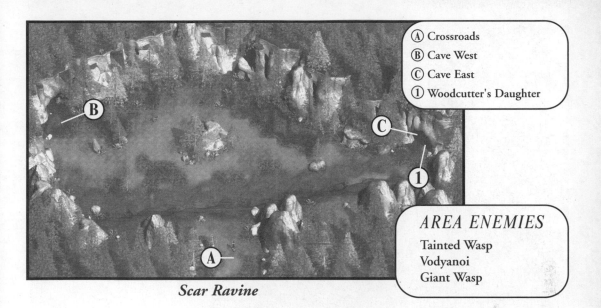

(A) Crossroads
(B) Cave West
(C) Cave East
(1) Woodcutter's Daughter

AREA ENEMIES

Tainted Wasp
Vodyanoi
Giant Wasp

Scar Ravine

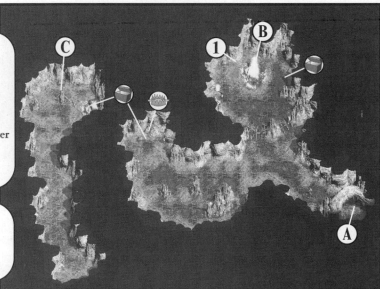

(A) Scar Ravine
(B) Magic Crystal to Ravine Cave West (Left Passage)
(C) Magic Crystal to Ravine Cave West (Near Entrance)
(1) Chest with Magnetized Silver
◉ Chest
◉ Trap

AREA ENEMIES

Tainted Wasp
Giant Wasp

Ravine Cave West

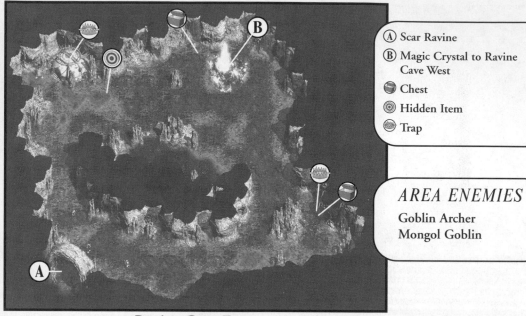

(A) Scar Ravine

(B) Magic Crystal to Ravine
    Cave West

Chest

Hidden Item

Trap

AREA ENEMIES

Goblin Archer
Mongol Goblin

Ravine Cave East

(A) Crossroads

(B) Lago Del Rio Ebro

(C) Rio Ebro

(D) Darkwood Cave

(1) Felipe the Woodcutter

AREA ENEMIES

Black Wolf
Brown Wolf
Goblin Archer
Mongol Goblin
Tainted Wasp
Giant Wasp

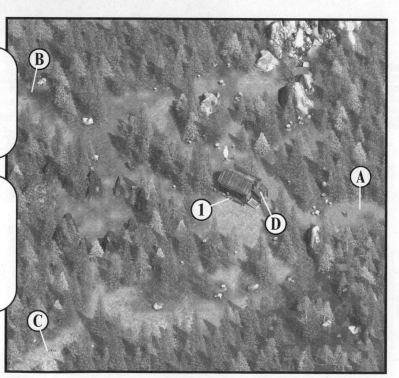

El Bosque

Lago Del Rio Ebro

(A) El Bosque
(B) Waterfall Passage
(C) Slave Pit Exterior
(D) Magic Crystal to River Dryad
(E) Magic Crystal to
Northeast Corner

(F) Skeleton Trap
(1) Goblin Grumdjum
(2) River Dryad
(3) Spaniard
Chest
Trap

AREA ENEMIES

Black Wolf
Brown Wolf
Goblin
Goblin Archer
Goblin Shaman
Mongol Goblin

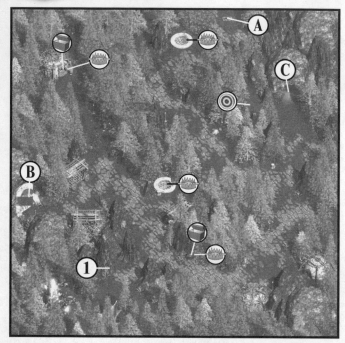

Ⓐ Lago Del Rio Ebro
Ⓑ Slave Pits
Ⓒ Wererat Cave
① Relican
◓ Chest
◉ Hidden Item
▨ Trap

AREA ENEMIES

Alpha Wererat
Goblin Archer
Mongol Goblin
Wererat

Slave Pit Exterior

Ⓐ Slave Pit Exterior
① Slaver Captain
◓ Chest
◉ Hidden Item
▨ Secret Wall

AREA ENEMIES

Elite Thug
Elite Thug Archer
Grey Wolf
Thief
Thug Archer
Thug Bowman
Slaver Captain
Vodyanoi Spawn

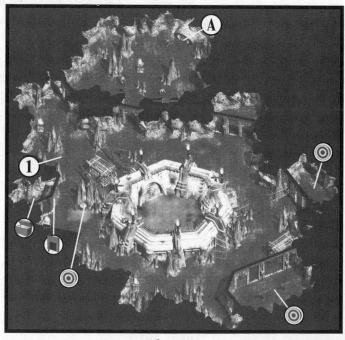

Slave Pits

Earn the Trust of Sir Auric

If the life of the Knights Templar appeals to you, speak to Sir Auric in the Temple District. To gain favor with Sir Auric, agree to track down and deal with a Thief named Benito. Sir Auric believes Benito operates in the alleys of the Port District.

You find Benito in an alley on the west side of the Port District. If your Speech skill is high, persuade him to leave peacefully or bribe him. If you fight him, Benito calls upon his comrades for aid. When you eliminate Benito, return to Sir Auric for your reward. He refers you to Lord Javier in the Cathedral for your next quest.

Knights Templar Initiation Quests

Tell Lord Javier you wish to join the Knights Templar. Before you can become an initiate, you must donate 1,000 gold pieces to the cause. If you don't have enough gold, complete some of the easier quests to earn some. Pick up everything your enemies drop and sell it to the local merchants. When you have the 1,000 gold donation, you can begin the initiation quests to become a Knight Templar.

ASSIST SIR ESTEBAN AT THE CROSSROADS

Lord Javier tasks you to find Sir Esteban, and offer your assistance. He can be found just inside the wilderness area known as the Crossroads, which is west of the Gate District beyond the walls of Barcelona.

ELIMINATE THE GOBLIN SCOUTS IN THE CROSSROADS

Sir Esteban tasks you to destroy all the Goblins in the Crossroads. The first Goblins appear when your conversation with Sir Esteban ends, so save your game before speaking to him.

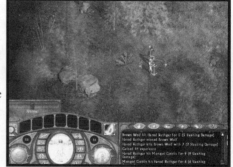

Travel to the southwest part of the Crossroads to destroy the remaining Goblins. Beware of Wolves that attack as you advance toward the Goblins. When you have eliminated all the Goblin Scouts, report to Sir Esteban and collect your reward.

NOTE *Esteban will also reward you if you find Goblin Blood Bracers. Keep in mind that Blood Bracers are rare.*

ELIMINATE THE GIANT WASPS IN THE CROSSROADS

Speak to Sir Esteban again to learn of Giant Wasps plaguing the Crossroads. This time, you must eliminate the Giant Wasp threat in the area.

Travel northwest from Sir Esteban to find the Giant Wasp nest. Giant Wasps are dangerous, because they swarm. Magic users can pick Giant Wasps off from a distance. Warrior types should use a bow to avoid being surrounded. When you've eliminated the Giant Wasps, return to Sir Esteban and collect your reward.

HELP SIR ESTEBAN DEAL WITH THE THIEVES OF THE CROSSROADS

Sir Esteban asks that you deal with a band of Thieves plaguing the Crossroads, led by a scoundrel named Ramon, the laughing bandit. Esteban believes the bandit hides somewhere within the woods of the Crossroads.

Find Ramon and his band of Thieves in the southeast corner of the Crossroads. If your Speech skill is high enough, you can talk Ramon into leaving the Crossroads. If not, a bribe or even a battle is necessary. If you walk into the camp without talking to the leader, the Thieves attack automatically. Report back to Sir Esteban, inform him that you have dealt with Ramon and the Thieves, and claim your reward.

Return to Barcelona's Temple District and inform Lord Javier that you have completed Sir Esteban's quests. Claim your reward from Lord Javier, then report to Sir Auric in the Armory. Offer Sir Auric your assistance and complete his tasks.

FIND THE LOST KNIGHT IN THE SEWERS

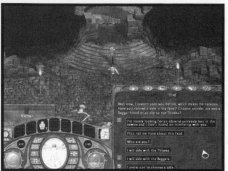

Sir Auric is concerned that a knight patrol has been lost in the Sewers. You agree to search the Sewers beneath Barcelona to learn the fate of the missing knight. Enter the Sewers through the grate on the northeast wall in the Temple District. As you enter, you witness a battle between resident Thieves and Beggars. At the end of the battle, you must choose one side to follow. If you have enough Speech skills, you can persuade the Thief that you don't wish to choose a side.

If you side with the Thieves, be prepared to battle the Beggars as you head through the twisting paths of the Sewers. If you side with the Beggars, you must defeat all the Thieves you encounter in your underground travels.

> NOTE *You can perform miscellaneous quests to assist the Thieves or the Beggars. If you choose one side or the other, you cannot undertake the quests that benefit the opposite side.*

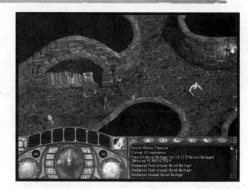

Travel to the lift. To activate it, pull the chain next to it. Enter the lift and descend to the lower level.

Leave the lift and head first north, then south to the lost knight. If you sided with the Beggars, you must defeat many Thieves in this area before you reach your destination.

If you are battling your way through the Sewers, pick up any items your enemies drop. Merchants in the Sewers have a limited supply of items for sale. More important, selling some of the items gets rid of excess weight.

Don't go directly to the lost knight. Instead, go south of his location, clearing a path that leads to a door Unlock that door and clear traps from the path leading to the lift. When you clear the area, return to the lost knight.

Escort the lost knight down the south path you just cleared. Be prepared for Thieves to attack as you lead the lost knight out of the Sewers. Keep the lost knight alive, or you fail your quest.

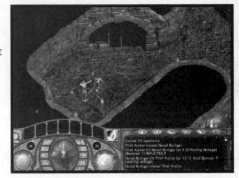

When you re-enter the Sewers, travel north, battling past Thieves to reach the exit. The lost knight leaves the Sewers and resumes his duties. Report back to Sir Auric that you found the missing knight in the Sewers and escorted him safely back to the service. Report back to Lord Javier and tell him you have completed Auric's tasks.

FORGE THE LION SHIELD

For your next task, Lord Javier tells you to forge a Lion Shield, a symbol of honor and commitment to the Knights Templar. To create the shield, you must seek out the expertise of Eduardo, the blacksmith in the Gate District.

Your Speech skill level has a dramatic effect on this task. If your Speech skill is not high enough, you may have to complete additional side quests to get Eduardo to make your Lion Shield.

Eduardo says you must perform a test of bravery to give the shield its strength. Unless you can talk him out of it, you have to retrieve Eduardo's sword from a Beggar named Felgnash. If you can dissuade Eduardo from insisting that you perform this task, he asks for gold instead. Whether you choose to demonstrate bravery or spend money, this is a comparatively easy quest to accomplish.

Travel back to the Sewers and head to the Hall of Beggars. Speak with Felgnash and persuade him to give you Eduardo's sword. If your Speech skill is high enough, you can talk Felgnash into selling you the sword for 500 gold. Return to Eduardo with the sword. If you choose to fight Felgnash for the sword, you become an enemy of the Beggars and are attacked by any Beggar you encounter.

Whether you choose to retrieve Eduardo's sword or not, another complication arises before Eduardo can work on your Lion Shield. Eduardo has all the materials he needs except for magnetized silver. Before he can complete your Lion Shield, you must retrieve the magnetized silver for Eduardo.

Recover a Supply of Silver for Eduardo

From the center of the Crossroads, travel north to Scar Ravine. Don't worry about encountering enemies when you return to the Crossroads. With a few exceptions, eliminated enemies do not return.

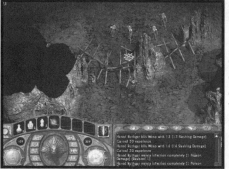

Enter Ravine Cave West and use a bow or magic to eliminate Goblins from behind the barricade. This makes it easier to clear the East Cave. You can see chests and an obelisk behind the barricade, but no way to reach this area. When you have fully explored this cave, return to Scar Ravine and travel east.

Use whatever buffs you have before entering Ravine Cave East. As soon as you enter, multiple Goblin Archers and Mongols attack. Defeat these enemies as you make your way to the Magic Crystal to travel to Ravine Cave West.

THE WOODCUTTER'S DAUGHTER

As a side quest, you can rescue the Woodcutter's daughter for experience and gold. Before traveling to Scar Ravine, travel west from the center of the Crossroads to reach El Bosque, the Woodcutter's forest. Speak with the Woodcutter and he tells you his daughter has disappeared. Offer to find her for him.

Head back to Scar Ravine, then east toward East Cave. A Goblin holds the Woodcutter's daughter captive. Defeat the Goblin and the girl runs home.

You appear behind the barricade, and must defeat all the Goblins in this area. Retrieve the magnetized silver from the chest. Touch the Magic Crystal to return to Ravine Cave East, then exit to Scar Ravine, returning to Eduardo in Barcelona.

NOTE *If you undertook the quest to rescue the Woodcutter's daughter, visit the Woodcutter after completing your task in this area to claim your reward.*

When you return the magnetized silver to Eduardo, he crafts your Lion Shield. Return to the Temple District and inform Lord Javier that you have your Lion Shield.

ELIMINATE THE SLAVER MENACE

For your final test, Lord Javier asks you to find and disrupt a slaving operation that is plaguing Barcelona. The slavers have a hidden compound in the wilderness west of Barcelona. Travel west through El Bosque to reach Lago Del Rio Ebro.

As soon as you enter Lago Del Rio Ebro, Goblin Grumdjum confronts you. Grumdjum proposes that you destroy the River Dryad located nearby. You can perform this side quest if you wish. If you refuse Grumdjum, battle him and every other Goblin in this area to the death.

For now, it's best to accept his offer. Grumdjum is a tough enemy and you aren't ready for a fight the first time you encounter him. Come back later when you're more experienced, and bring friends if possible.

> NOTE *When you eliminate the Goblins in the northeast corner, use the Magic Crystal to reach the River Dryad. This quest is outlined in detail later in this chapter.*

In the southeast corner of this area lies a Goblin camp. Beware of additional enemies that you can lure to your location from across the bridge leading to the west. Many Goblin Archers lie in wait in the Goblin camp. After you clear the area, talk to the Spaniard waiting in the compound. You can release him to find his way back home, or have him accompany you on your quest. Make your decision, then continue south to the Slave Pit Exterior.

Once more, battle the Goblins as you travel south. When you come upon a battle between Goblins and Wererats, don't think for a second that either is on your side. Hang back until the battle is over so you have fewer enemies to confront.

As you near the entrance to the Slave Pits, you may encounter Relican standing by the side of the road. Relican is part of another quest. At the level you're at now, make your salutations and continue down the road to your appointed quest.

Another, smaller Goblin camp is nestled in the northwest corner of this area. Rid the area of these fiends before entering the Slave Pits.

Returning to the Slave Pits isn't like coming home again. Your welcoming committee isn't happy to see you and tries to prevent you from traveling even a foot farther. Dispatch the Thugs as you make your way around the Slave Pits to confront the Slaver Captain.

If your Speech skill is high enough, you can initiate a conversation with the Slaver Captain, although the outcome is predictable. Even if you agree to let him flee, he turns on you. Kill the Slaver Captain and any nearby Thugs, then clean the area of chests and hidden treasures.

TIP *Showing mercy only makes the battle more challenging. The Slaver Captain frees several guard dogs to fight by his side.*

When you've cleared out the Slave Pits, return to Lord Javier Fernandez in the Temple District and tell him you have completed the task. He bestows upon you the title of knight and welcomes you to the order of the Knights Templar.

Your quest, however, is just beginning. Lord Javier convenes a council of his most trusted knights to see what can be done about a matter that imperils all of Europe. You must journey to Montserrat Abbey to ensure the safety of one of the relics. Lord Javier indicated the location of Montserrat on your map, so you can use a Magic Crystal to teleport there directly. You can find a Magic Crystal in the southwest corner of the Crossroads.

INQUISITOR

Established in 1231 to eradicate spirits, magic, and their taint from Earth, the Inquisition is an order of warriors, clergy, and justices. The Inquisition is both feared and revered among the general population, and its methods are harsh indeed. Somewhat hypocritically, the Inquisition practices Divine Magic without regret to find and imprison any beings tainted with magic. These beings are often killed, usually tortured, and always held with no hope of release or escape.

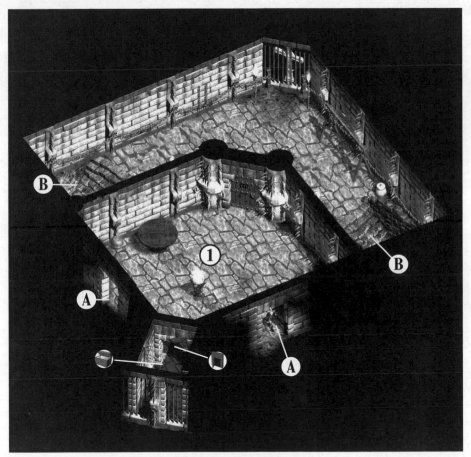

Inquisition Foyer

Ⓐ Barcelona Temple District	🛡 Chest		
Ⓑ Inquisition Chamber	◼ Secret Wall		
① Inquisitor Raphael			

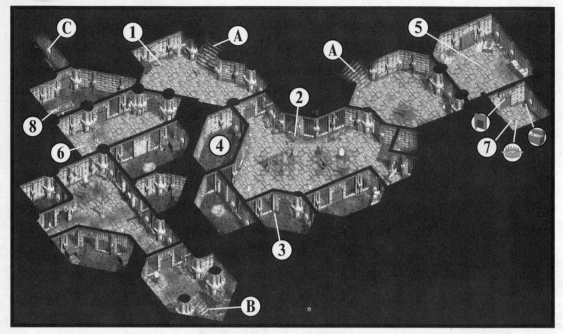

Inquisition Chambers

Ⓐ Inquisition Foyer

Ⓑ Inquisition Dungeon

Ⓒ Inquisition Exterior

① Inquisitor's Chalice in Chest

② Scepter of the Chambers in Chest

③ Jailed Inquisitor

④ Jailed Wielder

⑤ Grand Inquisitor Tomas de Torquemada

⑥ Destroyed Artifact

⑦ The *Centuries* (Rare Book)

⑧ Ring of the Undead

◉ Chest

◉ Trap

◉ Secret Wall

Ⓐ Inquisition Chamber

Ⓑ Crossroads

◉ Hidden Item

AREA ENEMIES

Black Wolf

Grey Wolf

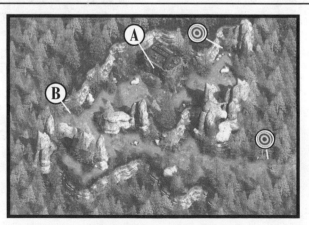

Inquisition Exterior

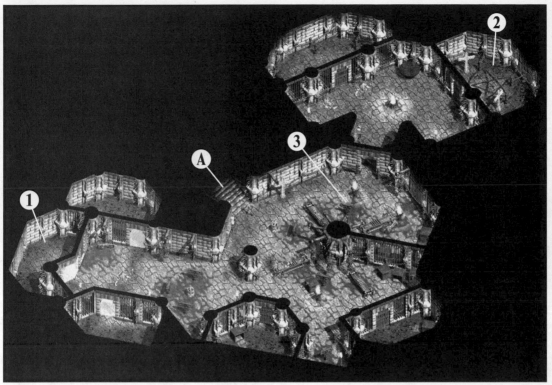

Inquisition Dungeon

(A) Inquisition Chamber
(1) Galileo
(2) Daeva of Pain
(3) Renaldo

AREA ENEMIES
Weak Terror

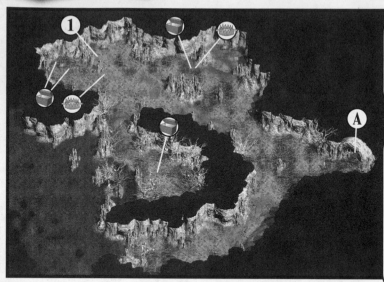

Ⓐ El Bosque
① *History of Necromancers*
  (Rare Book)
  Chest
  Trap

AREA ENEMIES

Decayed Ghoul
Decayed Zombie
Frail Ghoulish Hag
Ghoul Titan
Huge Brittle Skeleton
Lesser Brimstone Reaver
Weak Screaming Terror
Weak Terror

Darkwood Cave

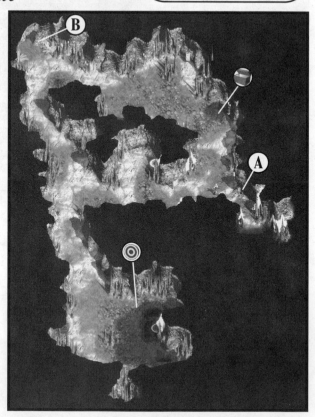

Ⓐ Lago Del Rio Ebro
Ⓑ Mongol Camp
  Chest
◎ Hidden Item

AREA ENEMIES

Vodyanoi

Waterfall Passage

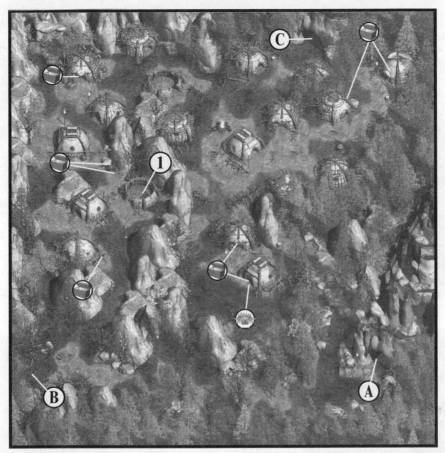

Goblin Camp

(A) Waterfall Passage
(B) Bounty Hunter's Camp
(C) Goblin Khan's Cave
(1) Inquisitor
Chest
Trap

AREA ENEMIES

Goblin Archer
Goblin Shaman
Mongol Goblin

Earn the Trust of the Inquisitors

Speak to Acolyte Garcia about joining the Inquisitors. Inform the Temple Gate guard that you wish to speak with Inquisitor Raphael in the Temple District, and he opens the gate. Before you can be considered for a position as an Inquisitor, you must prove yourself worthy. You are to speak with Inquisitor Dominguez in the Temple District, south of the Inquisition Chambers, and assist him in whatever task he asks of you.

Assist Inquisitor Dominguez

Inquisitor Dominguez asks that you remove the taint of the spirits from the Temple District. Collect these blue spirits from the streets by selecting them, which allows you to absorb the spirit and convert it into Mana for spells. Wander around the Temple District and collect 10 of these floating Mana spirits. When you collect all of them, return to Inquisitor Dominguez and receive your reward. Return to Inquisitor Raphael in the Inquisition Chambers and tell him that you have completed Dominguez's task.

NOTE *You can do this quest as the precursor to the Inquisition quest, or as a stand-alone side quest.*

When you return to Inquisitor Raphael, you are asked to donate 1,000 gold pieces to demonstrate your unwavering dedication. (If you are a tainted race, the fee is higher). If you have 1,000 gold pieces, pay the fee, speak with Inquisitor Raphael, and receive your first task to prove your worthiness as an Inquisitor. If not, go into the nearby wilderness and earn gold by completing some of the side quests available to persons of all factions.

DEAL WITH THE AFFLICTED IN THE SEWERS

Inquisitor Raphael first asks you to deal with the Afflicted, a dangerous group of lycanthrope creatures hiding in the Sewers beneath Barcelona. Seek out the Afflicted and eliminate them as a threat to the Inquisition. You may enter the Sewers through the northwest corner in the Temple District.

When you first enter the Sewers, you witness a battle between the Thieves and the Beggars. As your quest with the Inquisition is to rid the Sewers of the lycanthrope, siding with the Thieves is a likely choice, as the Beggars are Wererats. If, however, your Speech skill is high enough, you can convince the Thief to let you pass without choosing a side.

If you decide to side with the Thieves, your greeter directs you to speak to Juanita, the leader of the Thieves Guild. You can do this side quest at any time.

Travel west inside the Sewers to confront and defeat the roaming lycanthropes. The entrance to the Hall of Beggars lies to the west. Enter and clear the area of Wererats. After defeating the Wererats, return to the Inquisition Chambers and tell Raphael you have ended the threat of the Afflicted.

CREATE A ROD OF THE INQUISITOR

Your next task is to construct a Rod of the Inquisitor, a powerful item that serves you well against magic-using heretics. To make the Rod, seek out a supply of Darkwood. Raphael has heard of a supplier in the western wilderness. Once you have the Darkwood, return to Raphael.

Travel west through the Crossroads to reach El Bosque. You find Felipe the Woodcutter standing near his home.

THE WOODCUTTER'S DAUGHTER

When you speak to Felipe, you learn he is troubled because his daughter is missing. If you travel to Scar Ravine and save the Woodcutter's daughter before speaking with Felipe, you can save time.

Felipe is willing to provide you with the Darkwood, but he has a problem. Spirits overrun the cave below his house where he stores the Darkwood. The cave has been sealed off and he does not go down there. If you could exorcise the spirits, Felipe could get you the Darkwood you need. Destroy all the undead in the Darkwood Cave.

Take your time and draw out the spirits a few at a time. Don't charge into a fray, or you'll be outnumbered. The Lesser Brimstone Reaver is a nasty enemy. Don't let this undead creature get the upper hand, or the Darkwood Cave may be your final resting point.

Return to Felipe when you have cleared the cave, and he retrieves a piece of Darkwood for you. Take the Darkwood back to Inquisitor Raphael in Barcelona's Temple District and tell him that you have the first component for the Rod of the Inquisitor.

You must now acquire a true relic of a saint. All true Inquisitor's Rods have a relic fused in their structure. The relic is the source of the Rod's heavenly powers. The holy remains of Saint Bartholomew lie underneath Barcelona's Cathedral. You're stopped by the Cathedral guard when you try to enter the Cathedral. Inform him you are there on business for the Inquisition and he quickly grants passage.

Have your Detect Trap skill ready so you can locate the trap beneath the sarcophagus. When you disable the trap, open the coffin and retrieve the Hair of a Saint. Return to Inquisitor Raphael in the Inquisition Chambers.

After speaking with Inquisitor Raphael, you learn the Darkwood must be shaped and blessed to turn it into the Rod of the Inquisitor. Seek an audience with Grand Inquisitor Tomas de Torquemada. He is within the Inquisition Chambers, behind a hidden door. You must find the secret door or find someone who can reveal it to you.

Go downstairs and speak with Tithe Inquisitor. Tell him you are looking for the Grand Inquisitor Torquemada. Tithe may not be convinced you are ready for such an audience. Assure him you are, and he reveals the hidden door nearby.

Inside Torquemada's chambers, ask him to shape the Darkwood into a true Rod of an Inquisitor. After the Grand Inquisitor infuses the hair of Saint Bartholomew into the Darkwood, the Rod of the Inquisitor is yours.

RESCUE INQUISITOR DARSH

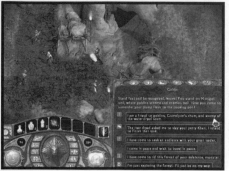

Cross through the Waterfall Passage west of Lago Del Rio Ebro to the Goblin camp, slaying any Vodyanoi in your path.

As you enter the Goblin camp, confront the Goblin that greets you, or, if your Speech skill is high enough, persuade the Goblin of your peaceful nature so that it allows you to pass. Because your ultimate goal is to free Inquisitor Darsh, the generosity of this Goblin evaporates once you make a break for it.

Explore the Goblin camp, and you find Inquisitor Darsh being held captive. When you eliminate the Goblin threat, talk to the Inquisitor and accompany him back to Barcelona. As you pass through the Waterfall Passage, several Goblins chase you. Darsh can hide you from the enemies with a spell, or you can attack them. If you choose to fight, lure the Goblins away from Darsh. If he dies, your quest fails.

At the gates of Barcelona, Inquisitor Darsh leaves your company, rewarding you with the Amulet of the Grand Inquisitor. Return to the Inquisition Chambers in Barcelona's Temple District and tell Inquisitor Raphael that you have saved Darsh from the Goblins.

LA CALLE PERDIDA (THE LOST STREET)

Inquisitor Raphael wishes you to perform another task. Unknown to many, wizards are hiding in Barcelona. The Inquisitors have heard whispers of a secret haven called La Calle Perdida, the Lost Street, where these wizards are said to gather. Inquire discreetly, find La Calle Perdida, and report back to Inquisitor Raphael so that the Inquisition may bring these heretics to justice.

The only insight Inquisitor Raphael can offer you in this quest is the knowledge that Signor Leo may associate with some Wielders. Also, seek out Quinn the Herbalist to see if he has knowledge of this area.

You can question Da Vinci about the wizards, but his knowledge is not as helpful as that of Quinn the Herbalist. Asking Quinn directly about the Wielders ends the conversation swiftly; Quinn is very protective of the group. You must lie to Quinn about why you want to know the Wielders' location before he reveals anything to you.

On a chair near Quinn is a tome with magic inscriptions that only a person touched with magic can comprehend. Luckily, you have such magic inside of you, and you can read a passage from the book to prove to Quinn that you wield magic. Approach the book in his shop and read it to activate the magic within its pages.

Now that you have proven to Quinn that you have magic inside of you, Quinn gives you an amulet called the Wielder's Charm that grants you the ability to pass through the hidden entrance to La Calle Perdida. Now you must search the Gate District to find the secret entrance along one of the western walls.

Travel north of the merchant in the west part of the Gate District. Because you bear the Wielder's Charm, the wall blocking the doorway to La Calle Perdida flashes. Pass through this wall to reach the doorway beyond.

Once you enter La Calle Perdida, your goal is accomplished. Return to Raphael and tell him you have found La Calle Perdida—or not, if you don't feel like betraying the Wielders. Whether you inform Raphael about the hidden location of the Wielders or lie to him, you are officially welcomed into the Inquisition and bear the title Inquisitor.

THE WIELDERS

Those who believe magic should be used for the good of mankind are known as Wielders. They congregate in hidden places, helping those imprisoned by the Inquisition to escape, and planning for the day when the world accepts them again.

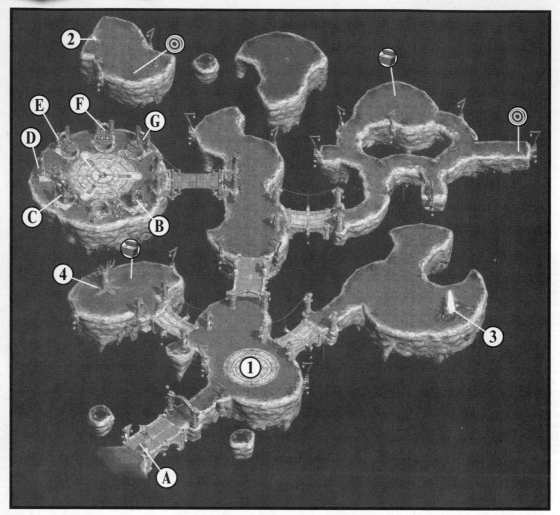

La Calle Perdida

Ⓐ Barcelona Gate District   Ⓕ La Calle Perdida (North Island)   ④ Brambles

Ⓑ Quinn the Herbalist   Ⓖ Crossroads   🗝 Chest

Ⓒ Trapped Ether Plane   ① Cedric Alsen   ◎ Hidden Item

Ⓓ Inquisition Chambers   ② Portal

Ⓔ Port District   ③ Modifier

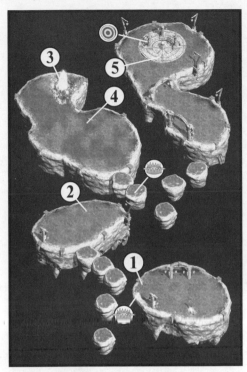

① Switch
② Spirit of Sir Earl Thomas Jameson II
③ Portal
④ Disembodied Spirit of Marco Polo
⑤ Mad Enchanter
◎ Hidden Item
◉ Trap

AREA ENEMIES

Decayed Zombie
Huge Brittle Skeleton
Lesser Brimstone Reaver
Mad Enchanter

Trapped Ether Plane

Find the Well-Concealed Wielders

If following the path of the magic Wielders interests you, you must follow a more shadowy existence than that of the Knights Templar or Inquisitors. Hunted because of their use of magic, the Wielders cannot be easily found along the brick-lined streets of the Barcelona Temple District. To locate the elusive Wielders, speak to Signor Leonardo Da Vinci and inquire about the "smaller groups" and wizards. Signor Leo suggests you speak with Quinn the Herbalist, who may be able to provide more information.

You must be open with Quinn when you inquire as to the location of the Wielders. Their location is a closely held secret, and Quinn isn't about to give up that kind of information easily for fear of retribution by the Inquisition. To prove you are interested in learning more about the magic within you, Quinn asks you to activate a tome lying on a chair nearby. Activate the tome, and Quinn provides you with the Wielder's Charm, which allows you to "see" the hidden wall on the west side of the Barcelona Gate District.

Walk through the hidden wall and go through the door to reach La Calle Perdida. Speak with Cedric Alsen and tell him you want to join the Wielders. Before you can join, you must prove your loyalty.

THE WAND OF SPIRITS

Your first test is to create a Wand of Spirits. To do this, you must collect Darkwood from the Woodcutter in the forest west of Barcelona. Seek out the Woodcutter in El Bosque.

Felipe the Woodcutter is happy to supply you with the Darkwood you need for your Wand of Spirits, but there is trouble in the caves below, where the Darkwood is stored. The Woodcutter cannot enter the Darkwood Cave below his house because undead creatures haunt the cave. You must destroy the undead to obtain the Darkwood.

CAUTION *The Darkwood Cave has many powerful creatures. Do not attempt this quest until you are more seasoned and can handle the enemies you find here.*

If you can obtain a weapon that causes additional damage to the undead, equip it before entering this cave. Also, buy scrolls to help defend against the disease attacks of the Decayed Zombies. Finally, any electrical buffers you can equip yourself with are helpful against Weak Terror attacks.

After you clear the cave, return to Felipe, who returns to the cave and retrieves the Darkwood you need. Come back to Cedric Alsen in La Calle Perdida with your Darkwood. You must now bind a spirit to the wand to give it power. To do this, you must obtain a friendly spirit from Galileo. Unfortunately, Galileo is being held prisoner in the Inquisition Chambers.

You can enter the Inquisition Chambers in several ways. You can speak with either the Knight Templar or the Inquisitor in the Gate District before approaching one of the gate guards to request access to the Temple District. (You must speak with one of the accepted factions before approaching one of the guards to request entry.) Or you may use one of La Calle Perdida's northern portals. One of these portals takes you to the Inquisition Chambers.

Once in the Inquisition Chambers, fool the Inquisitor into believing you are there on business of the Knights Templar. Your Speech skill must be high, or your visit will be short.

When you obtain the three keys from the Inquisition Jailer, distract the guards so that you can access the nearby chest containing the Scepter of the Chambers. Unlock the door to the jailed Inquisitor and he attacks, drawing the guards to his location. While the guards are otherwise engaged, open the chest and retrieve the Scepter of the Chambers.

With the scepter in your possession, activate the destroyed cross on the west side to release the force field on the cells. Travel through to reach the stairs leading to the Inquisition Dungeon.

Before you can get to Galileo, rid the area of a few Weak Terrors that have escaped from their cells. Galileo is easy to find in his room of bars. Surprisingly, Galileo isn't interested in being rescued from the Inquisition Chambers, but he is happy to teach you a magical technique. First, you must aid a friend of his. Seek out Faust, a wizard imprisoned in the chambers above, and set him free.

Return to the Inquisition Chambers and speak to Faust. Unlock and open Faust's door, and Faust disappears. Return to Galileo's cell within the Inquisition Chambers and tell him that you helped Faust escape.

Speak to Galileo and he grants you the ability to see a hidden spirit within the Observatory. Go to the Observatory in the Temple District and obtain the spirit to complete your wand. The Observatory is under heavy guard, however, and to gain access, you must convince the guard on the south side of the Observatory that you are there as an investigator to gather evidence against Galileo.

Activate the orb in the center of the room to unleash a hidden spirit that binds to your wand. Now that your Wand of Spirits has been empowered, return to La Calle Perdida, speak with Cedric, and tell him you are ready to continue with the initiation.

TIP *Use the telescope before leaving. Doing so grants your character a permanent +1 bonus to Perception.*

BRING RELICAN TO JUSTICE

As your final task, you must bring the Arch Necromancer Relican to justice. He is a Dark Wielder who hides in the wilderness near the Slave Pits. Relican was once a pupil of the Wielders before he turned away. Now he hates all Wielders and proves a difficult foe. If you eliminate him, your initiation is complete and you are accepted as a Wielder.

Travel west through El Bosque, to reach Lago Del Rio Ebro. Don't wander far from the path unless you want to add experience to your character, although most of the enemies you meet here shouldn't pose much of a problem for you.

Your first encounter in Lago Del Rio Ebro is with Goblin Grumdjum. Grumdjum has a proposition for you: Slay the River Dryad. This quest is outlined in detail in the side quests at the end of this chapter. Refer to the side quests if you wish to perform this quest for Grumdjum; you always have the option of refusing his offer. At this point, you must either agree to Grumdjum's terms or prepare to battle Grumdjum and all other Goblins that cross your path in this area.

Travel south, battling past Goblins and Wolves. Cross the bridge and stay close to the east side of the path, avoiding the monsters across the bridge to the west.

As you near the southern area, you see a lighted arch. Be prepared for a Goblin mob to attack! A Goblin camp beyond the arch houses Goblin Archers and Mongols waiting to make you a permanent member of their camp. Clear the area of Goblins to go to the Slave Pit Exterior.

There's no rest for the weary when you enter the Slave Pit Exterior. As you travel south down the path, prepare for more battles against more Goblins and a Wererat or two. Keep your Search Trap icon activated to alert you to traps in and around the chests in the area.

Before approaching Relican, have every scroll and healing potion at the ready. Relican calls upon his minions to aid him in his attack. Be prepared for poison attacks from the Decayed Zombies while Relican attacks with powerful electrical blasts. You can easily eliminate the Huge Brittle Skeletons joining the battle if you're armed with a weapon that inflicts additional damage against the undead. When you're ready, speak to Relican.

Relican makes you a counteroffer that, unfortunately, would mean destroying your fellow Wielders. If you would follow the way of the Wielders, your choice is clear—you must defeat Relican.

Focus on eliminating Relican to stop those electrical blasts from zapping your health points. Use a scroll to protect you from the electrical spells. The Decayed Zombies should be your next target, as several well-placed attacks take them down quickly. Finish off the Huge Brittle Skeletons to emerge victorious from this perilous battle.

Now that you have defeated Relican, return to La Calle Perdida and tell Cedric that Relican threatens the Wielders no more.

Speak to Cedric Alsen and inform him of your success. You have now passed your initiation and are welcomed as one of the Wielders.

THE TRAPPED ETHER PLANE

If, while exploring Le Calle Perdida, you should happen to stumble across the portal promising untold wealth and power, pass it by. There's no such thing as a free lunch. If you want a challenge and a few juicy items to add to your inventory, however, go into Portal C and enter the Trapped Ether Plane.

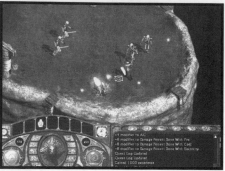

This area is not quest-driven, but you can't leave until you get past several obstacles. You must defeat the Mad Enchanter or, if your Speech skill is high enough, persuade him to take his own life. After the opening sequence with the Mad Enchanter, activate the switch to create a bridge and battle your way past the Huge Brittle Skeletons to the Spirit of Sir Earl Thomas Jameson II. Though he is a spirit, he can assist you by creating a bridge for you to reach the next island.

Have plenty of antidotes in your bag as you go past the Decayed Zombies and Lesser Brimstone Reavers to the next island. If you have a fire spell, use it to dispatch the Lesser Brimstone Reavers. Equip yourself with an undead weapon to help eliminate the onslaught of the undead. Talk to the disembodied spirit of Marco Polo. He can help you get to the next island, but only with the help of Sir Earl Thomas Jameson II. Return to Sir Jameson and enlist his aid to create another bridge.

On the final island, you confront the Mad Enchanter. If your Speech skill isn't high enough to talk him into taking his own life, you know what must be done: Destroy the Mad Enchanter.

The Mad Enchanter has electrical attacks that can inflict significant damage. Use whatever scrolls you have before you reach him to increase your resistances to electricity. If your attack skills are high, you can dispatch the Mad Enchanter quickly. Once you defeat him, collect all the items the Mad Enchanter drops, and what lies hidden nearby.

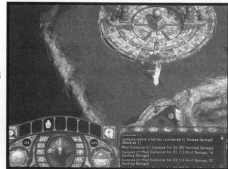

Joining the Dark Wielders

If, instead of helping Cedric all the way through, you decide to switch allegiance to Relican, he gives you a ring that summons him into La Calle Perdida. He must be summoned there, because he has been banned from there for life, and so cannot get there on his own. When you enter La Calle Perdida with the summoning ring, Relican teleports into La Calle Perdida, kills Cedric and the Wielders, and takes control.

He still puts you on the path to recover the relics, but his motivations are less altruistic.

> **CAUTION** *Agreeing to help Relican is the ultimate act of evil that has a profound effect on the end of the game. At some point, you should take on this role—but not the first time you play through the game.*

FIND THE SCEPTRE OF BONE

Before Lord Relican shares with you the dark secrets of Necromancy, you must prove yourself a worthy pupil. First, recover the Sceptre of Bone to help with your dark studies. Go to Da Vinci's workshop and examine the model horse, where you see the letters CECCA. Go to the organ and play the notes corresponding to those letters to be whisked away to Da Vinci's secret ethereal workshop.

In the chest near the siege engine is the Sceptre of Bone. Return to La Calle Perdida and deliver it to Lord Relican.

Although Relican now rules La Calle Perdida, a few wizards have refused to join your faction. The herbalist, Quinn, defies Relican's calling. Your final test is to persuade Quinn to join the order. When you confront him, he refuses you. You must either kill him or use your Speech skill, if it's high enough, to convince him that he would be a powerful Dark Wielder. Once Quinn acquiesces, return to Lord Relican and inform him that Quinn has joined the Dark Wielders.

There has been a great deal of activity within the city. The Inquisition and the Knights Templar are preparing for an important event involving relics that Lord Relican cannot yet see. Use your guile to discover what they are plotting. You may be able to convince Lord Relican to send one of the dark minions to do the job instead.

When the minion returns with news of the relics, Lord Relican commands you to travel to Montserrat Abbey and claim the Crown of Thorns to further the influence and power of the Dark Wielders.

SIDE QUESTING IN BARCELONA

Before, after, and during your initiation rites into one of the factions of Barcelona, you can undertake many sidequests to earn gold, experience, and special Perks.

> NOTE *At the end of chapter 3 in the game, quests from Barcelona and Montaillou cannot be completed, and thus you fail.*

These quests may gain you fortune or fame, but you always get valuable experience points. Some quests dovetail with others, so refer to your Quest Log to find out where you need to go and to whom you need to speak.

Not all quests are required. It is up to you to decide which quests to perform and which to skip, though completing every quest is the most advantageous path to take. Each quest has been graded by difficulty. Approach them with caution as your success or failure depends upon your character's level and skills.

The following quests have been broken up by starting area, though some take you to areas beyond the walls of Barcelona.

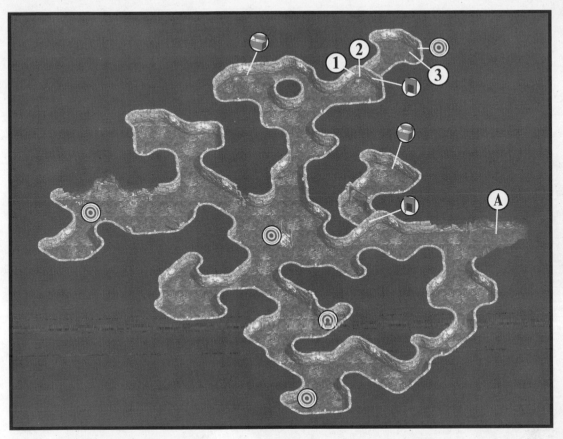

Troll Pit

Ⓐ Hall of Beggars
① Lava Troll Master
② Chest containing Red Ore
③ Thomas
⬙ Chest
◎ Hidden Item
▣ Secret Wall

AREA ENEMIES

Lava Trolls
Lava Troll Master

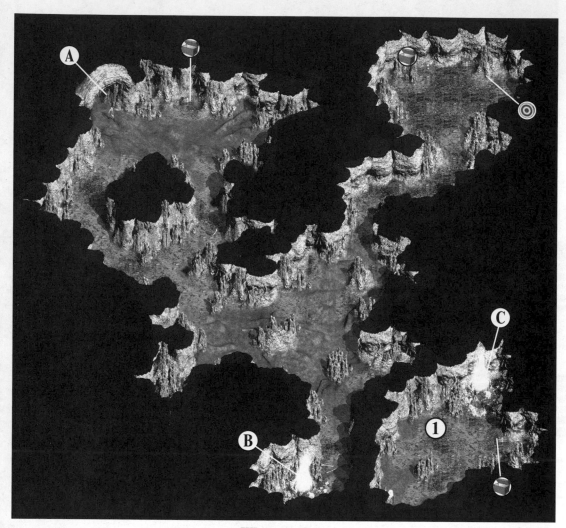

Wererat Cave

Ⓐ Slave Pit Exterior

Ⓑ Magic Crystal to
Aesma's Lair

Ⓒ Magic Crystal to Slave Pit
Exterior

① Aesma

◗ Chest

◎ Hidden Item

AREA ENEMIES

Aesma
Wererat
Wererat Minion

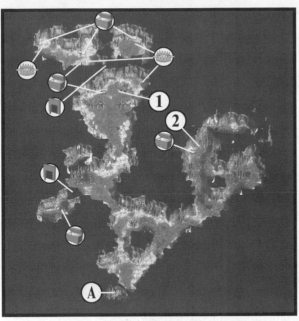

Goblin Warrens

Ⓐ Goblin Camp
① Goblin Kahn
② Rakeb
◉ Chest
▣ Secret Wall
◉ Trap

AREA ENEMIES

Goblin Archer
Goblin Khan Plumdjum
Mongol Goblin
Rakeb

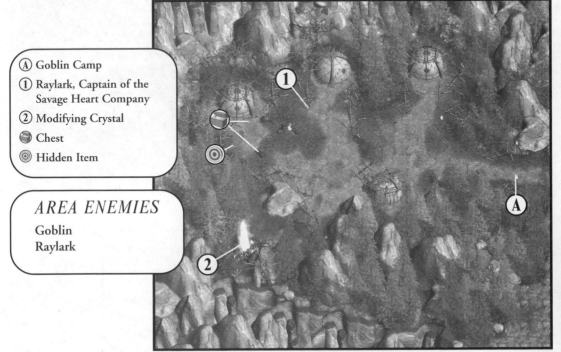

Bounty Hunter's Camp

Ⓐ Goblin Camp
① Raylark, Captain of the Savage Heart Company
② Modifying Crystal
◉ Chest
◎ Hidden Item

AREA ENEMIES

Goblin
Raylark

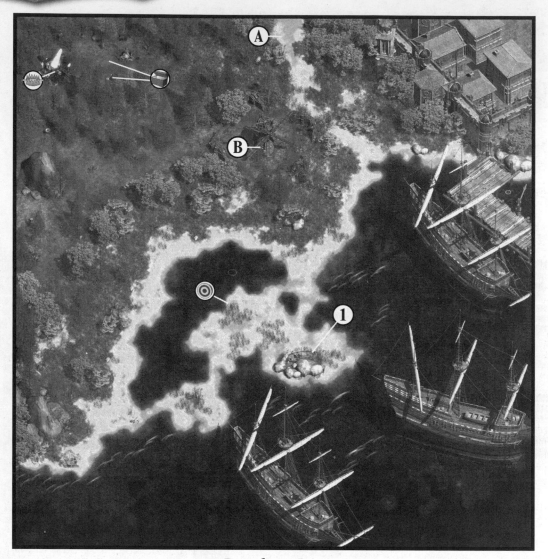

Barcelona Coast

Ⓐ Crossroads
Ⓑ Windmill
① Ghost of Captain Morales
🝰 Chest
◎ Hidden Item
🝰 Trap

AREA ENEMIES

Black Wolf
Goblin Archer
Mongol Goblin
Vodyanoi
Vodyanoi Spawn

BECOME A FAVORED ONE IN THE KNIGHTS OF SALADIN

Quest Synopsis

Challenge: Medium

Location(s): Barcelona Gate District, Barcelona Port District, Slave Pits

Quest NPCs: Amir ibn Shazid, Consuela the Barmaid, Dream Djinn

Type: Item Recovery

Reward: Experience

Principal Players

Amir ibn Shazid

Consuela the Barmaid

Dream Djinn

Quest Details

SEEK OUT ALI HUBAN

Talk to Amir outside of the Barcelona gates and ask him about the Knights of Saladin. Though you cannot join their order, you can perform trials to become a Favored One.

Your first test is to find Ali Huban and inquire if he has news for Amir. Ali is reported to be a wry rascal and difficult to find because he can cloak himself in disguises.

Travel to the Serpent's Bile in the Port District. Talk to the barmaid at the Serpent's Bile, commenting on her lip hair. Though you do have to suffer a slap or two, you can continue to speak to Consuela. If your Speech skill is high enough, you can find out that she is a man! This prompts Consuela to ask you to keep her secret and you can continue to ask her about any news she may have for Amir. If that option isn't available to you, you may be able to mention to her that Amir has sent you to find him. Return to Amir with the letter Ali Huban gives you.

Ali's note tells Amir about a group of Thieves who stole a priceless gem from Amir's tent. Your next quest for the Knights of Saladin is to find the stolen gem. Travel to the Slave Pits to retrieve the Shard of Dreams.

RECOVER THE SHARD OF DREAMS FROM THE SLAVERS

You must travel a great distance to reach the Slave Pits. If you have not previously cleared the path while completing other tasks, this mission may be dangerous. From Lago Del Rio Ebro, travel south to reach the Slave Pit Exterior. Battle past the Goblins and Wererats to reach the Slave Pits entrance.

Once inside the Slave Pits, defeat the Thugs to reach the Slaver Captain. Collect the Shard of Dreams and return to Amir in Barcelona.

DONATE A GEM TO THE KNIGHTS OF SALADIN

For your final test, you must complete the Dream Djinn's trials. Before you can participate in the trials, you must donate part of your wealth. If you completed the quest for the River Dryad, you may contribute the River Dryad Pearl. If you purchased a rare gem from the man in the Barcelona Port District or from Weng Choi in the Barcelona Gate District, you may donate that.

The choice is yours, but you can get the gem from the man in the Port District with minimal effort if your Find Traps/Secret Doors skill is high enough. Make your donation and prepare to meet the Dream Djinn.

COMPLETE THE DREAM DJINN'S TRIALS

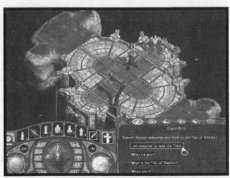

The Dream Djinn gives you a choice of being tested by either your intellect or your physical prowess. To be successful in the intellectual test, you must correctly answer three riddles. If you answer even one question incorrectly, you are returned to Amir and must make another donation to return. If you choose the physical prowess test, you must defeat three waves of enemies the Dream Djinn conjures.

When you successfully complete the Dream Djinn's tests, you receive the title of Scholar of the Crescent, a great honor among the people of the east, and are returned to Amir. Speak to Amir and he bestows upon you the title of Favored One.

SPY FOR HRUBRUB THE GOBLIN

Quest Synopsis

Challenge: Easy
Location: Barcelona Gate District
Quest NPC: Hrubrub the Goblin
Type: Task
Reward: Experience

Principal Player

Hrubrub the Goblin

Quest Details

Explore outside the eastern part of the Barcelona wall, and you see two Goblins fresh from killing a guard. You have a couple of options when you speak to Hrubrub, but only one completes this quest. You can either kill both Goblins and report their deaths to the Barcelona gate guards, or tell Hrubrub you're interested in the task she mentions.

If you take Hrubrub's offer, scout inside the Barcelona Gate District (walk through the gate) and report to Hrubrub. Tell Hrubjub the gate is weakly guarded and few defenders wait within. Helping the Goblins brings negative Karma, which affects the end of the game. If you report the Goblins to the guards at the gate, you earn a reward.

WILLIAM SHAKESPEARE QUEST: THE MUSE

Quest Synopsis

Challenge: Easy
Location(s): Barcelona Port District, Barcelona Gate District, Barcelona Temple District
Quest NPCs: William Shakespeare, Shylock
Type: Item Recovery (No Fighting Required)
Reward: Experience and a copy of
Eloquent Works

Principal Players

William Shakespeare
Shylock

Quest Details

While exploring the Docks area, you can complete an easy quest by paying a visit to the renowned William Shakespeare. His house is in the north side of the Docks area.

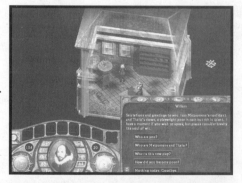

Speak to William and you discover he is working on a new play, though he is unable to finish it. The moneylender Shylock took Sytheria, William's muse, as collateral for a loan and William cannot complete his play without his muse. Agree to help William retrieve his muse to earn his gratitude.

NOTE *If you previously initiated a quest with Cortes in the tavern and sided against Shylock, you can still complete this quest. If you did not, go to the tavern in the Docks district and speak to Shylock. Whether you side with Shylock or Cortes, Shylock leaves the tavern and returns home.*

Return to the Temple District and go to Shylock's home. Speak to Shylock and demand Shakespeare's muse. Shylock requires a fee before discussing the matter further. Agree to pay. After payment, Shylock gives you a key that unlocks any of three chests before you. Use the key on the lead chest in the center to receive Shakespeare's muse.

TIP *If your Speech skill is high enough, talk Shylock into reducing his fee. If your Sneak and Lockpick skills are high enough, steal the muse and the other items from the chests.*

Return to Shakespeare's home and tell him that you have recovered his muse. In addition to the experience points you gain, Shakespeare rewards you with a copy of *Eloquent Works*, which you can use to increase your Speech skill or in the side quest with Weng Choi detailed later in this chapter.

Once you return Shakespeare's muse, speak to Shylock again. At this point, either talk Shylock into giving Shakespeare more time to pay his debt or, if you prefer, talk Shakespeare into repaying his debt to Shylock. You cannot do both these quests because the endings conflict, and you need high Speech skills to undertake either one.

PERSUADE SHYLOCK TO EXTEND SHAKESPEARE'S DEBT, OR PERSUADE SHAKESPEARE TO REPAY HIS DEBT

Quest Synopsis

Challenge: Easy
Location(s): Barcelona Port District, Barcelona Gate District, Barcelona Temple District
Quest NPCs: Shakespeare, Shylock
Type: Speech
Reward: Experience

Principal Players

William Shakespeare
Shylock

QUEST DETAILS

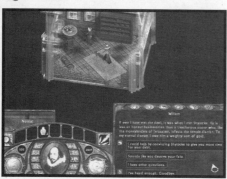

When you return Shakespeare's muse, speak to Shylock again. Either talk Shylock into giving Shakespeare more time to pay his debt or, if you prefer, talk Shakespeare into repaying his debt to Shylock. You cannot do both quests because their endings conflict. You need high Speech skills to undertake either quest.

If you assist Shylock, he rewards you with *Art of Barter*, a book you can use to increase your Barter skill. If your Speech skill isn't high enough to persuade Shylock to forgive Shakespeare's debt, you can complete the quest by killing Shylock and his cronies.

WENG CHOI'S BOOKS

Quest Synopsis

Challenge: Easy to Difficult
Location: Barcelona Gate District
Quest NPC: Weng Choi
Type: Recovery
Reward: Gold

Principal Player

Weng Choi

Quest Details

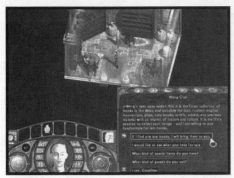

Weng Choi, a merchant in the Gate District, has rare items for sale, but only for his special customers. Give Weng Choi a book and he allows you to purchase items from this special collection. If you give him seven books, you're rewarded with Weng Choi's Shaolin Secret Perk, which is essential for those who fight with their hands. Here's where to find eight of the books.

Book of Death—Cortes's Quest
History of the Crusades—Shylock's Chest
Eloquent Works—Recover Shakespeare's Muse
History of Necromancers—Woodcutter's Basement
Centuries—Torquemada's Hidden Room
Tome of Geomancy—Brambles' Chest
History of Dragons—Da Vinci's Workshop
Art of Barter—Shylock's Quest

SAVE FERNAND'S BROTHER, JUAN

Quest Synopsis

Challenge: Easy
Location: Barcelona Port District
Quest NPCs: Fernand Desoto, Juan Desoto
Type: Rescue Juan
Reward: Experience, Gold, and Armor

Principal Player

Fernand Desoto

Quest Details

Explore the northern tip of the shoreline in the Barcelona Docks and Fernand Desoto calls to you to aid him in saving his brother.

Continue north along the beach to see Vodyanoi Spawn. Kill them and continue north across the sandy expanse to the next land mass. Fernand's brother, Juan, lies on the sand, under attack by more Vodyanoi Spawn. Slay the Vodyanoi. Unfortunately, regardless of your heroic efforts, you cannot save Juan. Although you could not reach Juan in time, the quest is still a success because you responded to Fernand's call for help.

In appreciation for trying to rescue Juan, you receive experience points and the items Juan dropped.

THE WIND SCROLL

Quest Synopsis

Challenge: Medium
Location(s): Barcelona Port District, Barcelona Gate District, Barcelona Temple District
Quest NPCs: Captain Isabella, Weng Choi, Sir Auric
Type: Retrieve a Wind Scroll
Reward: Experience and Gold

Principal Players

Captain Isabella
Weng Choi

Quest Details

Talk to Captain Isabella on her ship at the docks. If your Perception skill is high enough, Captain Isabella enlists your aid in her quest against the English. Captain Isabella needs a Wind Scroll.

Speak to Weng Choi, who sells rare and exotic items in the Gate District. He does have a Wind Scroll, but will only sell it to his most valuable customers. Weng Choi is also a collector of rare books. If you bring a rare book to Weng Choi and your Speech skill is high enough, he may be persuaded to sell you a Wind Scroll. You can also bribe Weng Choi into selling you a Wind Scroll.

Purchase the Wind Scroll, (Weng Choi gives away nothing for free) and return to Captain Isabella. Talk to Captain Isabella. Give her the Wind Scroll to receive experience points and gold.

RESCUE THE LOST BOY, TOMAS

Quest Synopsis

Challenge: Difficult

Location(s): Barcelona Port District, Sewer
Main Entrance, Hall of Beggars, Troll Pit

Quest NPCs: Marisol, Tomas

Type: Rescue

Reward: Experience

Principal Players

Marisol

Tomas

Quest Details

Talk to Marisol in the Port District and agree to enter the Sewers and search for her lost brother, Tomas.

If you have ventured into the Sewers while doing your initiation quests, the area is still cleared, except for the Vodyanoi. Travel from the Sewers' Main Entrance to the Hall of Beggars, finally reaching the Troll Pit.

Before entering the Troll Pit, use whatever scrolls of Fire Resistance you may have to help protect your character. The Trolls in this area blast the ground, causing it to shudder and damage anyone who nears them. Your main goal is to save the lost boy, so avoid the Trolls in the southwest area unless you want additional experience.

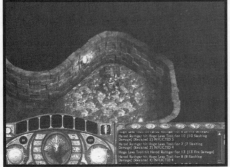

As you near the northeast corner, confront the Lava Troll Master. This monster can crush for an impressive amount of damage, and is capable of causing the underground fire damage that his smaller counterparts cause. When you defeat the Lava Troll Master, unlock the nearby chest to retrieve the Red Ore. You need this to complete the quest for Cortes, so grab it.

If your Find Traps/Secret Doors skill is low, bring a Master Thievery potion, so you can find where the boy is hidden. Detect the hidden wall behind the Lava Troll Master, enter it, and find the lost boy. This young man wastes no time leaving the Troll Pit. Follow his lead and head back to the Port District. Speak to Marisol and let her know her brother has been rescued.

RESCUE RENALDO FROM THE INQUISITION CHAMBERS

Quest Synopsis

Challenge: Medium
Location(s): Barcelona Port District, Barcelona Temple District, Inquisition Chambers, Inquisition Dungeon
Quest NPCs: Bartolome, Renaldo
Type: Rescue (Fighting Required)
Reward: Experience and Gold

Principal Players

Bartolome
Renaldo

Quest Details

Talk to Bartolome in the Port District and he tells you of the injustices being inflicted on his brother, Renaldo, by the Inquisitors. Agree to take a potion to Renaldo to begin this quest.

Travel to the Temple District and enter the Inquisition Foyer. If you completed earlier quests involving the Inquisitors, you shouldn't have any trouble reaching the Inquisition Chambers. If you haven't completed any initiation quests involving the Inquisitors, you may have some difficulty reaching the Inquisition Chambers.

When you reach the Inquisition Chambers, inform the Inquisitor you wish to examine the cells on behalf of the Knights Templar. Once you have possession of three keys, you can begin.

Unlock the jailed Inquisitor's cell. When the door opens, he attacks anyone in sight, including you! While the jailed Inquisitor has the full attention of the guards, open the chest nearby to get the Scepter of the Chambers.

Scepter in hand, move to the cells in the north and resurrect the crumbled cross lying in a heap near the west wall. As you do, the energy fields keeping the prisoners within their cells drop. Watch out for the escaping inmates! They couldn't care less that you are their benefactor, and attack as soon as they see you. Once past them, head to the Inquisition Chambers stairs and descend.

If you overheard the conversation of the guards in the hall leading to the Dungeon, you already know that some of the captive creatures have escaped. Destroy the Weak Terrors wandering the Dungeon, and then speak to Renaldo.

Renaldo is shackled to the stocks in the Dungeon's east side. Talk to him, and he asks you about the potion from his brother, Bartolome. Give Renaldo the potion and he disappears. Return to Bartolome in the Port District and tell him that his brother has been freed.

ASSIST INQUISITOR DOMINGUEZ

Quest Synopsis

Challenge: Easy
Location: Barcelona Temple District
Quest NPC: Inquisitor Dominguez
Type: Search
Reward: Experience

Principal Player

Inquisitor Dominguez

Quest Details

Inquisitor Dominguez has tasked you to remove the spirit taint from the Temple District. You can collect these blue spirits from the streets by selecting them, allowing you to absorb the spirit and convert it into Mana for spells.

Wander about the Temple District collecting 10 of these floating Mana spirits. Then return to Inquisitor Dominguez, tell him that you have cleansed the Temple District of the spirit taint, and receive your reward.

NOTE *This quest can be done as the precursor to the Inquisition quest, or as a stand-alone side quest.*

GIVE CORTES A HAND

Quest Synopsis

Challenge: Difficult

Location(s): Barcelona Port District, Barcelona Gate District, Sewers' Main Entrance, Hall of Beggars, Troll Pit

Quest NPCs: Cortes, Da Vinci, Eduardo the Blacksmith

Type: Recovery (Fighting Required)

Reward: Experience, Gold

PRINCIPAL PLAYERS

Cortes

Da Vinci

Eduardo the Blacksmith

Quest Details

Share a pint with Cortes in the Serpent's Bile and he tells you his story of the lost treasure. Cortes wants to retrieve his treasure to fund his future voyages, but cannot do it with only one arm. Cortes has spoken with Da Vinci about a mechanical arm. Tell Cortes you will find Leonardo and ask if his mechanical arm invention is complete.

Speak to Signor Leo and ask about the progress being made on the mechanical arm. Leonardo has finished the design for the arm, but Eduardo the Blacksmith needs Red Ore supply to build it. If you rescued Marisol's brother from the Troll Pit, you already have the Red Ore in your possession and can take it to Eduardo right away. If not, refer to the Marisol quest to learn how to navigate through the Troll Pit safely.

With Red Ore in hand, go to Eduardo's shop in the Gate District of Barcelona. Give Eduardo the Red Ore so that he may assemble the gears necessary for the mechanical arm. Take the gears to Da Vinci so that the new arm can be completed.

When it is complete, Da Vinci asks you to deliver the new arm to Cortes at the Serpent's Bile. Armed with his new appendage, Cortes asks you to join him on an expedition to retrieve his treasure. When you are ready, agree to travel with Cortes.

Travel south from the Crossroads to Rio Ebro. Battle past the enemies to reach the island in the southwest where the lone cross stands. Once there, Cortes forms a bridge, allowing you to cross the water to reach the cave beyond.

Inside the cave, Cortes claims his share of the treasure and leaves. You can explore the cave further, battling the undead within. Check the dragon's eye to locate the real treasures within the cave. When you leave the treasure room, however, all the spirits in the cave become hostile.

AID THE BEGGAR GUILDMASTER

Quest Synopsis

Challenge: Difficult

Location(s): Sewers' Main Entrance, Hall of Beggars, Thieves Congregation

Quest NPC: Enrique Garcia, the Beggar Leader

Type: Recovery (Fighting Required)

Reward: Experience and Gold

Principal Player

Enrique Garcia, the Beggar Leader

Quest Details

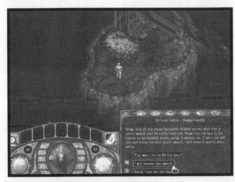

While traveling through the Hall of Beggars, speak to Enrique Garcia, the Beggar leader. Enrique asks that you help him by retrieving a sword belonging to him. You must find a Thief and defeat him to secure Enrique's sword.

TIP *If you have agreed to complete quests for the Thieves, complete them before undertaking this quest for Enrique. Any Thief quests that are outstanding automatically fail if you complete a quest for a Beggar.*

Refer to the map to find the Thief holding Enrique's sword and defeat him. When you have the sword, return to Enrique to claim your reward.

KILL THE THIEF CAPTAIN

Quest Synopsis

Challenge: Difficult
Location(s): Sewers' Main Entrance, Hall of Beggars, Thieves Congregation
Quest NPCs: Enrique Garcia, the Beggar Leader, and Juanita Suarez, the Thief Captain
Type: Recovery (Fighting Required)
Reward: Experience

Principal Players

Enrique Garcia, the Beggar Leader
Juanita Suarez, the Thief Captain

Quest Details

If you retrieved Enrique's sword, the Beggar leader asks you to perform another task. To prove your loyalty to the Beggars, Enrique asks you to search the Sewers and eliminate Juanita Suarez, the Thief captain.

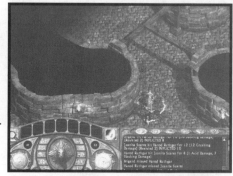

Juanita Suarez is in the northern part of the Thieves Congregation. Other Thieves are nearby, so be prepared to battle multiple enemies. Don't underestimate Juanita. She hits hard, so have healing potions on hand. Report to Enrique, tell him you have slain Juanita, and get your reward.

> **TIP** *Complete any outstanding quests for the Thieves before performing this quest. Any outstanding quests for the Thieves automatically fail if you attempt this quest.*

STEAL FROM THE INQUISITION

Quest Synopsis

Challenge: Medium
Location(s): Thieves Congregation,
Inquisition Chambers
Quest NPC: Enrique Garcia, the Beggar
Leader
Type: Recovery
Reward: Experience

Principal Player

Enrique Garcia, the Beggar Leader

Quest Details

Another task Enrique asks you to perform is to enter the Inquisition Chambers in the Temple District and steal a valuable chalice. He promises to pay well for the chalice.

To retrieve the chalice, your Speech skill must be high enough to convince the guard standing nearby that you are allowed to take the contents of the chest. If your Speech skill is not high enough, the guard attacks, and you have to battle all guards in the Chambers from this point forward. If your Sneak skill is high enough, you may be able to steal the chalice. Try a Sneak potion to ensure success.

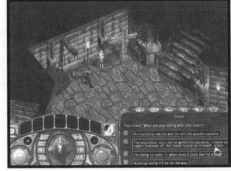

Once you have the chalice, return to the Sewers. Tell Enrique that you have stolen the chalice and receive your reward.

DESTROY THE LAVA TROLL MENACE

Quest Synopsis

Challenge: Difficult
Location(s): Thieves Congregation, Hall of
Beggars, Lava Troll Pit
Quest NPC: Enrique Garcia, the Beggar
Leader; Aesma
Type: Assassination
Reward: Gold

Principal Player

Enrique Garcia, the Beggar Leader

Quest Details

Enrique wants you to clear the Lava Troll stench. Travel to the Lava Troll Pit and defeat the Trolls within.

If you cleared out this area previously by completing other quests, you can inform Enrique and receive your reward. Otherwise, travel to the Lava Troll Pit through the Hall of Beggars and eliminate all the Lava Trolls within.

DISCOVER A CURE FOR WERERAT LYCANTHROPY

Quest Synopsis

Challenge: Difficult

Location(s): Thieves Congregation, Barcelona Gate District, Slave Pit Exterior, Aesma's Lair

Quest NPCs: Enrique Garcia, the Beggar Leader; Aesma

Type: Recovery

Reward: Gold, Potion, Beggar Comrade Perk

Principal Players

Enrique Garcia, the Beggar Leader

Quinn the Herbalist

Quest Details

Enrique, the Beggar leader, asks you to find a cure for whatever causes the Afflicted to change into Wererats. He believes Quinn, the herbalist in the Gate District, might be of help.

Tell Quinn that you need a cure for someone not completely turned into one of the Afflicted. Quinn knows that such a cure is possible, but grave risks are involved. Quinn possesses some of the components to brew the cure, but he needs a fur patch from the Prime Wererat who is in the wilderness beyond the Barcelona walls.

To obtain the fur patch, you must travel to Aesma's Lair, which can only be entered through the Slave Pit Exterior. Travel through Lago Del Rio Ebro to reach the Slave Pit Exterior. If you have not traveled here earlier while completing initiation quests, this is a difficult area. You must battle past Goblin camps in Lago Del Rio Ebro to reach the Slave Pit Exterior. Have an ample supply of healing potions in your inventory and keep a sharp eye on your health points.

Wererats comb the cave where Aesma resides. Increase your Poison and Disease Resistance before entering the cave. Aesma is a powerful Wererat and can inflict substantial damage through direct attack and poison. If your Speech skill is high enough, you can convince Aesma to leave without battle. If you can't talk Aesma out of fighting, let the battle begin!

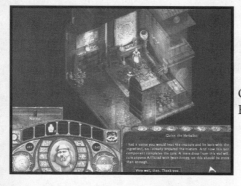

When you slay the Prime Wererat, deliver a fur patch to Quinn in the Gate District. Get the cure, then return to Enrique, the Beggar leader, in the Sewers for your reward.

RECOVER JUANITA'S STOLEN LOCKET

Quest Synopsis

Challenge: Difficult
Location(s): Sewers' Main Entrance, Thieves Congregation, Hall of Beggars
Quest NPC: Juanita Suarez, the Thief Captain
Type: Recovery
Reward: Experience and Gold

Principal Player

Juanita Suarez, the Thief Captain

Quest Details

If you did not side with the Beggars when you first entered the Sewers, you can complete this series of quests for the Thief Captain, Juanita Suarez. Talk to Juanita and she tells you that one of the Beggars stole a valuable locket from her. You must track down this Beggar and recover her locket.

Travel to the Hall of Beggars, defeating any Beggars who cross your path. The Beggar carrying Juanita's locket is near the center of the Dungeon by the wooden bridges. Return to Juanita and get your reward when you have the locket.

KILL ENRIQUE, THE BEGGAR LEADER

Quest Synopsis

Challenge: Difficult
Location(s): Sewers' Main Entrance, Thieves Congregation, Hall of Beggars
Quest NPCs: Juanita Suarez, the Thief Captain; Enrique Garcia, the Beggar leader
Type: Assassination
Reward: Gold

Principal Players

Juanita Suarez, the Thief Captain
Enrique Garcia, the Beggar Leader

Quest Details

Before Juanita can be certain you are trustworthy, you need to perform an assassination. Kill Enrique, the Beggar leader. If you kill Enrique, Juanita can be sure you are not in the enemy's employ.

If you killed Enrique while performing Juanita's previous task, inform her he is dead. If not, return to the Hall of Beggars, find Enrique to the south, and kill him. He's a tough enemy, so have healing potions on hand. Return to Juanita when he has been destroyed.

STEAL FROM A NOBLE'S HOUSE IN THE TEMPLE DISTRICT

Quest Synopsis

Challenge: Easy
Location(s): Sewers' Main Entrance, Thieves Congregation, Barcelona Temple District
Quest NPC: Juanita Suarez, the Thief Captain
Type: Recovery
Reward: Gold

Principal Player

Juanita Suarez, the Thief Captain

Quest Details

To welcome you into the fold, Juanita gives you a key to a house in the Temple District. Go to the house, remove whatever treasure you find there, and return to Juanita with her commission.

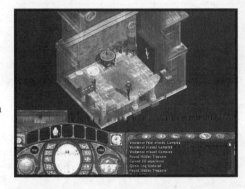

The house is next to the Cathedral. Go inside and use your Search skill to uncover the hidden treasure in the floor. Don't overlook the bookcase! Return to Juanita with her share.

COLLECT DUES IN THE PORT DISTRICT

Quest Synopsis

Challenge: Easy
Location(s): Sewers' Main Entrance, Thieves Congregation, Barcelona Port District
Quest NPC: Juanita Suarez, the Thief Captain
Type: Recovery
Reward: Gold

Principal Player

Juanita Suarez, the Thief Captain

Quest Details

For a fee of 70 gold pieces, Juanita tells you of a job you can perform. In the Barcelona Port District is a house that has a faulty lock. Inside is a man who has not paid his civic protection dues. Pay him a visit and collect those dues, returning half to Juanita.

The house is in the Barcelona Port District west of Shakespeare's house. It takes little convincing to get the citizen to pay his dues. Return to Juanita and inform her you have collected her dues and become a friend of the Thieves.

RETRIEVE EDUARDO'S SWORD

Quest Synopsis

Challenge: Difficult
Location(s): Barcelona Gate District, Sewers' Main Entrance, Hall of Beggars
Quest NPCs: Eduardo the Blacksmith, Felgnash
Type: Recovery
Reward: Experience and Gold

Principal Players

Eduardo the Blacksmith
Felgnash

Quest Details

You may have done this side quest if you followed the path of the Knights Templar. When you were attempting to obtain the Lion Shield, Eduardo the Blacksmith may have asked you to retrieve his father's stolen sword from a Beggar named Felgnash. If not, find Felgnash as you travel through the Sewers to the Hall of Beggars near the center of the Dungeon. Kill Felgnash to recover Eduardo's sword and return to the blacksmith for your reward. Beware that attacking Felgnash turns all Beggars against you.

RESCUE THE WOODCUTTER'S DAUGHTER

Quest Synopsis

Challenge: Difficult
Location(s): El Bosque, Scar Ravine
Quest NPCs: Felipe the Woodcutter, Gloria
Type: Rescue
Reward: Experience and Gold

Principal Players

Felipe the Woodcutter
Gloria

Quest Details

Speak to the Woodcutter in El Bosque and you find him troubled. His daughter, Gloria, has disappeared and the Woodcutter believes Goblins kidnapped her.

From the Crossroads, travel north to reach Scar Ravine. If you have traveled here earlier while completing tasks for your initiation, the area is still clear of enemies. Head east and approach the Goblin standing guard on a little girl.

If your Speech skill is high enough, you may be able to persuade the Goblin to let you take the child to the Goblin Khan as a gift from the Goblin guarding her. It's a lie, of course, but the Goblin doesn't know that. If your Speech skills is not high enough, you're forced to fight. Once the Goblin kidnapper is gone, Gloria can return home. Return to the Woodcutter, tell him you saved his daughter, and collect your reward.

SLAY THE RIVER DRYAD FOR THE GOBLIN GRUMDJUM

Quest Synopsis

Challenge: Difficult
Location(s): Lago Del Rio Ebro
Quest NPCs: The River Dryad, Goblin Grumdjum
Type: Assassination
Reward: Experience, Gold, Item, Dryad River Pearl

Principal Players

Goblin Grumdjum
River Dryad

Quest Details

When you enter Lago Del Rio Ebro, you won't have to travel far before being met by Goblin Grumdjum. If you have a mercenary's heart, you accept Grumdjum's offer for slaying the River Dryad near the center of this area. Use the Magic Crystal in the northeast corner just above Grumdjum to reach the River Dryad.

Your first option when speaking to the water witch is to have a change of heart about your quest. Opting out would be the nobler thing to do, but those of you with bloodlust in your heart choose the second option and complete the task you accepted by killing the River Dryad. Killing her brings negative Karma and affects the end of the game. If you choose to fight her, protect yourself from Fire and Electrical damage.

If you choose to side with the River Dryad and your Speech skill is high enough, you may have another option. You may be able to devise a plan to lure Grumdjum to the River Dryad so she may slay him. Keep in mind that as soon as you leave her protection, all Goblins have a death wish for you.

If you choose to deceive, return to Grumdjum and lie to him about her being dead. Grumdjum quickly travels back to the River Dryad's location to have a nice meal of brains. There he is destroyed, and you are rewarded for assisting the River Dryad.

If you opt to defeat the River Dryad, prepare for a few blasts of Electrical and Fire damage to come your way. The River Dryad is no piece of cake, but with increased Resistances you should be able to overtake her. Watch your back for Zombies to appear near the Magic Crystal. Have an antidote or two at the ready to cure you of any Poison damage inflicted by the Zombies.

RID THE DRYAD'S FOREST OF THE GOBLINS

Quest Synopsis

Challenge: Difficult
Location(s): Lago Del Rio Ebro, Waterfall Passage, Goblin Camp, Goblin Warrens
Quest NPCs: The River Dryad, Goblin Khan
Type: Assassination
Reward: Experience, Gold, Potion, Dryad River Pearl

Principal Players

River Dryad
Goblin Khan Plumdjum

Quest Details

Use the Magic Crystal in the northeast corner of Lago Del Rio Ebro to reach the River Dryad. The Dryad asks you to save her forest from destructive Goblin forces. To save the forest, you must slay the Goblin Khan who rules the Goblins in a village northwest of the lake.

NOTE *If you accepted the quest from the Goblin Grumdjum to destroy the River Dryad, you may still attempt this quest instead of fighting her.*

Use the Magic Crystal near the River Dryad to return to Lago Del Rio Ebro. Travel south, then west to the entrance to the Waterfall Passage. Defeat the Vodyanoi in the passage and exit through the west to reach the Goblin camp.

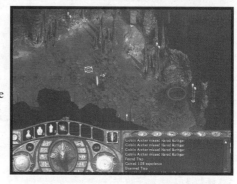

If this is your first visit to the Goblin camp, a Goblin greets you when you arrive. You can try to lie your way past this Goblin to travel through the Goblin camp unscathed, but it won't make any difference in the long run. When you return to camp after completing your quest to kill the Goblin Khan, you aren't received warmly. Battle your way past the Goblins to reach the Goblin Warrens.

> **TIP** *Duck in and out of the cave if you have difficulty eliminating the Goblins at the camp entrance. You can also use the Goblin huts to rest safely.*

The Goblin Khan is in the north part of the cave. You shouldn't have any problems reaching him—only a few Goblins stand between you and your goal. When you reach him, however, be prepared for an electrifying greeting. Several Goblin Shaman, ready to give their lives, attend the Goblin Khan. Boost your Electrical Resistance to endure their attacks. Defeat the Goblin Khan, return to the lake, and tell the Dryad that you have slain the Goblin Khan Plumdjum. The Khan is tough. Have lots of potions on hand and purchase the Everlasting from the Bounty Hunters west of the Goblin camp.

> **TIP** *Search the area for hidden walls after eliminating your enemies. There are treasures behind two hidden walls north of the late Goblin Khan's location.*

SLAY THE BOUNTY HUNTER FOR THE KHAN

Quest Synopsis

Challenge: Difficult
Location(s): Lago Del Rio Ebro, Waterfall Passage, Goblin Camp
Quest NPCs: Goblin Khan, Raylark the Bounty Hunter
Type: Assassination
Reward: Experience, Gold

Principal Players

Goblin Khan
Raylark the Bounty Hunter

Quest Details

When you reach the Goblin camp, tell the greeting Goblin that you have killed the River Dryad (lie if you must) to gain entry to the Goblin Khan's Cave.

Tell Khan you have killed the River Dryad (lie if necessary) to get this quest. Khan wants you to kill the Bounty Hunter. Travel to the southwest of the Goblin village in search of the Bounty Hunter.

Talk to Raylark the Bounty Hunter to learn about the Everlasting. You can ask Raylark to forge a similar weapon for you, but he won't. You can offer to pay for the weapon, but the price is exorbitant. The most attractive alternative is to take it from him. If this is the quest you wish to complete, kill the Bounty Hunter and the Everlasting is yours. Raylark is tough, so be careful. Have tons of healing potions ready and boost your defenses.

Return to Khan with the Everlasting. If you cower before him, ready to accept whatever he has to offer, Khan makes a meal of you.

SLAY GOBLINS FOR THE SAVAGE HEART

Quest Synopsis

Challenge: Difficult
Location(s): Bounty Hunter Camp,
Goblin Camp
Quest NPC: Raylark the Bounty Hunter
Type: Assassination
Reward: Gold

Principal Player

Raylark the Bounty Hunter

Quest Details

Speak with Raylark in the Bounty Hunter Camp and ask about his Goblin killing. If you agree to kill 12 Goblins, Raylark will share his bounty with you. Go into the Goblin village and kill 12 Goblins, returning to Raylark for your reward when you are done.

COLLECT THE GOBLIN SHAMAN RAKEB'S BOUNTY

Quest Synopsis

Challenge: Difficult
Location(s): Bounty Hunter Camp, Goblin Camp, Goblin Khan's Cave
Quest NPCs: Raylark the Bounty Hunter, Shaman Rakeb
Type: Assassination
Reward: Gold

Principal Players

Raylark the Bounty Hunter
Shaman Rakeb

Quest Details

Speak to Raylark the Bounty Hunter, and he engages you to slay the Shaman Rakeb. If you succeed, he'll split the bounty with you. Travel through the Goblin village to reach the Goblin Warrens and kill Rakeb. Return to Raylark and collect your reward.

ASSIST RAKEB THE GOBLIN SHAMAN

Quest Synopsis

Challenge: Easy
Location(s): Goblin Warrens, Waterfall Passage
Quest NPC: Rakeb
Type: Assassination
Reward: Gold

Principal Player

Rakeb

Quest Details

If you decide to befriend the Goblins instead of slaying them, travel through the Goblin camp into the Goblin Warrens and speak to the Shaman Rakeb. The Vodyanoi have prevented Rakeb from completing his work in the Waterfall Passage. Kill all the Vodyanoi in the Waterfall Passage and return to Rakeb for your reward.

COLLECT THE WOODCUTTER'S EYES

Quest Synopsis

Challenge: Medium
Location(s): Goblin Warrens, El Bosque
Quest NPCs: Shaman Rakeb, Woodcutter
Type: Assassination
Reward: Gold

Pricipal Players

Shaman Rakeb, Woodcutter

Quest Details

Completing this quest for the Shaman Rakeb has a serious impact on your Karma in the game. Think carefully before deciding to complete it. Rakeb is fascinated with the eyes of the Woodcutter in El Bosque. Agree to slay the Woodcutter and return his eyes and liver to Rakeb. When you return these items to Rakeb, she rewards you with gold and an opportunity to purchase weapons from her whenever you visit.

BUILD DA VINCI'S REPEATING CROSSBOW

Quest Synopsis

Challenge: Easy
Location(s): Barcelona Port District, Barcelona
Temple District
Quest NPC: Leonardo Da Vinci
Type: Recovery
Reward: Item (Repeating Crossbow)

Principal Player

Leonardo Da Vinci

Quest Details

Talk to Da Vinci in his workshop and ask him about his latest invention. Da Vinci purchased a crossbow from Weng Choi that he wants to improve upon, but he needs some final components to complete the design. Help Da Vinci by talking to the steam engine in Da Vinci's workshop to provide the gears Da Vinci needs. Be sure you have a potion in your inventory to give to the steam engine. Once you have the gears, return them to Da Vinci. The only other component Da Vinci needs is a lens. If you have not already retrieved the lens from the Observatory, travel to the Temple District and pry the lens from Galileo's telescope. Return it to Da Vinci to complete the bow. When Da Vinci is done, he gives the repeating crossbow to you.

RESCUE INQUISITOR DARSH

Quest Synopsis

Challenge: Difficult
Location(s): Lago Del Rio Ebro, Waterfall
Passage, Goblin Camp
Quest NPC: Inquisitor Darsh
Type: Rescue
Reward: Experience

Principal Player

Inquisitor Darsh

Quest Details

If you completed the River Dryad's quest, you may have spotted Inquisitor Darsh as you battled through the Goblin camp. If not, search the west side of the Goblin camp, eliminating any enemies you may have missed, and find Inquisitor Darsh. The Goblins are holding him prisoner. Agree to escort him safely to the Gate District of Barcelona.

Once you enter Waterfall Passage, the Inquisitor offers to use his magic to help you elude the Goblins. Either agree to his offer and leave the Waterfall Passage when the way is clear, or prepare for battle. If you choose to fight, lure the Goblins away from Darsh. If he dies, your quest fails.

If you destroyed the enemies on your way to the Goblin camp, you shouldn't have any problems getting Inquisitor Darsh to Barcelona. Watch out for Wolves that may have respawned in the areas you travel through. Upon reaching Barcelona, Inquisitor Darsh thanks you and rewards you for your bravery.

NOTE *If you followed the path of the Inquisition, you complete this quest as part of your initiation.*

RELEASE THE SPIRIT OF THE PRISONER'S WIFE

Quest Synopsis

Challenge: Easy
Location: Inquisition Chambers
Quest NPCs: Prisoner, Spirit of Prisoner's Wife
Type: Rescue
Reward: Experience

Principal Players

Prisoner
Spirit of Prisoner's Wife

Quest Details

While in the Inquisition Chambers, speak to the prisoner lying on the floor. The soul of the prisoner's dead wife is trapped in her cell, begging for release. Promise the prisoner you will find his wife and release her spirit. The prisoner has imbued you with his powerful spirit to help you breach his wife's locked cell.

Open the jammed door while the spirit is within you. It fades, and if it goes before the door is open, the quest fails.

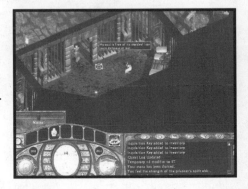

Return to the prisoner and tell him that you freed his wife's spirit. Knowing that his wife's spirit has been freed, the prisoner can now leave this plane of existence.

RESCUE FAUST FROM THE INQUISITION

Quest Synopsis

Challenge: Medium

Location(s): Inquisition Dungeon, Inquisition Chambers

Quest NPCs: Galileo, Faust

Type: Rescue

Reward: Experience, Galileo's Magical Battery Perk

Principal Players

Galileo

Faust

Quest Details

Take advantage of completing another simple quest by reaching deeper into the bowels of the Inquisition's headquarters. If you have not been here before as part of an initiation, you must complete a few minor steps to proceed.

From the Inquisition Chambers, release the jailed Inquisitor. This may be accomplished by either lying to the Inquisitor standing nearby to acquire three cell keys, or by using your Lockpick skill on the door. Either way, open the door and the Inquisitor attacks everyone nearby—even you!

While the guard's attentions are drawn to the escaped prisoner, use your Lockpick skills on the chest nearby, which contains the Scepter of the Chambers. Use the scepter on the destroyed artifact to the west to release the force fields over the prisoner's cells. The prisoners mistake you for one of their jailers, so be prepared to battle past them to reach the stairway to the Inquisition Dungeon.

Defeat any roaming Weak Terrors nearby and speak with Galileo. To your surprise, Galileo does not wish to be set free, but he does have a friend imprisoned upstairs in the Inquisition Chambers whom he wishes you to release.

Return upstairs and speak with the jailed Wielder. Unlock his cell and he disappears. Don't worry about the guards. They are too busy yawning to notice that most of their prisoners are gone. Return to Galileo to inform him that his friend has been set free, and receive your reward.

QUEST FOR LA BESTIA

Quest Synopsis

Challenge: Difficult
Location(s): Barcelona Temple District,
Barcelona Port District, El Bosque, Rio Ebro,
Barcelona Coast
Quest NPCs: Cervantes, Da Vinci
Type: Rescue
Reward: Experience

Principal Players

Cervantes
Signor Leonardo Da Vinci

Quest Details

As you wander about the Temple District of Barcelona, you can't help overhearing the nonsensical ramblings of Miguel Cervantes. He is seeing "La Bestia" (the beast) around the Temple District.

Speak to Cervantes and he tells you about his quest, though most of it won't make sense. Agree to help Cervantes track the dangerous monster known as "La Bestia." Follow Cervantes so he can lead you to the creature.

After following Cervantes for a while, if your Speech skill is high enough you can suggest to him that you should lead the hunt. If not, a Knight Templar decides to take care of Cervantes. Persuade him that Cervantes is mad but not criminal, and he puts Cervantes in the Inquisition Dungeon. Any other response gets Cervantes killed and the quest fails.

To free Cervantes, you need to use the Scepter of the Chambers from the Inquisition Chambers and fix the destroyed cross to the west. This allows you to reach the Dungeon and Cervantes, who is locked in a cell. Use either the jailer's keys or pick the lock to free him. Cervantes suggests you take the lead from now on.

With Cervantes following you, go to Da Vinci's workshop in the Port District. Talk to Da Vinci, to learn that Cervantes must have used Da Vinci's enchanted quill to bring one of his legendary creations to life. To help Cervantes, you must have him accompany you to the Barcelona Coast to confront the beast.

TIP *Before you attempt this quest, travel to the Barcelona Coast and rid the areas of enemies. Otherwise, traveling to the coast is dangerous to Cervantes.*

When you reach the Barcelona Coast, go to the windmill, where you discover the beast of Cervantes is the Shade of Don Quixote. Quixote believes that Cervantes is a monstrous dragon and stalking him. Talk to Quixote and persuade him to dissolve. Fight him if your Speech skill isn't high enough.

TASK FOR MACHIAVELLI

Quest Synopsis

Challenge: Medium
Location: Barcelona Temple District
Quest NPC: Machiavelli
Type: Rescue
Reward: Gold

Principal Player

Machiavelli

Quest Details

Talk to Machiavelli in the Barcelona Temple District, and he hires you as a personal guard to protect him against any would-be assassins seeking to end his political ambitions. You must search inside and outside his home to ensure his safety.

When you exit Machiavelli's home, you hear screams coming from inside. Re-enter the house to see Machiavelli being attacked. Ignore the enemies nearest the door and rush to Machiavelli's side to draw the attention of his would-be assassins, saving his life. After the battle you learn of Machiavelli's betrayal. Either slay him or take the high road and let him go.

FIND THE CURE TO RESTORE BRAMBLES

Quest Synopsis

Challenge: Difficult
Location(s): La Calle Perdida, Slave Pit Exterior
Quest NPCs: Brambles, Relican
Type: Recovery
Reward: Gold, Brambles' Patience Perk

Principal Players

Brambles
Relican

Quest Details

Talk to the tree in La Calle Perdida and you discover it is actually a person, cursed and transformed into the tree. Brambles, the tree, believes that Relican, the exiled Necromancer, can undo the curse. Relican has fled Barcelona and may be hiding in the western forest.

To find Relican, you must travel to the Slave Pit Exterior. Relican is in the southwest corner of the area. Before engaging Relican, increase your Electrical and Disease Resistances. When you speak to Relican, tell him you are there to recover the cure for Brambles. Unfortunately, Relican isn't interested in helping Brambles, or anyone else for that matter. Defeat Relican and the minions he spawns. When he has been defeated, pick up the Potion of Transformation, return to La Calle Perdida, and speak with Brambles, who is thrilled to have the cure.

The potion drains into the ground and Brambles absorbs it. To show his thanks, Brambles not only rewards you with gold, but also teaches you Brambles' Patience Perk.

SEARCH FOR THE FIVE WAYS CRYSTALS

Quest Synopsis

Challenge: Easy to Difficult
Location: La Calle Perdida
Quest NPC: Wielder
Type: Discovery
Reward: Modifying Crystals

Principal Player

Wielder

Quest Details

Speak to the Wielder on the east side of La Calle Perdida. Use the Ways Crystal nearby to permanently modify some of your skills. Speak to the Wielder again and ask about the Ways Crystal. Finding and using all five Ways Crystals bestows upon you an additional Wielder faction Perk. The other four Ways Crystals are in the Bounty Hunter Camp, the exterior forest of Nostradamus Caverns, the Shrine Dungeon, and in Alamut.

HELP THE CONSPIRATOR AGAINST THE SPANISH ARMADA

Quest Synopsis

Challenge: Medium
Location(s): Barcelona Port District, Barcelona Gate District
Quest NPC: Guitterez
Type: Assassination
Reward: Experience, Gold

Principal Players

Guitterez
Captain Isabella

Quest Details

Have a drink with Guitterez in the Serpent's Bile. When he makes a toast to Spain, you toast England. Though Guitterez finds your toast curious, he does not initiate a battle. Instead, he questions you more. Tell him your allegiance is with England and Guitterez whispers he wants a discreet meeting with you outside of the Barcelona gates. Go to the west side of the outside gates to meet with Guitterez.

Speak to Guitterez and he tells you his real name is Guy Fawkes. Though once opposed to England's royalty, he is now an agent of Queen Elizabeth. The Queen has ordered Guy to infiltrate the Spanish Armada and learn what secrets he can of their invasion plans. Agree to speak with Captain Isabella to learn of the Spanish invasion, then return to Guy Fawkes with the information.

Guy asks that you perform another task for England. He has plotted to kill the Duke of Medina Sidonia and needs your help to see his plot to fruition. To help Guy with his plot, you must lure the Duke to Guy's trap in the Port District. Speak to the Duke and tell him a man claiming to possess knowledge of the English fleet wants to meet with him. This prompts the Duke to leave his ship and go to the Port District.

When he passes a fenced-in area near Da Vinci's home, a bomb explodes, killing the Duke. Return to Guy, tell him of the Duke's death, and receive your reward.

You have the option of changing the outcome of this quest. When you speak to the Duke, tell him your conscience forces you to tell him the truth about the plot against his life. Because you are the only one who knows the conspirator's identity, the Duke asks that you end the threat by dealing with him yourself. Return to Guy Fawkes and tell him you have exposed his deception to the Duke. After defeating Guy, return to the Duke for your reward.

SOLVE THE MURDER OF CAPTAIN MORALES

Quest Synopsis

Challenge: Difficult
Location(s): Barcelona Coast, Barcelona Port District
Quest NPCs: The Ghost of Captain Morales, Captain Isabella, Mute Sailor, Sailor
Type: Task
Reward: Experience

PRINCIPAL PLAYERS

Ghost of Captain Morales
Mute Sailor
Sailor
Captain Isabella

Quest Details

If you completed the quest for Cervantes, your quest took you to Rio Ebro. Travel west from Rio Ebro to reach the Barcelona Coast. Travel south near the water's edge to see the ghost of Captain Morales. Your initial meeting isn't smooth, as Captain Morales believes you are the murderer who stabbed him and threw him in the ocean, where the sharks had him for an hors d'oeuvre.

Morales believes there was a witness to his murder, another who was on the deck at the time of his demise. It was dark, and Morales didn't see who the crewmember was. The captain's ship is docked at the Barcelona port, so agree to search the Port District to find the witness.

Talk to the mute sailor on the dock. This is the man who witnessed the murder of Captain Morales, but he will not reveal the killer's identity to you. He mentions, however, that he "spoke" to another member of the crew—a horned sailor, likely a tainted Demokin.

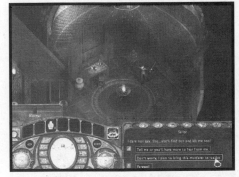

Go to the Serpent's Bile in the Port District and talk to the sailor in the darkened corner. The mute sailor, Aidan, told this sailor that the killer stabbed Captain Morales in the back and pushed him overboard during last month's storm. The sailor will not reveal the murderer's name, in fear that "she" may find out and kill him.

The only seafaring "she" in the area is Captain Isabella aboard La Libertad de Espana. Tell Captain Isabella you spoke with the witnesses and that you believe she is Captain Morales's killer. You have several options to finish this portion of the quest, including being paid for your silence, rendering swift justice by the use of your own sword, or, if your Speech skill is high enough, persuading Captain Isabella to turn herself in and explain her story to the authorities.

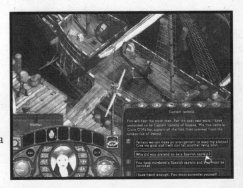

Return to the coastline outside of Barcelona and tell Captain Morales's spirit that Isabella killed him to take over his command. Relieved to know the truth, the spirit of Captain Morales can rest in peace.

SLAY THE GOBLIN KHAN

Quest Synopsis

Challenge: Difficult
Location(s): Inquisition Chambers, Goblin Camp
Quest NPCs: Torquemada the Grand Inquisitor, Goblin Khan
Type: Assassination
Reward: Experience, Gold

Principal Players

Torquemada the Grand Inquisitor
Goblin Khan

Quest Details

The Grand Inquisitor Tomas de Torquemada tells you of the evil that has taken root in the forests outside of Barcelona, threatening to devour the fruits of the Inquisition's labor. If you wish to aid the continuing cause of the Inquisition, seek out Khan of the Goblin tribes and deal with him.

When you reach Lago Del Rio Ebro, Goblin Grumdjum confronts you. Grumdjum wants you to destroy the River Dryad, a water witch living in these parts who has caused his clan trouble. This quest is listed in detail earlier. If you decide to destroy the River Dryad, this quest is added to your Quest Log.

If you refuse Grumdjum's proposal, be prepared to do battle with not only Grumdjum, but also with all Goblins you encounter from this point on. Because your ultimate goal is to slay the Goblin leader, Khan, throwing down the gauntlet now just hastens the Goblin enmity you'll feel when you slay Khan.

It pays to slay the Goblins in this area now. When the northeast corner is cleared of the Goblin threat, use the Magic Crystal in the northeast corner to reach the River Dryad.

THE RIVER DRYAD

When you speak with the River Dryad, she asks you to save her forest from the destructive Goblin forces. To save the forest, you must slay the Goblin Khan who rules the Goblins in a village northwest of the lake. The Goblin Khan is the target of your current quest, so these two overlap well.

Agree to the River Dryad's request, and this quest is added to your Quest Log.

Cross the Waterfall Passage, slaying any Vodyanoi you encounter on the way to the Goblin camp. As you enter the Goblin camp, either confront the Goblin that greets you, exposing your intent to slay their Goblin Khan, or, if your Speech skill is high enough, persuade the Goblin of your peaceful nature so he allows you to pass through the area.

Because your ultimate goal is to destroy the Goblin Khan, the current generosity of this Goblin vanishes when you emerge victorious from Goblin Khan's Cave.

Instead of traveling north through the Goblin camp, continue east, battling Goblins as you go to the Bounty Hunter Camp. Once there, speak with the Bounty Hunter and learn his strategy for slaying Goblins. The Everlasting, though expensive, is worth the gold the Bounty Hunter wants for it.

Don't bother asking him to forge one for you; he hasn't the time or the inclination to help you. If you can afford it, purchase the Everlasting. When it comes to destroying Goblins, there is no better weapon in the entire game.

With the Everlasting in hand, return to the Goblin camp and battle with the roaming Goblins before entering Goblin Khan's Cave. Have your Find Traps detector at the ready whenever you're in a new area. Damage suffered from these traps could be hazardous to your health and could make the difference between success and failure in the upcoming battle.

The Goblin Khan is not alone. Goblin Archers and Shamans home in on you, ready to pay the ultimate price to prevent you from fulfilling your destiny. Do not underestimate the Goblin Shamans. They can blast you with magic that freezes you in your tracks, providing ample opportunities for Goblin Khan to inflict damage on your character. Have lots of healing potions on hand. The Goblin Khan is a strong enemy and lethal in battle.

Even if you cleared the Goblin camp before entering the Goblin Khan's Cave, Goblins wait for you to exit the cave. More Goblin Shamans may wait outside the cave, so have your health maxed out before you leave the cave.

When you've slain Goblin Khan Plumdjum and fought through the Goblin village, return to the Inquisition Chambers in Barcelona, and tell the Grand Inquisitor that your quest is complete.

SEARCH FOR THE RELICS

BATTLE TO THE ABBEY

Having completed the first part of your quest, you must travel on. Regardless of the faction you join, all roads lead to Montserrat. You must travel to Montserrat to ensure that the relic hidden within the Abbey walls is safe. Use the portal in La Calle Perdida or the Crossroads to access the world map; select Montserrat.

> **NOTE** *Don't be surprised if you get to this point in the game with little experience—as early as Level 10 or as late as Level 20. Your level depends largely on the number of quests you complete in and around Barcelona. Getting this far at a low level isn't a bad thing, because the game adjusts to your level, but it isn't recommended. You benefit greatly by completing as many quests as possible.*

MONTSERRAT

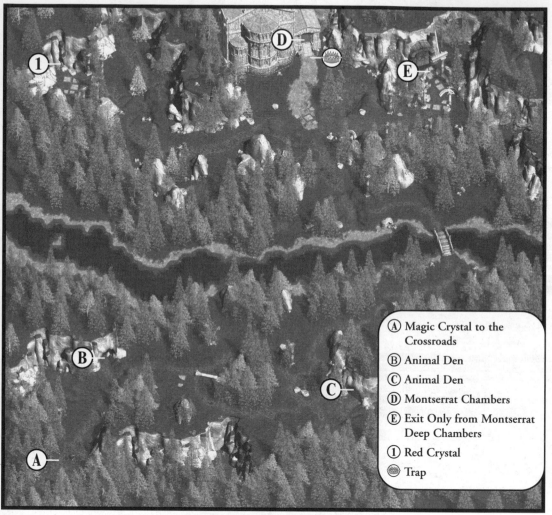

A — Magic Crystal to the Crossroads
B — Animal Den
C — Animal Den
D — Montserrat Chambers
E — Exit Only from Montserrat Deep Chambers
1 — Red Crystal
⬤ — Trap

Montserrat Grove

AREA ENEMIES

Black Wolf	Tainted Wasp
Grey Wolf	Vodyanoi
Snakebreed	Vodyanoi Feral
Snakebreed Crusher	Vodyanoi Spawn
Snakebreed Viper	

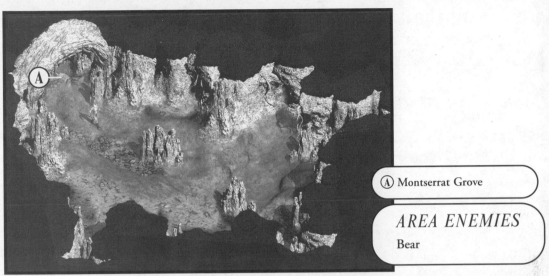

Ⓐ Montserrat Grove

AREA ENEMIES
Bear

Animal Den (Bears)

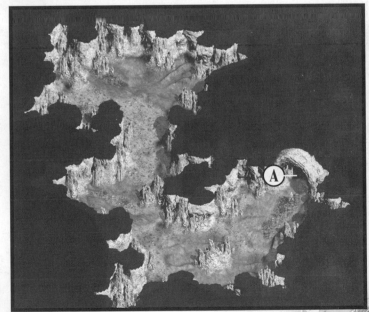

Ⓐ Montserrat Grove

AREA ENEMIES
Tainted Wasp
Wasp

Animal Den (Wasps)

Reaching the Abbey

The path to the Abbey is dangerous. Prepare for your journey by increasing your Poison Resistance. Snakebreeds attack when you near the Animal Den entrance. Travel the path slowly, drawing out these creatures a few at a time to avoid being overwhelmed. If you are inflicted with poison, let it run its course, and heal fully from any battle damage before continuing up the path.

Gain experience by entering the Animal Den northwest of the crystal. The cave has no chests or hidden treasures, but any experience that helps you increase your level is beneficial.

Defeating the bears in the cave nets you a fair amount of experience points. More important, the life orbs you absorb from the slain bears help you heal faster for your journey farther up the path to Montserrat Abbey. Search the entire cave for Mana orbs that may be tucked away in the corners of the cave.

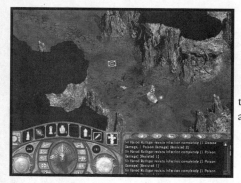

The second cave holds no chests or hidden treasures, but there are plenty of Wasps. Arm yourself against Poisoning and defeat all Wasps in the cave.

Back on the path to the Abbey, you hear the all-too-familiar sounds of nearby Vodyanoi, typically keeping to the shoreline. Prepare for the Vodyanoi's Poison attacks.

Just up the path from the Vodyanoi, more Snakebreeds attack from the south as you near the bridge. A camp of Snakebreeds is farther south if you veer from the path. Avoid this area to conserve any antidotes you may be carrying.

From the bridge to the entrance of the Abbey, Snakebreeds and Vodyanoi try to prevent you from continuing your journey. Defeat them. Once you reach the Abbey steps, keep your Find Traps skill active to identify a trap at the Abbey steps. Use the Magic Crystal to return to Barcelona and restock your antidote supply before entering the Abbey. When you return, the creatures previously slain have not respawned, so you have safe access to the Abbey.

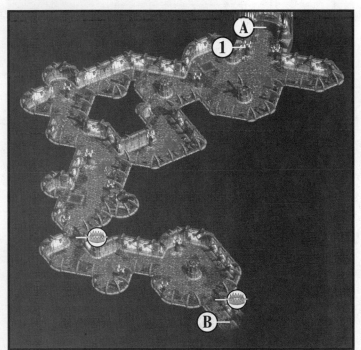

Montserrat Chambers

- Ⓐ Montserrat Grove
- Ⓑ Montserrat Deep Chambers
- ① Door Switch
- Trap

AREA ENEMIES

Snakebreed
Snakebreed Crusher
Snakebreed Viper

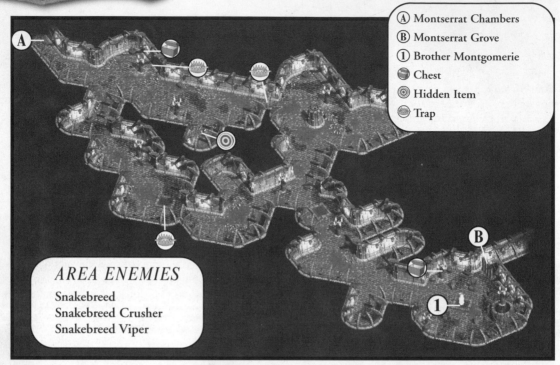

A — Montserrat Chambers
B — Montserrat Grove
1 — Brother Montgomerie
— Chest
— Hidden Item
— Trap

AREA ENEMIES

Snakebreed
Snakebreed Crusher
Snakebreed Viper

Montserrat Deep Chambers

Staying Alive

Arm yourself with any spells at your disposal to help you defeat the Snakebreed menace that roams the halls of Montserrat Abbey. Use the orbs available from any slain enemies to keep your health and Mana at their max.

Beware of the many vicious Snakebreed Crushers. These creatures are devastating, so avoid fighting more than two at a time or you rapidly consume your stock of healing potions.

TIP *Activate your Find Traps skill after every battle. Although the first floor of the Abbey has no hidden treasures, be prepared for traps that may block your path. Refer to the map to see trap locations and disable them.*

A large group of Snakebreeds is near the Montserrat Deep Chambers entrance. Lure the Snakebreeds out a few at a time to thin their numbers and decrease your risk. Snakebreeds expel poison a long distance. Pulling the enemy out and around a corner allows you to battle one or two at a time rather than drawing too many enemies at once.

Brother Montgomerie

Besides the Snakebreed threat in the Abbey, the Deep Chambers has traps. Keep your Find Traps skill active to avoid these dangerous pitfalls.

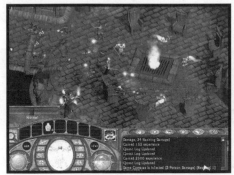

You must defeat all of the Snakebreeds in the Montserrat Deep Chambers before speaking to Brother Montgomerie. Cautiously approach the area where Brother Montgomerie lies. Multiple Snakebreeds surround him. Lure out the Snakebreeds, reducing the number you must battle at one time. After you eliminate the threat, approach Brother Montgomerie.

Brother Montgomerie tells you with his dying breath that he is the last survivor of Montserrat. Horrible beasts charged in, stealing the relic he was guarding. The creatures that took the relic went north, seeking more relics. Brother Montgomerie tells you to travel north to seek the guidance of Brother Michel in Montaillou.

Return to your guildmaster to report your findings. Back at Barcelona and the Crossroads, restock your supply of antidotes, which has probably diminished since you first entered the Abbey. Purchase all the weapon and armor upgrades you can afford. Travel to La Calle Perdida if possible, or go to the Crossroads and use the Magic Crystal to reach the Plains.

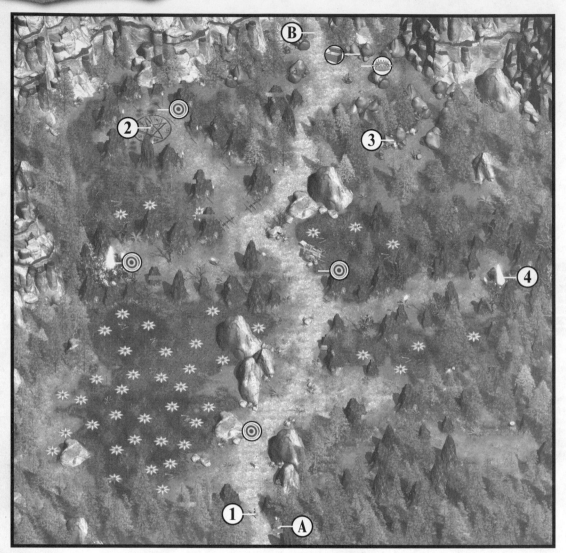

Duero Plains

(A) World Map
(B) Pyrenees Mountains
(1) Inquisitor Diego
(2) Mauldo the Wilderness Merchant
(3) Dark Inquisitor Leader
(4) Red Crystal
◎ Hidden Item
⬚ Trap

AREA ENEMIES

Black Wolf
Dark Inquisitors
Goblin Archer
Hired Beastman
Hired Goon
Mongol Goblin
Poisonous Plant

BRING THE DARK INQUISITORS TO JUSTICE

Quest Synopsis

Challenge: Medium
Location: Duero Plains
Quest NPCs: Inquisitor Diego, the Dark Inquisitor
Type: Assassination
Reward: Experience, Gold

Principal Players

Inquisitor Diego
The Dark Inquisitor

Quest Details

When you appear in Duero Plains, Inquisitor Diego begs for your assistance with a task. A cult of heretics masquerading as Inquisitors is committing atrocities against the people. Inquisitor Diego asks that you walk with him and bring these Inquisitors to justice. Inquisitor Diego believes the Dark Inquisitors are camped in the northern area of the Plains.

CAUTION *Avoid the plants in the area. As you near them they explode, shooting poisonous thorns at anyone unfortunate enough to be standing nearby.*

TIP *As you head off to complete this quest, leave Inquisitor Diego at the crystal to protect him from harm.*

As you start your walk, hired goons block your path, demanding your gold. No matter how accommodating you are, these goons aren't satisfied. Get rid of them and save yourself the aggravation of trying to appease them. After dealing with the Snakebreeds, these guys seem like marshmallows to defeat.

As you near the ritual circle, the Dark Inquisitor stops you. Confront him and prepare to do battle with the Dark Inquisitor and all of the Inquisitors in his circle. Lightning blasts abound as the Dark Inquisitors attempt to thwart your quest of execution. Protect yourself against Fire and Electrical damage before fighting. Defeat the Dark Inquisitors and keep Inquisitor Diego alive to successfully complete this quest. If you left Inquisitor Diego behind, return to him to complete this quest.

NOTE *If your Speech skill is high enough, you can aid the Dark Inquisitors by accepting their quest to slay Inquisitor Diego. Naturally, if you accept this task, your quest for Inquisitor Diego fails.*

Mauldo the Wilderness Merchant

East of the Dark Inquisitors, you see Mauldo the Wilderness Merchant. Mauldo's stock is limited, but he has some powerful weapons for sale. Consider them. Also, sell off any excess items you're carrying.

The Goblin Camp

Travel carefully as you head north from Mauldo. There is a camp nearby that is full of bloodthirsty Goblins hungry for a meal of misguided travelers. Lure Goblins away from the camp, reducing the number attacking you to a more manageable number. Use Arrow Deflection potions to help ward off the Goblin Archer's well-aimed arrows.

THE PYRENEES MOUNTAINS

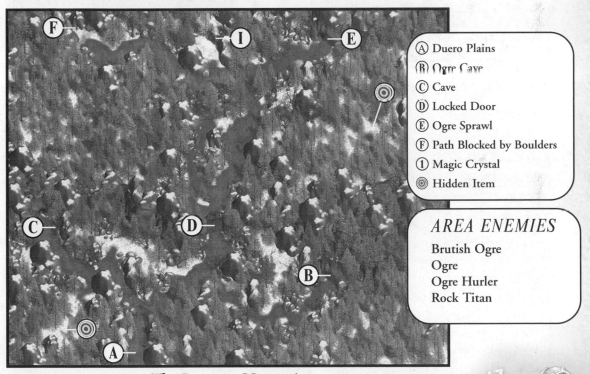

Ⓐ Duero Plains
Ⓑ Ogre Cave
Ⓒ Cave
Ⓓ Locked Door
Ⓔ Ogre Sprawl
Ⓕ Path Blocked by Boulders
① Magic Crystal
◎ Hidden Item

AREA ENEMIES

Brutish Ogre
Ogre
Ogre Hurler
Rock Titan

The Pyrenees Mountains

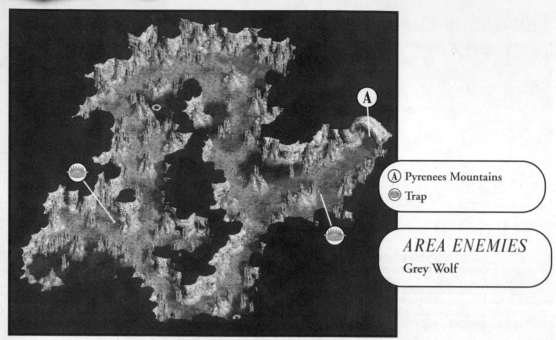

Ⓐ Pyrenees Mountains

Trap

AREA ENEMIES

Grey Wolf

The Cave

Ⓐ Pyrenees Mountains

Ⓑ Ogre Sprawl

Chest

Hidden Item

Trap

AREA ENEMIES

Brutish Ogre

Ogre

Ogre Hurler

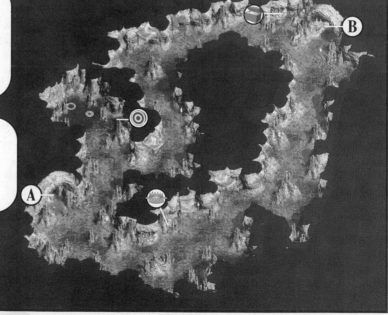

Ogre Cave

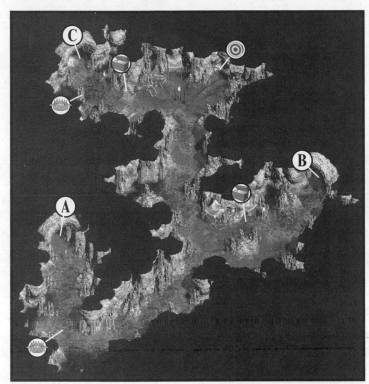

Ⓐ Ogre Cave
Ⓑ Aka Manah's Lair
Ⓒ The Wilderness Pass
🛢 Chest
◎ Hidden Item
🛡 Trap

AREA ENEMIES

Brutish Ogre
Ogre
Ogre Hurler

Ogre Sprawl

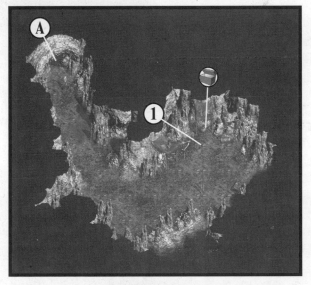

Ⓐ Ogre Sprawl
① Aka Manah
🛢 Chest

AREA ENEMIES

Aka Manah

Aka Manah's Lair

The Titans

Cold and desolate, the Pyrenees Mountains pose challenges far beyond the bitterly cold winds sweeping down their sides. Travel cautiously in this rocky landscape, listening for the growls of the inhabitants.

Explore the cave northwest of your starting point, destroying the Grey Wolves that roam within. Look for hidden traps and treasures as you clear the cave.

Ignore the main path heading north through the center of the Pyrenees Mountains—a massive door blocks the path and cannot be opened. Travel east instead. Ogres of awesome strength wander about the area, attacking all who dare pass. Arm your most devastating weapon to combat the Ogres and reach the Ogre Cave. Increase your resistance to Crushing damage to make the battles easier.

Whether you select the northeast or northwest path, you cannot escape the Ogres residing in Ogre Cave. Because of the cave's close confines, it's easy to lure out one or two Ogres at a time. Watch for traps in this cave as you wind your way around to the Ogre Sprawl.

TIP *Ogres are very resistant to Crushing damage. If you usually sport a mace, hammer, or morning star, arm yourself with a sword to carve your way through this area.*

Keep your Find Traps skill up and running after each battle in the Ogre Sprawl. A trap blocks your way just south of the entrance. Disarm it lest you accidentally trip it in the heat of battle.

Near the entrance to Aka Manah's Lair, speak to the Ogre and learn of his confused state just before he runs off. You don't have to enter the lair immediately, but if you try to leave this area without visiting Aka Manah's Lair, you're automatically teleported there.

The short path leading to Aka Manah is safe from attack, as no other being inhabits the lair. When you speak with Aka Manah, you discover he has no interest in letting anyone leave. Aka Manah splits into three identical creatures to aid in the bloodletting about to begin.

Two of the creatures fall quickly, but the real Aka Manah is not easily defeated. Use any spell at your disposal to eliminate this Daeva. He splits several times during the battle. Keep your Fire and Electricity resistances boosted throughout the battle, and keep potions on hand for quick healing.

Exit Ogre Sprawl to return to the Pyrenees Mountains. More Ogres wait for you as you exit the cave. Battle your way to the Magic Crystal and teleport to Montaillou.

MONTAILLOU

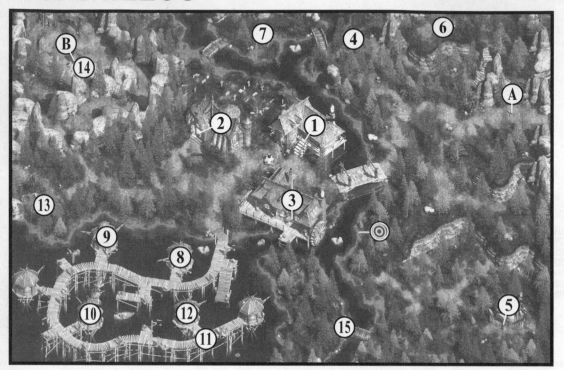

Montaillou

Ⓐ World Map	⑧ Beatrice the Woman		
Ⓑ Strange Cave	⑨ Marlin		
① Tavern of the Bright Sword	⑩ Merchant Adelie		
② Church	⑪ Lucius		
③ Mayor's House	⑫ Brother Michel		
④ Beatrice the Chicken	⑬ Merchant Guillaume		
⑤ Na Roqua	⑭ Nanghaithya		
⑥ Signor Leo	⑮ Maury the Shepherd		
⑦ Charmed Sculpture	◎ Hidden Item		

AREA ENEMIES

Black Wolf
Grey Wolf
Vodyanoi
Vodyanoi Spawn

FIND THE TEMPLAR CRYPT AND RECOVER THE SACRED LANCE

Seek out Brother Michel on the dock. Before you can enter, you must defeat his companion, the Rock Titan Lucius. If your Diplomacy skill is high enough, you may be able to persuade Lucius to allow you to pass. If not, you must defeat him (which isn't difficult). After he takes a few good hits, he concedes.

Tell Brother Michel that the relic was stolen from Montserrat Abbey. Another relic is hidden within the Crypt of the Knights Templar. Brother Michel believes the crypt is no longer a secure resting place for the Holy Lance. You must journey there, defeat the undead sealed within, and recover the lance. After you speak to Brother Michel, the crypt appears on the world map.

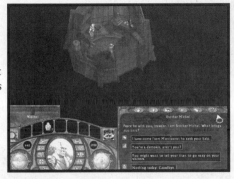

Ⓐ World Map
Ⓑ Crypt Antechamber

AREA ENEMIES

Brittle Skeleton
Screaming Terror
Skeleton
Zombie

Crypt Entrance

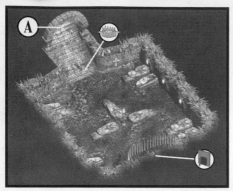

Ⓐ Crypt Entrance
Ⓑ Retreat of Souls
◉ Secret Wall
◉ Trap

Retreat of Souls Entry

AREA ENEMIES

Greater Skeleton

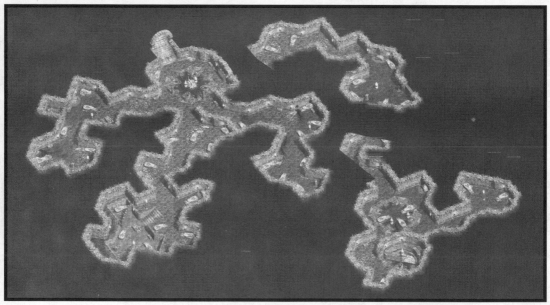

Retreat of Souls

Ⓐ Antechamber
Ⓑ Mausoleum of Clovis
Ⓒ Main Switch to Lower Wall
Ⓓ Defiled Vault of Remigius
Ⓔ Doomed Plateau

① Ivory Mace of Divinity
◉ Chest
Ⓢ Switch
◉ Secret Wall
◉ Trap

AREA ENEMIES

Brimstone Soul Reaver
Disemboweled Gangler
Festering Ghast
Ghoul
Greater Skeleton
Huge Ghoul
Second Guardian
Skeleton
Terror
Zombie

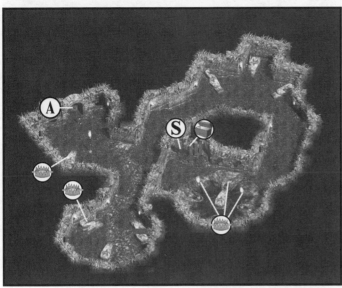

Mausoleum of Clovis

Ⓐ Retreat of Souls
🛢 Chest
Ⓢ Switch
⬜ Trap

AREA ENEMIES

Screaming Terror
Skeleton
Zombie

Ⓐ Retreat of Souls
① Blade of the Berserker
🛢 Chest
⬜ Trap

AREA ENEMIES

Revenant
Screaming Terror
Zombie

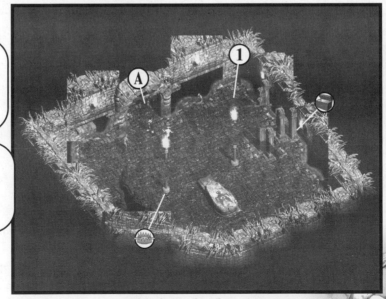

Defiled Vault of Remiquis

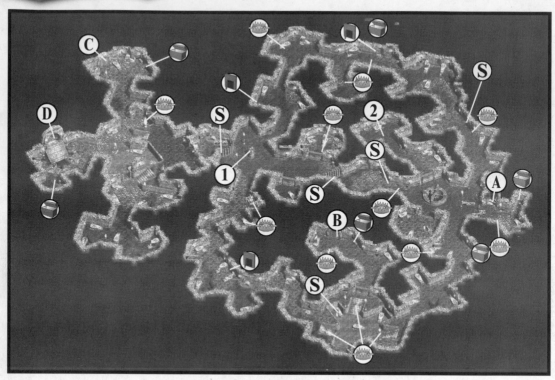

Doomed Plateau

Ⓐ Retreat of Souls
Ⓑ Crypte De Trois
Ⓒ Merovingian Crypt
Ⓓ Burial Chambers
① Jehanne D'Arc
② Spirit Council
Ⓢ Chest
Ⓢ Secret Wall
Ⓢ Switch
Ⓢ Trap

AREA ENEMIES

Arctic Succubus
Brimstone Soul Reaver
Charred Terror
Disemboweled Gangler
Ghoul
Greater Skeleton
Huge Ghoul
Mana Reaver
Revenant
Screaming Terror
Zombie

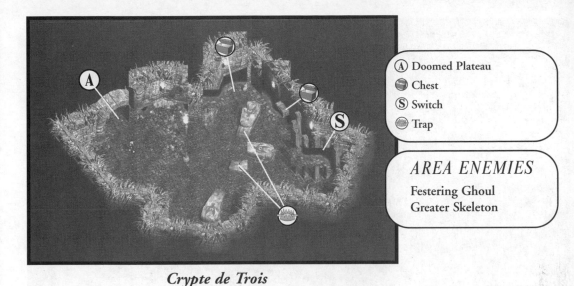

Ⓐ Doomed Plateau
🔘 Chest
Ⓢ Switch
▦ Trap

AREA ENEMIES

Festering Ghoul
Greater Skeleton

Crypte de Trois

Ⓐ Doomed Plateau
🔘 Chest
🔳 Secret Wall
Ⓢ Switch
▦ Trap

AREA ENEMIES

Disemboweled Gangler
Ghoul
Ghoulish Hag
Greater Skeleton
Huge Ghoul
Revenant
Screaming Terror

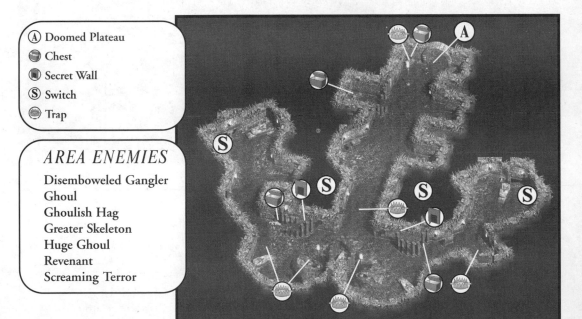

Merovingian Crypt

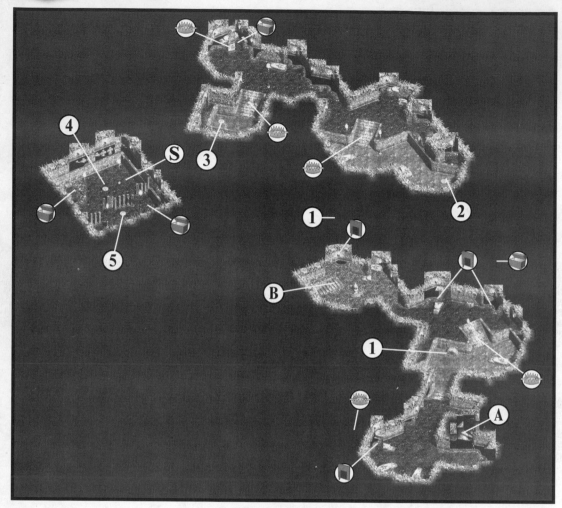

Burial Chambers

Ⓐ Doomed Plateau
Ⓑ Crypt of the Lance
① Magic Crystal to #2
② Magic Crystal to #1
③ Magic Crystal to #4
④ Magic Crystal to #3
⑤ Magic Crystal to Crypt of
   the Lance

Chest
Secret Wall
Ⓢ Switch
Trap

AREA ENEMIES

Arctic Succubus
Brimstone Soul Reaver
Frozen Terror
Ghoul
Ghoulish Hag
Greater Skeleton
Huge Ghoul
Skeleton
Zombie

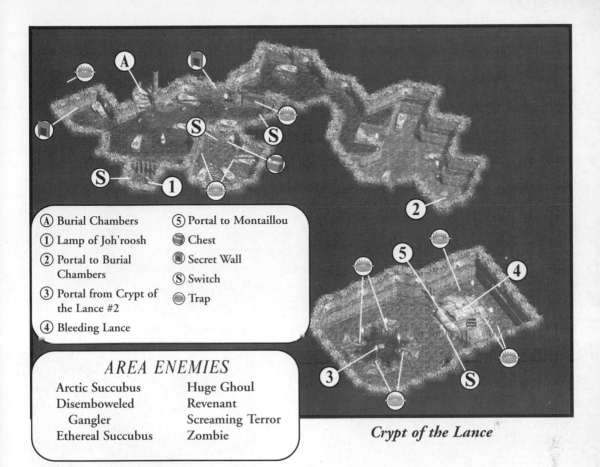

- **Ⓐ** Burial Chambers
- **①** Lamp of Joh'roosh
- **②** Portal to Burial Chambers
- **③** Portal from Crypt of the Lance #2
- **④** Bleeding Lance
- **⑤** Portal to Montaillou
- Chest
- Secret Wall
- **Ⓢ** Switch
- Trap

AREA ENEMIES

Arctic Succubus	Huge Ghoul
Disemboweled Gangler	Revenant
Ethereal Succubus	Screaming Terror
	Zombie

Crypt of the Lance

Retreat of Souls

Talk to the guard in the entry for the Retreat of Souls who asks you to make a choice. If your Find Traps/Secret Doors skill is high enough, however, you won't have to. Enemies attack from within any of the sarcophagi in the room's center. Watch for the Guardian of the Lance, which spawns from behind the spiked wall. Defeat it to claim the Bleeding Lance, or at least a reasonable facsimile. Have your Find Traps/Secret Doors skill up and walk to the spiked wall. The secret wall appears, and the spiked wall drops. Go into the Retreat of Souls.

Expect an unfriendly welcome when you enter. Keep your distance from the Disemboweled Ganglers or suffer the consequences of their combustible behavior.

TIP *Almost every sarcophagus throughout the crypt can be opened, revealing treasures or enemies trapped inside. If you open every sarcophagus, be careful. Many contain multiple creatures, including as many as three of the fierce Revenants. Save before opening any secret room or sarcophagus or before entering a new area.*

Refer to the map of this area often. Almost every path is lined with traps. Keep your Find Trap skill active!

Activate three switches on this floor to lower the spikes surrounding the switch in the center of the first room. Activating the center switch lowers a nearby wall, which leads to another hidden area. Be ready for an attack. When the barricade drops, the crypt's Second Guardian attacks with a horde of undead creatures. When you have all the treasures on this and the surrounding floors, head to the Doomed Plateau.

> **TIP** *In the Mausoleum of Clovis, opening a nearby sarcophagus lowers a barricade. Be ready with potions and save before triggering this trap! It spawns a Revenant, which is quickly followed by a storm of undead creatures. If you last that long, the cycle ends with a second Revenant.*

> **TIP** *Opening the sarcophagus in the Defiled Vault of Remiquis spawns three Revenants and lowers the barricade along the side. The treasure in the chest isn't usually worth the risk, but the decision is yours.*

Doomed Plateau

Talk to one of the knights guarding the area, who advises you to speak with Jehanne. As enemies attack, the guards assist you in slaying them. The number of enemies on these floors can be daunting. Take advantage of the extra blades whenever you can.

Speak to Jehanne, who dismisses your claim of wanting to protect the lance. Don't aggravate the situation. Instead, seek out the Spirit Council by heading down the central corridor. Tossing the second switch opens a path to the council.

The Spirit Council

As you approach the council, the spirits appear. Speak to them and hear the tale of Jehanne and her attempt, with the Saracen, to solicit protection for the lance with the aid of a lamp. Jehanne and all the knights who served her were cursed into undeath, condemning them to keep the relic safe for all time. The Spirit Council refers to Jehanne as the "Pious Child."

Return to Jehanne and mention "Pious Child" to prove that you have spoken with the Spirit Council. This is the only way to convince Jehanne you are there to protect the relic. When you have done so, Jehanne raises the gate, allowing you to pass to the tomb at the bottom of the crypt. Continue clearing this floor of enemies and looting treasures. When you're ready, enter the Burial Chambers.

NOTE *In the Merovingian Crypt, the two switches on the sides drop the barriers in front of the secret rooms. The switches in the secret rooms drop the barrier on the coffin in the center and in front of the chest near the stairs.*

The Burial Chambers

NOTE *In the Burial Chambers, use the portals to travel to various areas. Use the stairs B to reach a more protected area of the Crypt of the Lance.*

The Crypt of the Lance

If you used the stairs to reach this area, undead knights will help you slay enemies. Take advantage of the added strength, destroying all that attack.

Activate the switches to drop a wooden wall that protects another switch and the Lamp of Joh'roosh. Fazzad, the Spirit of the Lamp, offers to fulfill one wish exactly. You have the options of increasing your strength, your intelligence, or even your gold. You may even destroy all the enemies within the crypt. Choose the more altruistic wish to undo the curse laid upon Jehanne and her fellow knights. Any other choice is fulfilled with disastrous results.

Use the portal ② to reach the final stage for the crypt. When you materialize, you face the Assassin Master. The Assassin is a powerful foe with an unusual defense—he disappears and reappears at will. Keep your guard up, move constantly, and prepare for the Assassin to reappear behind you. Watch out for the traps in the immediate area and disarm them quickly. Once you vanquish the Assassin, activate the switch.

Disarm the traps surrounding the sarcophagus and open it, retrieving the Bleeding Lance. A portal materializes when you pick up the lance. Walk through it and you appear in Montaillou. Inform Brother Michel that you recovered the Bleeding Lance. You can speak to Brother Michel at length about the war, but promise him you will guard the lance and don't speak with him about it again.

SIDE QUESTING IN MONTAILLOU

You can complete several side quests in Montaillou to gain experience and gold before continuing your quest. You can complete most of these side quests within Montaillou, but a few require you to travel beyond the borders of this city on the water.

AREA ENEMIES

Black Wolf
Grey Wolf
Vodyanoi
Vodyanoi Spawn

Montaillou

Ⓐ World Map	⑤ Na Roqua	⑪ Lucius
Ⓑ Strange Cave	⑥ Signor Leo	⑫ Brother Michel
① Tavern of the Bright Sword	⑦ Charmed Sculpture	⑬ Merchant Guillaume
② Church	⑧ Beatrice the Woman	⑭ Nanghaithya
③ Mayor's House	⑨ Marlin	⑮ Maury the Shepherd
④ Beatrice the Chicken	⑩ Merchant Adelie	◎ Hidden Item

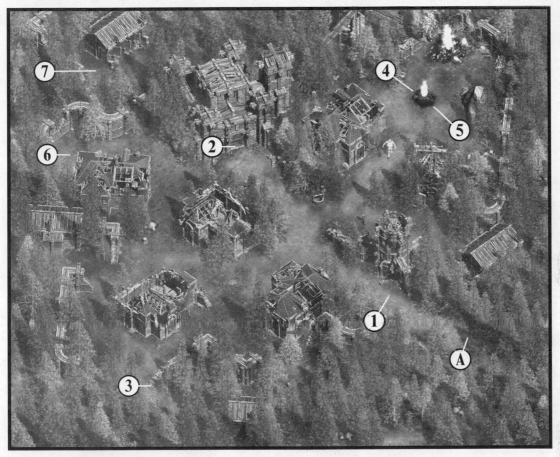

Toulouse

- Ⓐ World Map
- ① Tereo
- ② Lethos
- ③ Rhea
- ④ Menoetius
- ⑤ Iapetus
- ⑥ Thierrey
- ⑦ Thierrey's Cache

AREA ENEMIES

Rock Titans

RESCUE THE SHEPHERD

Quest Synopsis

Challenge: Easy
Location: Montaillou
Quest NPCs: Small Boy, Marlin
Type: Rescue
Reward: Experience, Gold

Principal Players

Henri
Marlin

Quest Details

As you approach the bridge south of Montaillou, a small child enlists your aid to save his father, Marlin. Marlin is across the bridge, protecting his herd from the attacking Vodyanoi. Cross the bridge and defeat the Vodyanoi.

THE CHARMED STATUE

Quest Synopsis

Challenge: Easy
Location: Montaillou
Quest NPCs: The Ghost, The Innkeeper,
    Inquisitor
Type: Discovery
Reward: Experience, Items, Gold

Principal Players

Ghost of the Innkeeper
Innkeeper
Inquisitor

Quest Details

Speak with the Innkeeper at the Tavern of the Bright Sword. The Innkeeper, always hospitable, asks if you're hungry. You have a choice of meat or vegetables. Meat-eaters aren't taken to kindly in Montaillou. If you ask for meat, the Innkeeper directs you down the steps to an Inquisitor happily munching on meat.

> **CAUTION** *If you ate meat with the Inquisitor, you are mugged when you leave the tavern. To avoid a nasty confrontation, convince the muggers that you side with the "good men" and have a spirit within you.*

Most first-time visitors happily accept the nonmeat dish to appease the villagers. Ask the Innkeeper about the previous owner and he recounts a mysterious tale of a treasure long lost. Accept wine from the Innkeeper and travel to the graveyard.

You can pour the wine on the grave, but the ghost isn't interested. Instead, he presents a puzzle for you to solve: He who lives the way he lived will be rewarded the secret of his treasure. It's time to go back to the tavern.

This time, head down the steps and ask the Inquisitor for a helping of meat. Return to the graveyard after you've finished your meal.

When you speak with the ghost, the faint scent of roasted meat does not escape him. Tell the ghost you shared a plate of meat, and you receive the secret of his treasure. Travel north from the ghost's grave and utter the secret words given to you by the ghost. The secret chamber containing the ghost's treasure opens.

HELP THE MAYOR RESTORE THE SOUL OF BEATRICE

Quest Synopsis

Challenge: Easy
Location: Montaillou
Quest NPCs: Mayor, Beatrice, Weird Woman
Type: Rescue
Reward: Experience, Gold

Principal Players

Mayor
Beatrice
Na Roqua (the Weird Woman)

Quest Details

Go to the Mayor's house in the center of Montaillou. The Mayor is upset about a personal matter. Talk to him and he enlists your aid to help him with a small task. The friend of a young woman accidentally transplanted the young woman's mind into the head of a chicken to protect her from the Inquisitors. You must find Beatrice and take her to Na Roqua, a witch who lives southeast of town. Na Roqua's magic can undo the blunder inflicted upon Beatrice.

Find Beatrice scratching the dirt northeast of the secret chamber that belongs to the ghost. Persuade Beatrice to travel with you to be saved. You must protect Beatrice from the attacking wolves as you make your way to Na Roqua. Tell Na Roqua the poor chicken you have is in need of her magic. When Beatrice's restoration is complete, return to the Mayor and tell him the curse has been undone.

OBTAIN THE SPIRIT GEM FOR DA VINCI

Quest Synopsis

Challenge: Easy to Difficult
Location: Montaillou
Quest NPCs: Da Vinci, Guillaume, Inquisitor Fournier
Type: Item Retrieval
Reward: Experience, Gold

Principal Players

Da Vinci
Guillaume
Inquisitor Fournier

Quest Details

Climb the stairs west of the guards near the crystal to see Da Vinci standing beside his inoperable flying machine. Ask Da Vinci what brings him to Montaillou. A merchant named Guillaume has promised to deliver a rare spirit bound with a special gem. Da Vinci needs this spirit to power one of his new inventions.

Guillaume is near the road on the town's west side. Unfortunately, he no longer has Da Vinci's gem. The Inquisitor Fournier stopped Guillaume, searched him, and took the gem. Speak to Inquisitor Fournier to retrieve the spirit gem.

The Inquisitor is in the church, but he isn't interested in your crusade to safeguard the relics. To prove your worthiness to him, you must perform certain tasks, like finding the witch Na Roqua for the Inquisitor to kill. You can decline the Inquisitor's offer. If you do, another task is offered to you, regarding the Mayor. You can tell the Inquisitor the Mayor is a heretic and adulterer.

If you complete both these tasks for the Inquisitor, you win his confidence and he gives you the gem. You will not be able to seek out Na Roqua to help you with further quests. If you deny any assistance to the Inquisitor, he dismisses you as a nuisance.

You can speak to the Inquisitor again and ask if he confiscated a magical gem from Guillaume. If your Speech skill is high enough, you can persuade him you will take the gem and destroy it. If you are successful in your lie, Fournier gives you a key to the chest nearby so you can retrieve the gem. If your Speech skill is not high enough, but your Sneak skill is high, you can pick the lock and steal the gem without attracting anyone's attention.

Your only other alternative is to kill Inquisitor Fournier and all the knights within the church, and steal the gem from the chest. Go to the tavern and return the gem to Da Vinci.

RESCUE THE PEOPLE OF TOULOUSE

Quest Synopsis

Challenge: Difficult
Location(s): Montaillou, Toulouse
Quest NPCs: Esclarmonde, Thierrey
Type: Rescue
Reward: None

Principal Players

Esclarmonde
Lethos
Rhea
Thierrey
Lucius

Quest Details

As you pass through Montaillou after speaking with Brother Michel, you overhear a conversation between Esclarmonde and the Mayor. Talk to Esclarmonde to learn that Titans have taken over Toulouse. Esclarmonde asks that you travel to Toulouse and talk to Thierry, a prisoner of the Titans. Devise a plan to free him and the other prisoners.

As you near Toulouse, Tereo, the guard, stops you. Tereo allows you to pass if you tell him you are there to talk—not fight. Go up the path and speak to Lethos.

Lethos dispels any rumors about the Titans eating villagers. They are looking for someone who has left their tribe. Speak to Rhea, and she explains about the person they are seeking and why it is important he be found. Return to Lethos after speaking to Rhea.

Now that you know what the Titans are doing, you can help them find their Memnosesthion in exchange for releasing the prisoners of Toulouse. Agreeing to assist them means you must kill Lucius. Return to Montaillou and speak to Lucius.

If you accept the quest of the Rock Titans and kill Lucius, your agreement to the Titans is fulfilled. You can return to Toulouse with the Mneme Crystal and inform Lethos the job is done. The prisoners are set free and the Titans leave.

If you decide instead to aid Lucius, refer to the "Help Lucius with His Problem" quest.

NOTE *Either way you play this quest, the villagers are set free, completing the quest for Esclarmonde. Speak with Thierrey after the humans are safe to claim your reward.*

DESTROY THE SHAPESHIFTING DAEVA

Quest Synopsis

Challenge: Difficult
Location(s): Montaillou, Toulouse
Quest NPCs: Iapetus, Na Roqua,
    Nanghaithya
Type: Assassination
Reward: Gems

Principal Players

Iapetus
Na Roqua
Nanghaithya

Quest Details

If you accepted the offer from Lethos to help find Lucius, speak with Iapetus near the campfire on the town's east side. Iapetus denies rumors that the Titans are eating the villagers of Toulouse and insists that a shapeshifting Daeva is responsible for the killings. Agree to locate and confront the shapeshifter, which is hiding somewhere in Toulouse. He is up near Thierry's stash, if you haven't already met him in Montaillou.

If you cannot find the Daeva in Toulouse, return to Montaillou and travel to the west, following the rocky path to a clearing where you meet Nanghaithya. You cannot defeat this Daeva now. Run from the battle before you are too injured to leave. The beast does not follow you when you return to the main path. You must seek help in destroying this creature.

Seek out the help of Na Roqua on the town's east side. Tell her you have found a foe you cannot defeat. There is only one way to kill this Daeva, and Na Roqua can help you. Na Roqua has relics blessed by an ancient Persian prophet. If you possess an item of the prophet, you can kill the shapeshifting Daeva. Step through the fire when instructed and retrieve the Ring of the Prophet from the chest within Na Roqua's secret room. Return to Nanghaithya. If you met Amir in Barcelona, and talked to him about the corpses outside the city walls to the southeast, he gives you an amulet. You don't need to seek Na Roque's help.

Battle Nanghaithya with confidence, but protect., but protect yourself against Crushing Damage and Disease before the battle begins. After defeating the shapeshifter, pick up the Stone Key that Nanghaithya dropped. This key allows you to enter a secret chamber Nanghaithya once stood watch over. Enter the room and activate the switch. This awakens a companion Lightning WarGolem that joins your party. Return to Iapetus in Toulouse and claim your reward.

TIP *The Lightning WarGolem is immune to magic. Take care of it, and it serves you well wherever you go.*

You also have the option of not battling Nanghaithya. If your Speech skill is high enough, you can convince him that he is being used by his masters. He will abandon his post, dropping the key that opens the secret chamber he guarded.

HELP LUCIUS WITH HIS PROBLEM

Quest Synopsis

Challenge: Difficult
Location(s): Montaillou, Toulouse
Quest NPC: Lucius
Type: Assassination
Reward: Gold

Principal Player

Lucius

Quest Details

Talk to Lucius about the Titans in Toulouse, and he asks you to help him with his problem. You can try to talk Lucius into fulfilling his destiny with the Titans, but he prefers living to self-sacrifice. If you help Lucius, you must return to Toulouse and kill the four elder Titans.

On the path to Toulouse, Tereo meets you again. Defeat Tereo and continue into Toulouse. Go up the path and battle Lethos. The elder Titans are powerful, with an Electrical spell they cast often. Strengthen your character with any spell that assists in deflecting this type of damage. Use whatever spells you have to inflict secondary damage on the Titans.

These battles are long and, depending upon your level, may well take you to the brink of death. Watch your health, casting a healing spell or using a potion whenever you get low.

West of Lethos, defeat the guard watching over the prisoners. Speak to Thierrey and agree to meet him in Montaillou.

Return to where you battled Lethos. Travel north to where two more Titans stand guard. Lure one of the Titans away from his post, close to where you battled Lethos, and defeat him. Repeat this for the second guard standing in the north.

To dispose of the last two Titans, lure them away from each other. Once the two northern guards have been vanquished, you shouldn't have any problems luring Menoetius from the fireside to where the guards previously stood. Recoup all of your health and Mana before battling the final elder Titan near the fire.

After you defeat the fourth elder, return to Lucius with the four stone hearts and receive your reward.

TIP *Other Titans are south of the campfire. Lure the elder Titans away from the fire to the north to prevent attracting the attention of other Titans.*

In Montaillou, speak to Thierrey for a reward. He is standing near Esclarmonde in the town center.

FIND THE LOCATION OF THE SEER NOSTRADAMUS

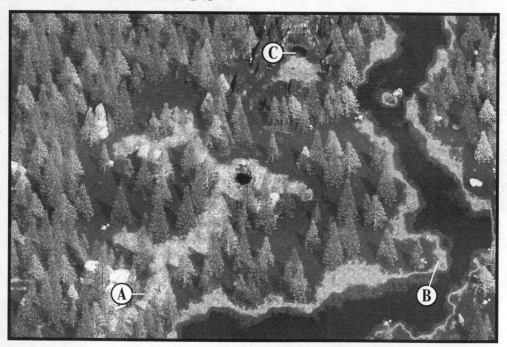

Nostradamus Heart of Fire Entrance

Ⓐ World Map
Ⓑ Ways Crystal
Ⓒ Clan of the Hand

AREA ENEMIES
Hujark Acolyte
Hujark Shieldsman
Hujark Warrior
Snakebreed Viper

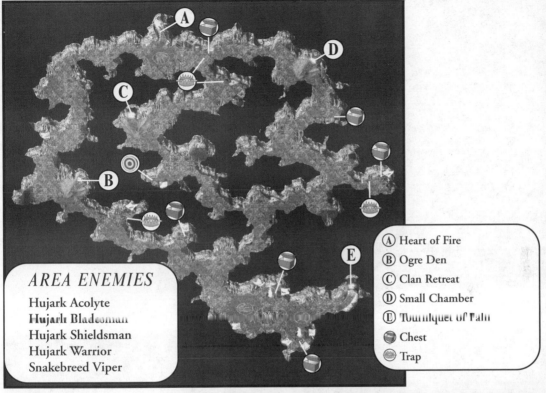

AREA ENEMIES

Hujark Acolyte
Hujark Bladesman
Hujark Shieldsman
Hujark Warrior
Snakebreed Viper

Ⓐ Heart of Fire
Ⓑ Ogre Den
Ⓒ Clan Retreat
Ⓓ Small Chamber
Ⓔ Tourniquet of Pain
Chest
Trap

Clan of the Hand

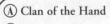

Ⓐ Clan of the Hand
Chest

AREA ENEMIES

Hujark Acolyte
Hujark Warrior
Snakebreed Crusher
Snakebreed Viper

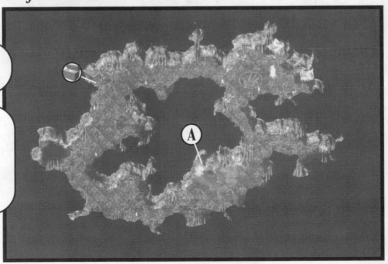

Ogre Den

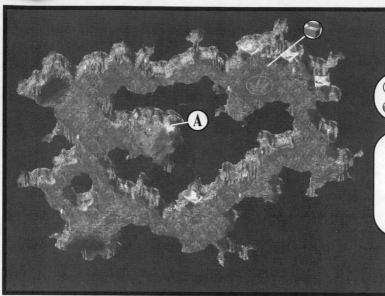

Ⓐ Clan of the Hand
⬤ Chest

AREA ENEMIES

Hujark Acolyte
Hujark Shieldsman
Hujark Warrior
Snakebreed Viper

Clan Retreat

Ⓐ Clan of the Hand

AREA ENEMIES

Hujark Blademaster
Hujark Shieldsman
Snakebreed Viper

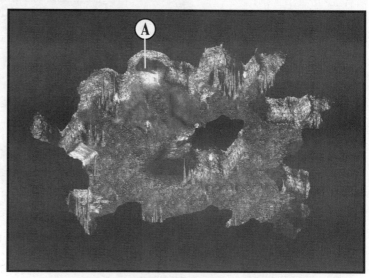

Small Chamber

A Clan of the Hand
B Clan of the Skull

AREA ENEMIES

Assassin
Hujark Acolyte
Hujark Blademaster
Hujark Shaman
Hujark Shieldsman
Snakebreed Viper

Tourniquet of Pain

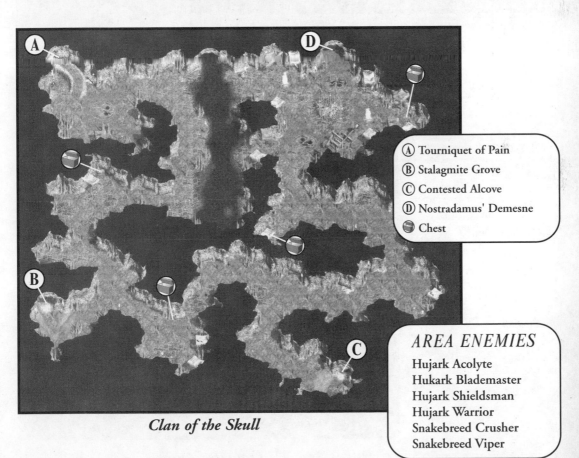

A Tourniquet of Pain
B Stalagmite Grove
C Contested Alcove
D Nostradamus' Demesne
⬜ Chest

AREA ENEMIES

Hujark Acolyte
Hukark Blademaster
Hujark Shieldsman
Hujark Warrior
Snakebreed Crusher
Snakebreed Viper

Clan of the Skull

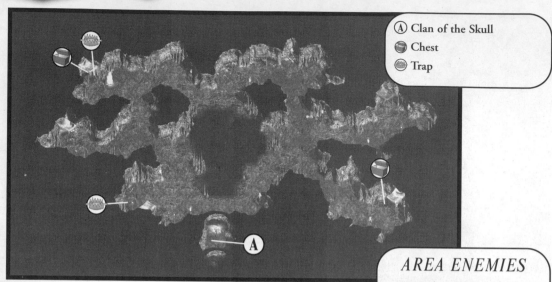

(A) Clan of the Skull
Chest
Trap

Stalagmite Grove

AREA ENEMIES

Hujark Acolyte
Hujark Blademaster
Hujark Shieldsman
Hujark Warrior

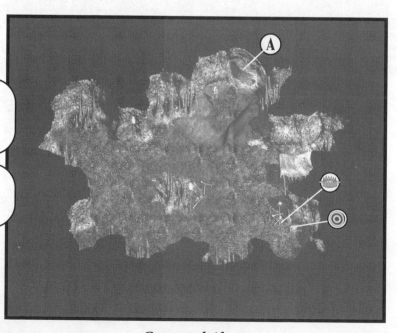

(A) Clan of the Skull
Hidden Item
Trap

AREA ENEMIES

Snakebreed Viper

Contested Alcove

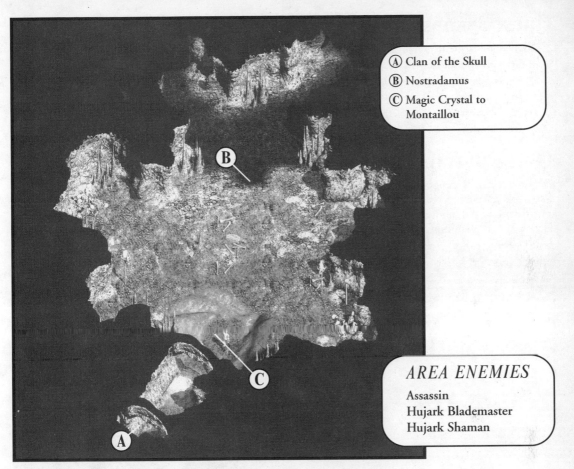

A Clan of the Skull
B Nostradamus
C Magic Crystal to Montaillou

Nostradamus's Demesne

AREA ENEMIES

Assassin
Hujark Blademaster
Hujark Shaman

Quest Synopsis

Challenge: Difficult

Location: Montaillou (Starting Point)

Quest NPCs: Da Vinci, Na Roqua, Nostradamus

Type: Discovery

Reward: None

Principal Players

Brother Michel

Da Vinci

Na Roqua

Nostradamus

Quest Details

This quest marks the beginning of the second half of the game. After you speak to Nostradamus, the areas you traveled to before are no longer available. If you have any side quests you want to complete in towns you visited before this point, go back and finish them now. Those cities are irrevocably changed after you complete this quest.

Talk to Da Vinci near his airship. Da Vinci believes that if you seek out the seer Nostradamus, he might hold useful knowledge for your quest. Da Vinci also believes there are others in Montaillou that may hold more information on the seer's whereabouts. Perhaps Na Roqua can aid you in your quest.

After warning you of the dangers, Na Roqua marks Nostradamus's hiding place on your map. When you are ready, use a Magic Crystal to teleport there to find Nostradamus.

When you arrive, one of Nostradamus's monks asks you to stop the "Old Man" and to save Nostradamus. You must make your way through the Hujark Assassins to save and consult Nostradamus.

The Hujark are tough to defeat. Use every spell you can to protect yourself. Also, increase your Poison resistance to combat against the Snakebreed attacks. Be careful and advance slowly to draw them out one at a time. When you reach the Clan of the Hand entrance, max out your health and Mana and save your game before entering.

NOTE *You can explore multiple caves as you battle your way to Nostradamus. Follow the legends on the maps to find your way. Cross the Tourniquet of Pain from the Clan of the Hand to reach the Clan of the Skull. Explore Multiple caves to gain experience and treasure. When you are ready, enter Nostradamus' Demesne.*

Prepare for battle when you enter Nostradamus's Demesne. Confronting Nostradamus for information is a Hujark Shaman, Hujark Blademaster, and an Assassin. When they realize you have entered, they turn their attention to you. Destroy the enemies and approach Nostradamus. Question Nostradamus about your path and destiny. His visions will assist you as you decide upon the paths before you. After you finish, a portal appears near the original door. You must enter this portal to leave.

THE ENGLISH INVASION

Montaillou Destroyed!

Ⓐ Cathedral
Ⓑ Na Roque
Ⓒ Portal to Barcelona
   Temple District

AREA ENEMIES

Bear	Guardsman
Druid	English Lieutenant
English Bowman	English Sergeant
English Captain	Royal Guardsman
English	

FIND THE PORTAL

After traveling through the portal from the crypt, you arrive in Montaillou. This is a different city from the one you left not long ago. You appear in the Cathedral, and the city lies in ruins around you. Buildings still smolder from the fires that raged throughout the city. Bodies litter every path. The English have invaded.

To reach Brother Michel, defeat the English holding parts of the bridge. Defeat each pocket of soldiers as you take the path along the dock. Unfortunately, all the homes have been destroyed and Brother Michel is nowhere to be found.

Whatever path you take, prepare for battle against English invaders. The bridge leading to the Magic Crystal has been destroyed, so you must travel west of the Church, through the graveyard, to cross the water.

TIP *Take advantage of friendly soldiers in the village and save them from the attacking English. You can drag enemies back to the surviving soldiers for a little assistance when taking on large groups.*

If you venture to Na Roque's home, you find she is safe and refuses to leave her home. Speak to Na Roque and purchase armor and supplies.

The original Magic Crystal has been destroyed. Climb the steps to Da Vinci's crippled flying machine, still lying near the ledge's edge, to find a nearby portal. Go through the portal to reach Barcelona.

SIEGE OF BARCELONA

Ⓐ The Cathedral
Ⓑ Barcelona Gate District

Barcelona Temple District

AREA ENEMIES

Bear
Druid
English Bowman
English Captain
English Guardsman
English Lieutenant
English Sergeant
Fire WarGolem
Ice WarGolem
Lightning WarGolem
Royal Guardsman

THE ASSASSIN

Like Montaillou, Barcelona is burning to the ground. The Inquisitors and Knight Templars fight bravely against the English invasion, but they are vastly outnumbered. Assist the Barcelona factions in fighting against the common enemy. The exit to the Temple District is barricaded. Instead, go into the Cathedral.

When you enter, you confront an Assassin, who mysteriously disappears. The Assassin has taken the relic. Leave the Cathedral and travel to the Gate District of Barcelona.

Dispatch the WarGolems quickly. Cold works well against the Fire WarGolem; fire spells are most effective against the Ice WarGolem. Boost your defenses versus these elements. Take advantage of the few troops that remain in the city to defeat entrenched English.

> **TIP** *Complete all the quests from the earlier game before reaching this point. Only the Barcelona Gate District and Barcelona Temple District are accessible.*

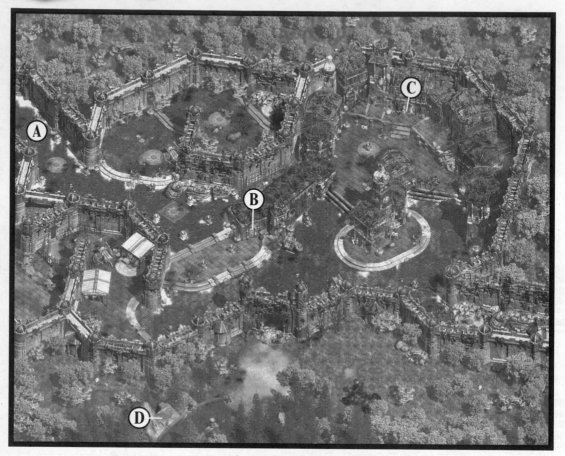

Battle to the Crossroads

Ⓐ Barcelona Temple District
Ⓑ Eduardo the Blacksmith
Ⓒ Weng Choi
Ⓓ Crossroads

AREA ENEMIES

Bear
Druid
English Bowman
English Captain
English
Guardsman
English Lieutenant

English Sergeant
Fire WarGolem
Ice WarGolem
Lightning
WarGolem
Royal Guardsman

FEW PEOPLE REMAIN

Like the Temple District, the Gate District is swarming with the English. Help Barcelona residents fight the assault.

Eduardo the Blacksmith and Weng Choi are the only two merchants left in Barcelona. Eduardo doesn't have a lot for sale, but you can purchase health potions if you need them. If you are working on the book quest for Weng Choi, you can still turn in works to him. Weng Choi is selling whatever he has to help repulse the English, including his special stock of powder kegs.

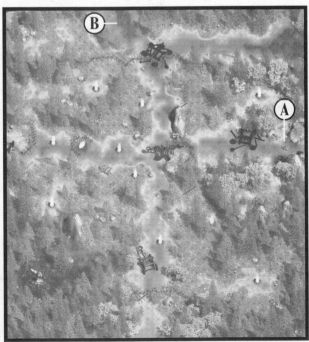

Ⓐ Barcelona
Ⓑ Portal to Ether Plane

AREA ENEMIES

Bear
Druid
English Bowman
English Captain
English Guardsman
English Lieutenant
English Sergeant
Fire WarGolem
Ice WarGolem
Lightning WarGolem
Royal Guardsman

Crossroads Seige

FIGHT TO THE PORTAL

There are pockets of resistance throughout the Crossroads, but you don't need to battle through them all unless you want the additional experience. If you travel north around the barricades, fighting back the English invaders, you can reach the portal to the Ether Plane. All other areas that used to branch from the Crossroads are blocked off. The portal you need to reach is west of the entrance to the Crossroads on the other side of the blockades.

TIP *Resistance in this area is extremely heavy. Move slowly and draw the enemies out in small groups. Large numbers of enemy archers hide behind the barricade that runs down the center of the area. It's difficult to lead them away from their barrier, but with a little patience you can slowly pull them to a safer location.*

Ⓐ Crossroads
Ⓑ Druid Shrine Exterior
① Surrey

AREA ENEMIES

Bear	English Sergeant
Druid	Fire WarGolem
English Bowman	Ice WarGolem
English Captain	Lightning
English	WarGolem
Guardsman	Royal Guardsman
English Lieutenant	

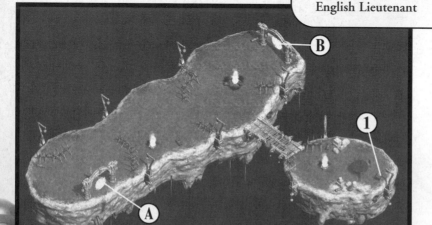

Ether Plane

DRIVE BACK THE ENGLISH

Defeat the English as you head toward the portal leading to the Druid Shrine. Beware of the archers as you enter this area. Protect yourself from Piercing damage and go back through the portal to heal if necessary. After you eliminate the enemy, trick the resident merchant into selling his wares to you.

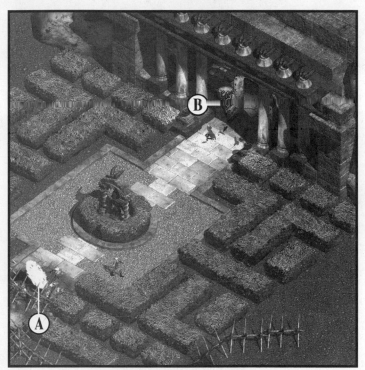

Druid Shrine Exterior

(A) Crossroads
(B) Temple of the Initiate

AREA ENEMIES

None

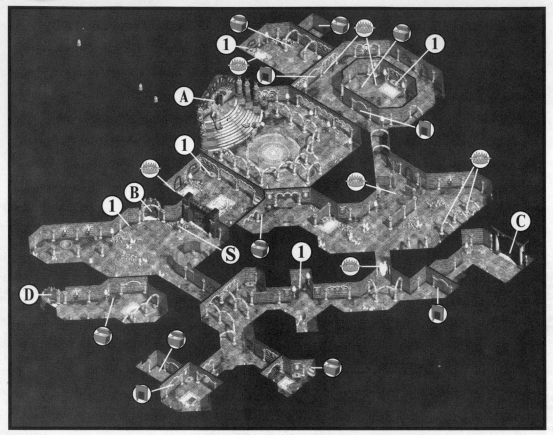

Temple of the Initiate

Ⓐ Druid Shrine Exterior

Ⓑ Stone Chamber of Wyrmkind

Ⓒ Meditation Chamber 1

Ⓓ Exalted Chambers

① Magic Tome

⬤ Chest

⬤ Secret Wall

Ⓢ Switch

⬤ Trap

AREA ENEMIES

English Bowman

English Bowmaster

English Captain

English Guardsman

English Soldier

Ice WarGolem

Lightning WarGolem

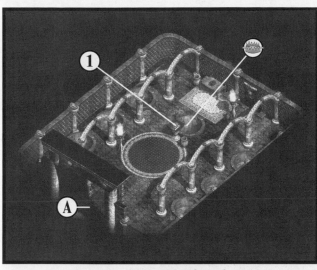

(A) Temple of the Initiate
(1) Magic Tome
⚙ Trap

AREA ENEMIES

Druid
Fire WarGolem
Ice WarGolem

(A) Temple of the Initiate
(B) Meditation Chamber 2
(C) Meditation Chamber 3
(D) Antechamber of Lore
(1) Magic Tome
⚙ Chest
⚙ Secret Wall
(S) Switch
⚙ Trap

Meditation Chamber 1

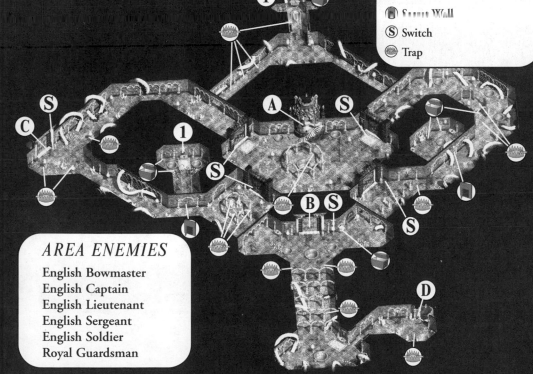

AREA ENEMIES

English Bowmaster
English Captain
English Lieutenant
English Sergeant
English Soldier
Royal Guardsman

Stone Chamber of Wyrmkind

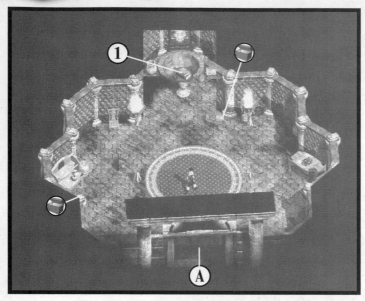

Ⓐ Stone Chamber of
Wyrmkind
① Magic Tome
Chest

AREA ENEMIES

Druid
Fire WarGolem
Lightning WarGolem

Meditation Chamber 2

Ⓐ Stone Chamber of
Wyrmkind
① Magic Tome
Chest
Trap

AREA ENEMIES

Druid
Lightning WarGolem

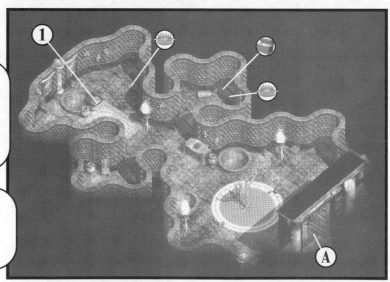

Meditation Chamber 3

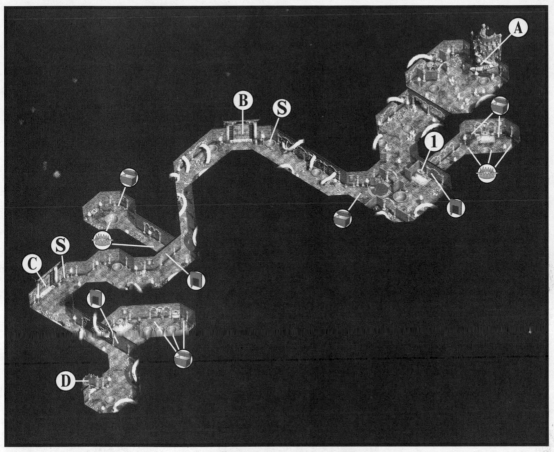

Antechamber of Lore

(A) Stone Chamber of Wyrmkind	
(B) Chamber of the Crystal	
(C) Inner Sanctum	
(D) Exalted Chambers	
(1) Magic Tome	
Chest	
Secret Wall	
(S) Switch	
Trap	

AREA ENEMIES

English Bowman
English Bowmaster
English Captain
English Guardsman
English Lieutenant
English Sergeant
Ice WarGolem
Lightning WarGolem
Royal Guardsman

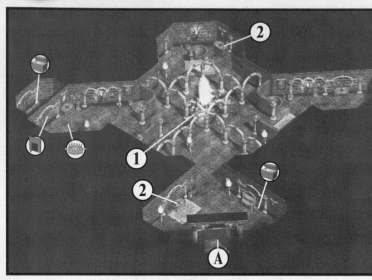

Ⓐ Antechamber of Lore
① Ways Crystal
② Magic Tome
◒ Chest
▨ Secret Wall
◉ Trap

AREA ENEMIES

Bowman
Bowmaster
English Captain
English Guardsman
English Sergeant
Fire WarGolem
Lightning WarGolem

Chamber of the Crystal

Ⓐ Antechamber of Lore
◒ Chest
Ⓢ Switch

AREA ENEMIES

English Bowmaster
English Captain
English Guardsman
English Sergeant

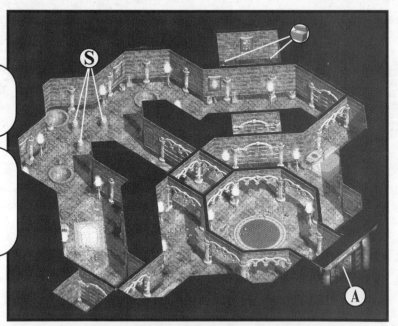

Inner Sanctum

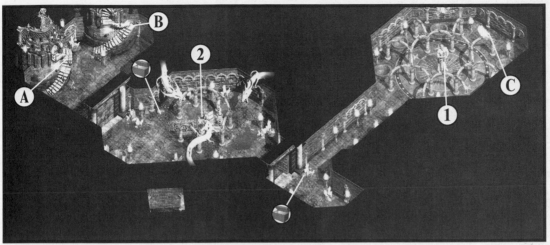

Exalted Chambers

Ⓐ Antechamber of Lore
Ⓑ Temple of the Initiate
Ⓒ Portal to Ether Plane
① Statue of Richard the Lionhearted
② Magic Tome
⬤ Chest

AREA ENEMIES

Assassin
Druid
Fire WarGolem
Ice WarGolem
Lightning WarGolem
Royal Guardsman

RECOVER THE RELICS

You don't need to defeat any enemies to reach the Temple of the Initiate. As you step around the bodies of fallen comrades, collect as many Mana orbs as you can before entering the Temple.

As you enter, you hear the all-too-familiar sounds of battle. Speak with Sir Roger Templeton and enlist his aid in fighting the English foe. The other Knight Templars fan out to fight their own battles as Sir Templeton joins you. Draw the attention of any enemies you meet to keep Sir Templeton alive.

You must stop the Druids from using the True Cross, and recover the stolen relics. The floors of the Druid Shrine are trap-laden and filled with English soldiers and powerful golems. The Druids have fled to their unholy shrine. Find the shrine and stop the Druids before they can escape.

TIP *Reading a Magic Tome restores a large quantity of Mana. Mana can be hard to find in this dungeon, but Magic Tomes are scattered throughout the structure. Look for them on desks.*

A path leads from the top floor to your final destination, the Exalted Chambers, but it isn't open at first. Enter the Stone Chamber of Wyrmkind, then head to the Antechamber of Lore. From there, you can enter the Exalted Chambers.

Be extra careful as you explore. The English wait around every corner. When you see a group, grab the attention of one or two fighters and lure them to you. If the entire group gives chase, quickly retreat through the halls. They slowly split up, and it is then possible to challenge them one at a time.

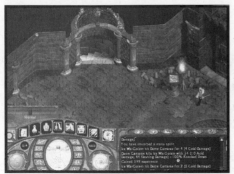

In addition to the main floors, there are several Meditation Chambers and other rooms. Explore them all, but be cautious. Some contain ferocious enemies and deadly traps. Don't miss the Chamber of the Crystal, which contains the fourth Ways Crystal.

TIP *In the Inner Sanctum are three switches in the back of the room. These switches open hidden alcoves on both sides of the room that contain enemies and treasure. Open them one at a time, so the enemies don't overrun the area.*

When you reach the Exalted Chambers, you overhear a conversation between an Assassin and an English Druid. Enter and be prepared for battle. WarGolems of each type appear, as well as an English Druid that tries to stop you in your tracks. Quickly back out of the room when the golems appear and boost all your elemental defenses, then attack. Healing is necessary, so have potions ready. When the golems are eliminated, finish off the English Druid and be on the lookout for a few English soldiers to the south.

TIP *After all enemies are defeated, take advantage of the Magic Tome in the center of the room to regain some much-needed Mana.*

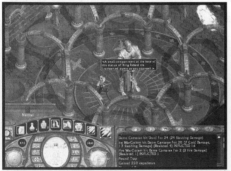

Dispatch the few remaining Englishmen in the outer hall to reach the statue of Richard the Lionhearted. Activate the statue, and a small compartment at the base of the statue opens, releasing the Blood Ring of Richard the Lionhearted. This ring gives you 10 percent more Crushing and Slashing damage and increases your Mana Pool by 30. Go through the nearby portal to reach the Ether Plane.

ASSAULT OF ALAMUT

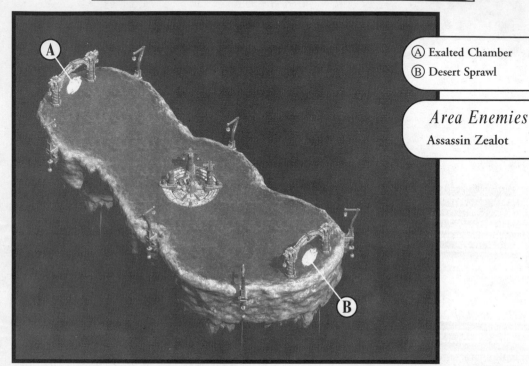

Ether Plane

> A Exalted Chamber
> B Desert Sprawl

> *Area Enemies*
> Assassin Zealot

Entering the Ether Plane

Assassin Zealots lie in wait as you enter the Ether Plane. Defeat them to reach the portal to the Desert Sprawl. Prepare yourself for the Desert Sprawl by increasing your Poison Resistance before going through the portal.

MIDDLE EASTERN DESERT TERRAIN

The sun beats down mercilessly on this dried and cracked desert land. A horde of dangerous creatures senses your arrival and attacks relentlessly. Monstrous Scorpions and other creatures roam the desert. You must traverse this inhospitable desert terrain to reach the Old Man's mountain fortress.

Combating Desert Scorpions

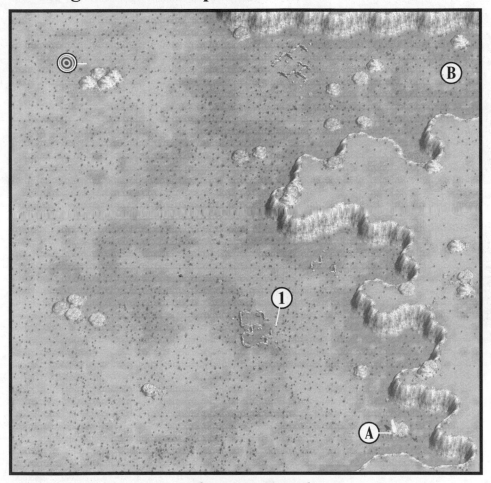

The Desert Sprawl

Ⓐ Ether Plane
Ⓑ Shifting Dunes
① Ali Akbah, Merchant
◎ Hidden Item

AREA ENEMIES

Desert Scorpion
Egyptian Sand Elder
Egyptian Sand Spirit
Monstrous Scorpion

Scorpions inflict a dangerous sting. Have plenty of potions on hand to counter their venomous bite. If you have some Poison Resistance, the poison isn't too damaging, but it lasts for a long time. The Scorpions, especially the Monstrous Scorpions, are very dangerous when they attack in groups. Try to split them up by running away. Slower characters have a tough time with this and may be in for some really nasty battles.

Do not let the limited vocabulary of the Egyptian Sand Spirits fool you. They're highly intelligent creatures. You can elude them by staying clear of the area to the north, but if you do, you miss out on the hidden treasure nearby. These creatures hit hard and are very resistant to damage. Running doesn't help, because they're also extremely fast. Save before taking them on—you may be surprised at how difficult the battle is. If necessary, run back to the portal to the Ether Plane. You can duck in and out of it while fighting the Egyptian Sand Spirits.

Crossing the Shifting Dunes

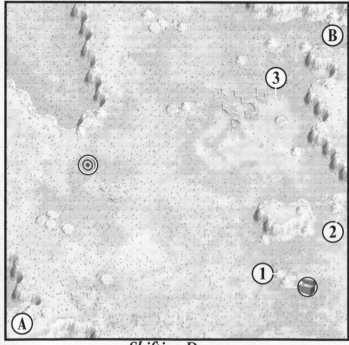

Shifting Dunes

Ⓐ Desert Sprawl
Ⓑ Azi Dahaka
① Ship
② Way Crystal
③ Knight of Saladin
🝑 Chest
◎ Hidden Item

AREA ENEMIES

Brimstone Soul Reaver
Charred Terror
Desert Scorpion
Festering Ghoul
Greater Skeleton
Monstrous Scorpion
Skeleton

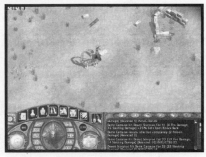

You must once again survive Scorpion attacks. Increase your Poison and Slashing defense against these creatures until you have dispatched them.

Don't overlook the chest near the ship in the southeastern area of the desert. Evil spirits wander the sand in that area, so be ready for a horde of undead to attack. The last of the Ways Crystals is north of the ship. Don't miss it! If you touch all five, you get a permanent statistics bonus.

Finally, before traveling to Azi Dahaka, speak to the Knight of Saladin to enlist his aid in the upcoming battle. Don't expect him to last long, but the assistance he provides is better than none at all.

Ali Dahaka, the Sand Dragon

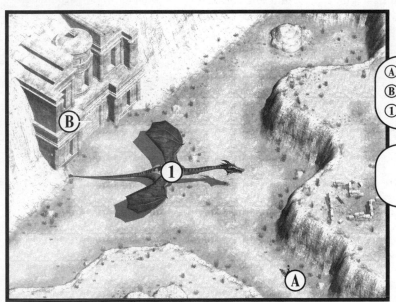

The Lair of Azi Dahaka

(A) Shifting Dunes
(B) Maw of the Assassin
(1) Azi Dahaka

AREA ENEMIES
Azi Dahaka

Azi Dahaka is a ferocious opponent, capable of using powerful magic to heal and launch powerful attacks against you. In addition to its magic, the dragon's Breath and Melee attacks can inflict terrible damage.

If your Speech skill is extraordinarily high, you may be able to appeal to Azi Dahaka's ego and convince him he is being used and not the revered creature he believes himself to be. If you can dissuade Azi Dahaka from attacking, bravo! If you cannot, prepare for a lengthy battle.

Equip your character with armor to help protect you against the dragon's Crushing, Slashing, and Fire attacks. Also use potions or scrolls to boost your Fire Resistance and defense. The dragon has two attacks. If you're close to its mouth, it strikes with its fangs, hitting you several times and pushing you back. If you stand a few feet back from the dragon, out of reach of its mouth, it shoots a spread of fireballs.

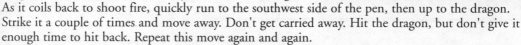

There's an easy way to defeat the beast, but it requires speed, so you need high Agility, speed potions, or light-weight armor to make it work. Stay back from the dragon. As it coils back to shoot fire, quickly run to the southwest side of the pen, then up to the dragon. Strike it a couple of times and move away. Don't get carried away. Hit the dragon, but don't give it enough time to hit back. Repeat this move again and again.

With a little luck it's possible to get through this battle without taking a scratch. If you're more of a magic caster, use whatever Cold spells you have at your disposal, or summon creatures against Azi Dahaka. Stay back and use the same duck-and-move strategy, but blast the beast from the side rather than rushing up to it.

FORTRESS OF ALAMUT

Atop the Alborz Mountains in Persia rests the daunting fortress of the Old Man and his secret sect of Assassins. After battling the terrible sand dragon, enter Alamut Mountain and the cave beyond. The Old Man has stocked these corridors with some of the most fearsome creatures released from the Disjunction. Deadly traps and puzzles slow your progress, and the Old Man sends waves of his minions against you.

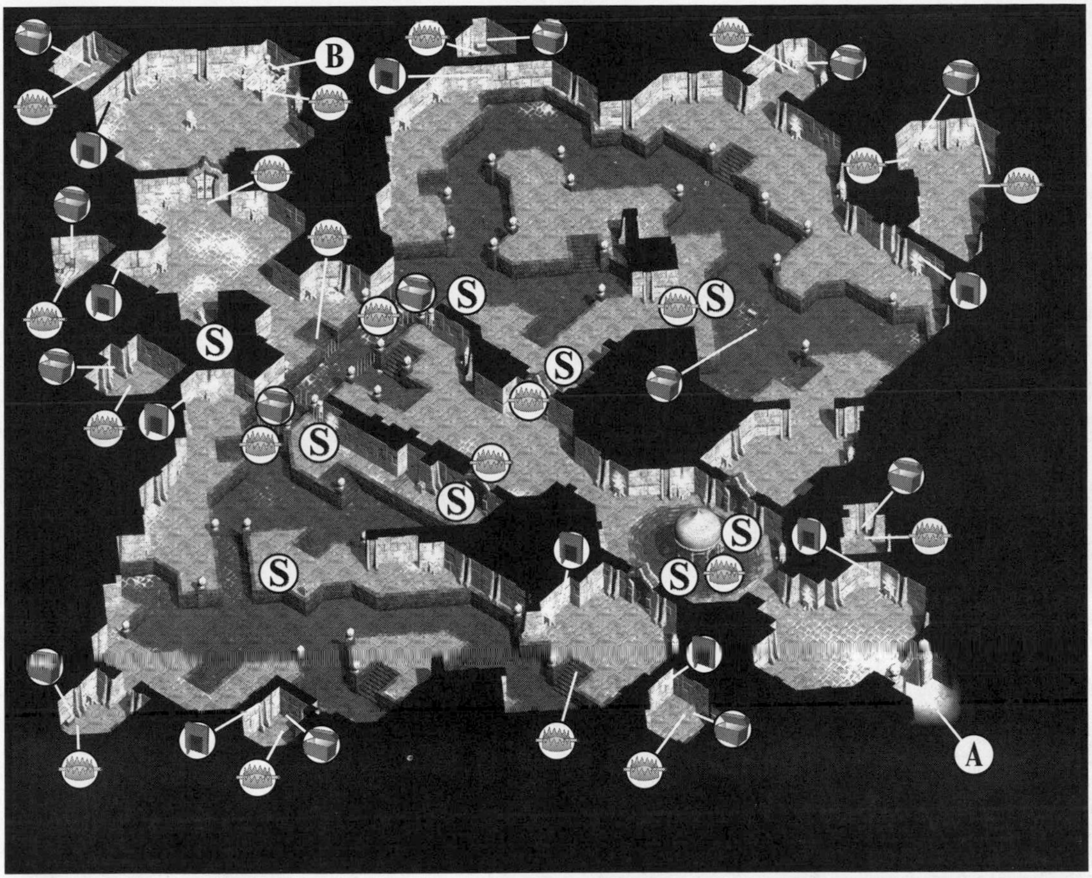

Maw of the Assassin

- (A) Lair of Azi Dahaka
- (B) Acid Wash
- Chest
- Secret Wall
- (S) Switch
- Trap

AREA ENEMIES

Assassin
Assassin Master
Assassin Zealot
Guard Dog

The Old Man in the Mountain

A large, trap-laden Dungeon lies before you. Don't let your guard down for even a second. Assassins lie in bloody wait for their prey, but the traps hidden deceptively all about this floor may prove to be your undoing if you're not constantly on the lookout for them.

The central hall leads to a steel barricade. The switches that lower the spikes are in the northeast and southwest halls. Each hallway is filled with nasty archers on ledges, making it very difficult to combat them with close-range weapons. Magic users and archers have a distinct advantage in this Dungeon. Save often.

The southwest hallway is easier than the northeast one, so enter it first. A shallow corridor runs down the center of the hall, with ledges on either side. The ledges on the south side of the hall have easy-to-reach staircases. If you're a fighter, suck it up and rush through the hail of arrows onto the ledges. Otherwise, pick the archers off from a distance.

CAUTION *Many traps here can't be deactivated normally. You must find a switch near the traps to stop them. Look for large grooves in the floor or on stairs. Blades pop out of them and cause serious damage to anyone standing too close.*

The northeast hall is much more challenging. A staircase leads up to the north ledge about halfway down the hall, and a second staircase is farther along, but the stairs onto the south ledge are at the very end. If you're a fighter, it's difficult to reach the last stair case because of the archers. Other character types can blast the archers from a safe distance.

If you run low on Mana, go back outside and collect spirit orbs from the sand. Boost your defense and use anything that blocks Piercing damage, and make a run for it if necessary.

When you flip the switches in both halls, the barricade drops and you can move on to Acid Wash.

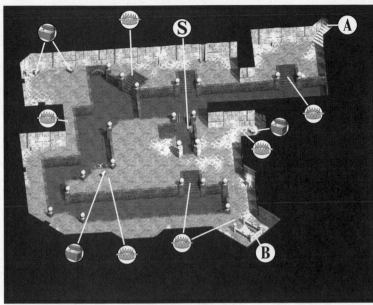

A Maw of the Assassin
B Chamber of Torment
Chest
S Switch
Trap

AREA ENEMIES

Assassin
Assassin Master

Acid Wash

The Maw of the Assassin

A new danger washes across the halls of this Dungeon that may prove as perilous as the Assassins that wait within. As you proceed down the corridors, acid begins to fill the path behind you! Don't linger in the halls, even if it means rushing headlong into the arms of waiting Assassins. You should have plenty of time to clear the path before the acid catches up with you. Shortly after it passes, the acid recedes, allowing you to proceed.

This area is just as challenging for fighters as the last. Getting past the first acid trap is easy, but the second requires running around the center island. There's no way to reach the enemy archers on either side, because there's only one way up to the ledge and it's at the end of the canal. Magic users and archers have an extreme advantage here.

Lure the enemies down the canal one at a time and pick them off. Fighters must be very brave. Boost your defenses against Piercing damage, Fire, and Cold, and then boost your Agility and Speed. You must be fast and resistant to make it through the gauntlet alive. Take a deep breath and run down the corridor to the stairs. Don't stop to fight, and have potions ready for emergency heals. When you reach the stairs, head north and quickly throw the switch next to the steel spikes you saw on your way in.

Head back to the stairs leading to the Maw of the Assassin. You haven't killed anyone and you're badly hurt, but you have opened a shortcut to the center aisle. Now you can lure the enemies out one or two at a time and safely eliminate them all.

The Chamber of Torment

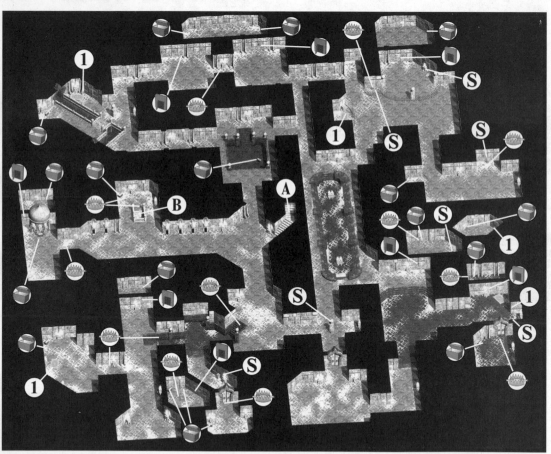

Chamber of Torment

(A) Acid Wash

(B) The Dark Temple

(1) Jeweled Tooth

(🛡) Chest

(▦) Secret Wall

(S) Switch

(⚙) Trap

AREA ENEMIES

Assassin Master

Assassin Zealot

Guard Dog

You enter this level of the mountain almost in the center of the room. Your instincts may lead you down the corridor to the west, but you won't travel far. As soon as you near the trap-laden hall, you are met by someone who tries to dispel any hope you may have of continuing with your quest. Do not try to pass the traps in this area. Travel to the north or the south instead. There is a lot you must do first.

Six Jeweled Teeth are tucked away in corners and chests on this floor. You must get all these teeth to pass through the traps in the center corridor. Note the locations of all these teeth, identified on the map by ①.

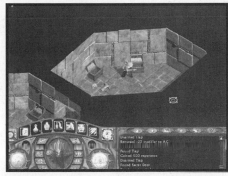

Activate your Find Traps skill to identify all the secret walls and traps. Without this skill, you may miss one of the areas hiding a Jeweled Tooth or succumb to one of the many traps blocking stairs and doors to which you need access. Bring several Master Thievery potions along to boost your skill when necessary, and maybe a couple of items that provide a bonus.

This part of the Dungeon has two problem areas. In the northeast corner, several areas are protected by steel spikes jutting out of the floor. To lower the spikes, enter the hall on the south side of the corner. A switch at the end lowers the spikes along the large alcove to the north. Beware of enemies in the hallway as you enter.

Slowly head back to the north. Several Master Assassins and Assassins are now free. Draw them out in pairs to make them easier to eliminate, then toss the switch behind the enemies to lower the barricade around the switch to the left. Deactivate the trap and toss the switch to lower the barricade around the Jeweled Tooth on the west side of the room.

The southwest corner has a lot of Master Assassins, blocking a tiny staircase. As you climb the stairs, they attack. Drop back behind the wall and lure them to you one at a time, so you aren't fighting four Master Assassins at once. If they won't come, bolster your Fire and Cold Resistance and charge in, but be ready to heal.

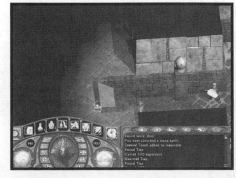

When you have all six Jeweled Teeth, return to the center near the entrance and head west down the corridor. Activate each of the heads lining the north wall. As you do, you disable the traps. If you don't have all six Jeweled Teeth, you suffer considerable damage trying to pass by the traps.

You only need four of the teeth to reach the stairs down to the Dark Temple, but if you have all six you can reach the chest and secret room at the end of the hallway. A chest within the secret room contains the Bow of Fiery Smite. If your Ranged Weapons skill is at least 125, arrows fired from this bow do 40 percent more Piercing damage than a regular bow.

Entering the Dark Temple

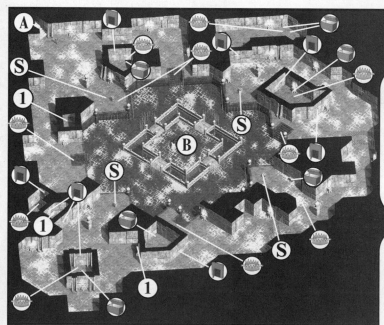

Dark Temple

Ⓐ Chamber of Torment

Ⓑ Final Encounter

① Ambush

⬚ Chest

⬚ Secret Wall

Ⓢ Switch

⬚ Trap

AREA ENEMIES

Assassin
Assassin Master
Assassin Zealot
Desert Scorpion
Guard Dog

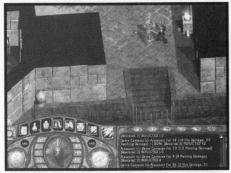

Steel spikes that stick out of the floor block the path ahead. To lower them, you must throw four switches. The first switch, in the area where you begin, allows you to access the lowered center area. The second and third switches are on the northeast and southwest sides. They lower the barricade on the southeast side of the area, providing access to the final switch, which lowers the barricades around the central island.

Secret walls in some areas open as you approach, releasing an enemy or two. Refer to the map to learn where these walls are, so you can prepare for attacks.

CAUTION *Be very careful heading into the lowered area for the first time. Several enemies roam around, but several Assassin Masters are trapped in the center island. Get too close and they light you up with fire and ice magic. Also beware of archers standing on the ledges. Move quickly and get onto the next ledge, where the walls offer some protection, rather than fighting in the lower section where anyone can see you.*

When you activate all of the switches, the spikes blocking access to the portal drop, allowing you to enter. Use the portal to reach the Final Encounter.

The Final Encounter

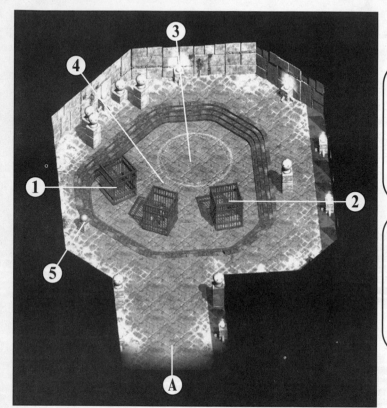

A Dark Temple
1 Galileo
2 Da Vinci
3 The Old Man of the Mountain
4 Holy Cross
5 Monster Generator

AREA ENEMIES

Assassin
Assassin Zealot
Chaos Dragon
Ethereal Succubus
Hujark Acolyte
Hujark Shaman

The Final Encounter

You end this game as you began it, held captive in a cell while your enemy stands nearby. You are reduced to a helpless bystander, part of the audience to witness what is about to happen. The sacred relics, including the Bleeding Lance you once held in your protective grasp, now lay strewn about the floor surrounding the Old Man. Next to you, also in cages, are your friends Galileo and Da Vinci, held captive by the same evil that is attempting to unleash a powerful spell and invoke another Disjunction.

If you've been working on your Speech skill since the very beginning, you may have a high enough level to talk the Old Man of the Mountain into ending this battle before it begins. Even if your Speech skill is high, however, you *must* have spoken with Na Roqua in Montaillou to glean some insight into the Old Man before this option is even available to you.

If you can talk him into ending the battle, the Old Man perishes, releasing your captive friends. You have thus prevented the Disjunction. If you cannot dissuade the Old Man from calling forth the dragon, you must prepare for battle.

Just as you begin to think all is lost, you hear a sound nearby. One of Da Vinci's creations has emerged from the darkness and releases you from your cell. To prevent the Old Man from summoning his spell, you must defeat him and whatever evil he may unleash.

The Chaos Dragon

This is a very challenging battle. When you first try it, it may even seem impossible. A few tricks make it manageable. The dragon spits fire across the room, which isn't too damaging, but can't be ignored. Protect yourself from fire damage using potions, scrolls, or armor with a magical fire-stopping enchantment.

If you get too close to the dragon, it attacks with its powerful jaws. These hits are very powerful and rapidly deplete your health. They also knock you down and make it hard to hit the dragon at close range.

You also must deal with the attacks of a seemingly never-ending wave of enemies. This is where the battle gets really difficult. Enemies continue to appear, and their attacks are even more damaging than the dragon's. Something must be done about them if you're going to stand a chance.

Keep an eye out for your friends during the battle. Magic users spawn near their cages and attack them directly. Get to these new threats quickly, drawing the attack away from Galileo and Da Vinci. Turn your attention back to the dragon, returning to assist your friends as needed.

As the battle begins, quickly pause the game and use scrolls and potions to protect yourself from the four elements. Boost Defense, Speed, and your Find Traps ability. Back in action, grab the Holy Cross from the floor in front of the dragon. It melds to your skin and provides a Strength and Endurance boost.

Avoid the temptation to fight, and search for traps instead. There's a stone orb on the northwest side of the pen that turns red. If it's not there, boost your Find Traps ability with potion and items until you see it. Deactivate the orb by clicking on it. This prevents most of the additional enemies from joining the battle. Spell casters still appear next to Galileo and Da Vinci, but no other creatures join the battle. This step alone makes the battle winnable.

When the orb is deactivated, spikes pop out of the floor along the back of the pen. Stay out of this area. If you use magic, stay back and fire away at the dragon with everything you've got. Fighters must charge in and take their lumps while dishing out the damage. Wait for the dragon to spit fire before charging in, and then quickly hit the dragon and back away before it can bite.

Keep an eye on Galileo and Da Vinci and protect them. The enemies that attack them also drop spirit orbs, so a quick refill is available if your Mana runs low. When you defeat the dragon, you release your captive friends and prevent the Old Man from invoking another Disjunction.

POSSIBLE ENDINGS

The battle with the Chaos Dragon offers a multitude of endings to the game, depending on the type of character you chose to play and how well you fared in battle.

Karma, which modifies the end-game sequence, also plays a large part in what ending you get. The possibilities are numerous. How you interacted with various characters as you traveled throughout your quests is part of your Karma. If you aided people in need, that adds to your good Karma. If you killed those people, that adds to bad Karma. Karma is added to and subtracted from at numerous points in the game.

There are also different dialogue possibilities, depending on who dies at the end. For the best possible ending, you want everyone to survive the battle, Galileo and Da Vinci to stay alive, and have no negative impact to your Karma throughout the game. If one of your friends died, depending on what happened, you get a different ending.

Spirit choices have no effect on the game ending, although they make a difference in what your spirit may say at the end.

Remember: You *must* speak with Na Roque in Montaillou after its destruction to talk the Old Man out of his plan to begin the next Disjunction.

MAGIC SKILLS

THE MAGIC OF LIONHEART

Every character, no matter what race and spirit, has access to the same basic set of spells. You get additional spells by spending earned skill points on the 12 spell branches under the three Magic Discipline: Divine, Thought, and Tribal. Given the limited skill points available to be earned throughout the game, it's impossible to master all three orders, or even one order to its full extent. You must be selective.

This section shows all the spells available in the game by order and branch. The number in parentheses after each spell indicates the level of the parent spell branch needed to learn the spell. Every spell has at least one or two attributes that improve over time as you spend additional skill points on the parent branch. The ranges listed here indicate an approximate starting and ending value for these variable attributes. The values are not exact, because many Perks, Racial Traits, and other item-related bonuses can alter them.

DIVINE MAGIC

This Magic Discipline gains its power from a spiritual source. This is the most physical of the spell types, and best complements fighter characters.

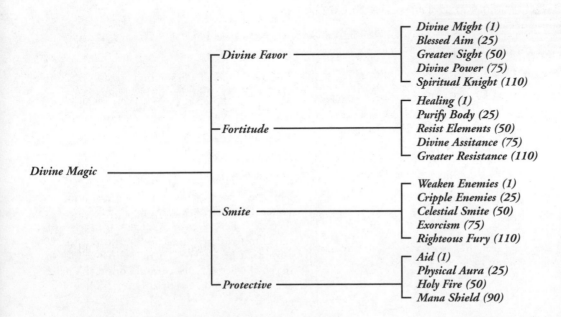

Divine Magic
- Divine Favor
  - Divine Might (1)
  - Blessed Aim (25)
  - Greater Sight (50)
  - Divine Power (75)
  - Spiritual Knight (110)
- Fortitude
  - Healing (1)
  - Purify Body (25)
  - Resist Elements (50)
  - Divine Assitance (75)
  - Greater Resistance (110)
- Smite
  - Weaken Enemies (1)
  - Cripple Enemies (25)
  - Celestial Smite (50)
  - Exorcism (75)
  - Righteous Fury (110)
- Protective
  - Aid (1)
  - Physical Aura (25)
  - Holy Fire (50)
  - Mana Shield (90)

Divine Favor Branch

These spells grant spiritual favor. They strengthen the sword, steady the hand, and can summon a goodly knight for assistance.

DIVINE MIGHT

Branch Level: 1

Mana Cost: 10

This spell increases the caster's Crushing and Slashing Damage (+10 percent at Level 1 to +40 percent at Level 300) for a limited time (30 seconds at Level 1 to 130 seconds at Level 300). At later levels, the caster's Strength is increased (+1 at Level 150), and allies within a radius of 15 feet of the caster gain Melee Damage (+10 percent Crushing and Slashing Damage at Level 40).

BLESSED AIM

Branch Level: 25

Mana Cost: 20

The caster gets increased Melee and Ranged Weapons Skills (+10 points at Level 1 to +50 points at Level 276), and a Bonus Chance to Hit (+3 points at Level 1 to +25 points at Level 276) for a limited time (30 seconds at Level 1 to 122 seconds at Level 276).

GREATER SIGHT

Branch Level: 50

Mana Cost: 40

The caster's Perception increases (+1 at Level 1 to +2 at Level 215) for a limited time (20 seconds at Level 1 to 240 seconds at Level 215). At higher levels, the caster's Find Traps/Secret Doors Skill also increases (+10 points at Level 20 to +56 points at Level 251).

DIVINE POWER

Branch Level: 75

Mana Cost: 80

The caster's Strength increases (+1 at Level 1 to +2 at Level 226) for a limited time (30 seconds at Level 1 to 219 seconds at Level 226). At higher levels, the caster's Endurance also increases (+1 at Level 40).

SPIRITUAL KNIGHT

Branch Level: 110

Mana Cost: 160

This spell calls forth a ghost Knight Templar to fight for the player for 3 minutes. The knight starts out with more Hit Points than it had in life (15 percent more at Level 1 to 110 percent more at Level 191). At higher levels, the knight gains a damage bonus (+1 at Level 50 to +6 at Level 191).

Fortitude Branch

These spells enable the caster to call upon divine power to fortify the caster's constitution, to heal, or to grant resistance to physical harm.

HEALING

Branch Level: 1

Mana Cost: 10

The caster and all allies within a radius of 20 feet are healed for a number of Hit Points (+3–6 at Level 1 to +20–30 at Level 300).

PURIFY BODY

Branch Level: 25

Mana Cost: 20

This spell increases the caster's Disease and Poison Damage Resistances by a percentage (+25 percent at Level 1 to +65 percent at Level 276) for a limited time (30 seconds at Level 1 to 229 seconds at Level 276). There is also a chance that the spell will cure Disease and Poison (25 percent at Level 1 to 100 percent at Level 276).

RESIST ELEMENTS

Branch Level: 50

Mana Cost: 40

The caster's Fire Damage Resistance is increased by a percentage (+25 percent at Level 1 to +75 percent at Level 251) for a limited time (30 seconds at Level 1 to 220 seconds at Level 251). At higher levels, the caster's Cold Damage Resistance is also increased (+25 percent at Level 25 to +70 percent at Level 251).

DIVINE ASSISTANCE

Branch Level: 75

Mana Cost: 80

Magical Damage Thresholds are increased (+1 at Level 1 to +4 at Level 226) for the caster and all allies within a radius of several feet (8 feet at Level 1 to 20 feet at Level 226). At later levels, Physical Damage Thresholds (+1 at Level 25 to +4 at Level 226), Armor Class (+10 percent at Level 40 to +29 percent at Level 226), and Mana Capacity (+10 percent at Level 70 to +30 percent at Level 226) are also increased.

GREATER RESISTANCE

Branch Level: 110

Mana Cost: 160

This spell increases the Acid, Electrical, Fire, and Poison Damage Resistances of the caster and all allies within a radius around the caster (10 feet at Level 1 to 25 feet at Level 191) by a percentage (+30 percent at Level 1 to +73 percent at Level 191) for several seconds (60 seconds at Level 1 to 98 seconds at Level 191).

Smite Branch

Calling upon the power of the celestial host, the caster can call down the wrath of the heavens to smite foes.

WEAKEN ENEMIES

Branch Level: 1

Mana Cost: 10

Up to 4 enemies within a radius of the caster (8 feet at Level 1 to 25 feet at Level 300) receive a penalty to their Armor Class (-5 percent at Level 1 to -25 percent at Level 300) and Chance to Hit (-5 percent at Level 1 to -25 percent at Level 300). Also, the spell lowers Crushing, Electrical, and Fire Resistances (-10 percent at Level 1 to -50 percent at Level 300) for a limited time (10 seconds at Level 1 to 30 seconds at Level 300).

CRIPPLE ENEMIES

Branch Level: 25

Mana Cost: 20

All enemies within a radius of the caster (8 feet at Level 1 to 13 feet at Level 276) take several points of Crushing Damage (3–5 at Level 1 to 15–20 at Level 276), and the amount of damage they can cause is reduced by 20 percent for a limited time (5 seconds at Level 1 to 15 seconds at Level 276).

CELESTIAL SMITE

Branch Level: 50

Mana Cost: 40

The targeted enemy takes points of Fire Damage and Electrical Damage (4–7 each at Level 1 to 24–35 each at Level 251). At higher levels, the spell also freezes the creature for a second (Level 55).

EXORCISM

Branch Level: 75

Mana Cost: 80

All enemies within a radius of the caster (8 feet at Level 1 to 12 feet at Level 226) take points of Crushing Damage (14–22 at Level 1 to 25–38 at Level 226). There is also a chance (10 percent at Level 1 to 20 percent at Level 226) that undead in the area of effect disintegrate.

RIGHTEOUS FURY

Branch Level: 110

Mana Cost: 160

All enemies within a radius of several feet of the caster (8 feet at Level 1 to 13 feet at Level 191) are wracked with pain, causing Crushing Damage (20–30 at Level 1 to 30–40 at Level 191). The caster gains 5 Hit Points every 5 seconds for 30 seconds.

Protective Branch

Spells from this branch wrap the caster in a divine cloak that protects the caster from enemies and harms those foolish enough to attempt to harm the caster.

AID

Branch Level: 1

Mana Cost: 10

The caster's Armor Class is increased (+5 at Level 1 to +30 at Level 300) for a limited time (25 seconds at Level 1 to 75 seconds at Level 300). At higher Levels, the caster's Hit Points are also increased (+10 at Level 50 to +35 at Level 300).

PHYSICAL AURA

Branch Level: 25

Mana Cost: 20

The caster's Crushing, Piercing, and Slashing Damage Resistances are increased (+10 percent at Level 1 to +35 percent at Level 276) for a limited time (45 seconds at Level 1 to 150 seconds at Level 276). At higher levels, the caster's Crushing, Piercing, and Slashing Thresholds are also increased (+1 at Level 50 to +3 at Level 276).

HOLY FIRE

Branch Level: 50

Mana Cost: 40

This spell creates a ring of fire around the caster (8 feet at Level 1 to 15 feet at Level 251) causing Fire Damage (1–3 at Level 1 to 6–12 at Level 251) every 2 seconds for several seconds (25 seconds at Level 1 to 125 seconds at Level 251) to all enemies in the area of effect.

MANA SHIELD

Branch Level: 90

Mana Cost: 80

Damage taken by the caster is split up between the Mana Pool and the Hit Points for a limited time (50 seconds at Level 1 to 200 seconds at Level 211). A percentage of the damage (15 percent at Level 1 to 50 percent at Level 211) is taken from the caster's Mana Pool and the remaining damage is taken from Hit Points.

TRIBAL MAGIC

This Magic Discipline is powered by the awakening of the Earth as the rocks, trees, and the natural environment release energy absorbed during the Disjunction.

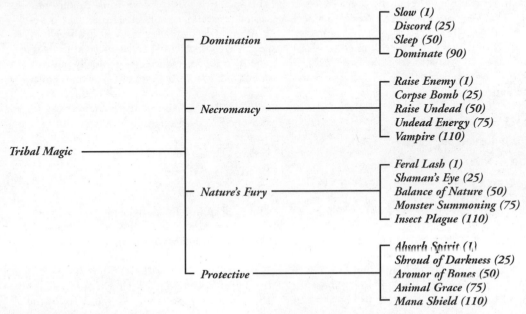

Tribal Magic

Domination
- Slow (1)
- Discord (25)
- Sleep (50)
- Dominate (90)

Necromancy
- Raise Enemy (1)
- Corpse Bomb (25)
- Raise Undead (50)
- Undead Energy (75)
- Vampire (110)

Nature's Fury
- Feral Lash (1)
- Shaman's Eye (25)
- Balance of Nature (50)
- Monster Summoning (75)
- Insect Plague (110)

Protective
- Absorb Spirit (1)
- Shroud of Darkness (25)
- Armor of Bones (50)
- Animal Grace (75)
- Mana Shield (110)

Domination Branch

This spell branch grants the power to control the minds of others.

SLOW

Branch Level: 1

Mana Cost: 10

All enemies within a radius of the caster (8 feet at Level 1 to 20 feet at Level 300) slow to a percentage of their base movement speed (85 percent at Level 1 to 50 percent at Level 300) for a limited time (10 seconds at Level 1 to 47 seconds at Level 300).

DISCORD

Branch Level: 25

Mana Cost: 20

This spell has a chance (25 percent at Level 1 to 95 percent at Level 276) to turn one enemy within a radius of 25 feet of the caster against its fellows. A controlled creature fights to the death for the caster, but not wholeheartedly. Its mental struggle to break the spell makes it clumsy and uncoordinated, reducing its Hit Points by 50 percent. You may not inflict Discord upon an enemy while holding one under the effects of Domination.

SLEEP

Branch Level: 50

Mana Cost: 40

All enemies within a radius of the caster (8 feet at Level 1 to 20 feet at Level 251) have a percentage chance (20 percent at Level 1 to 50 percent at Level 251) of falling asleep for a limited time (10 seconds at Level 1 to 30 seconds at Level 251). This spell has no effect on strong-willed creatures or the undead.

DOMINATE

Branch Level: 90

Mana Cost: 80

One enemy within a radius of 25 feet of the caster has a percentage chance (35 percent at Level 1 to 75 percent at Level 211) of falling under the charm of the caster for a limited time (60 seconds at Level 1 to 180 seconds at Level 211). Maintaining control of an enthralled creature drains the caster's Mana. You may not Dominate an enemy while holding one under the effects of Discord.

Necromancy

The dark, forbidden arts of Necromancy beckon to the intrepid wizard who dares to unlock them. These spells give casters the power to call forth frightful creatures from beyond the grave.

RAISE ENEMY

Branch Level: 1

Mana Cost: 10

This spell raises the targeted enemy corpse to fight for the caster. As the caster's skill increases, he or she can raise more powerful creatures from the dead. The raised enemy has a varying number of Hit Points (20 at Level 1 to 80 at Level 300) and deals a percentage of the damage that it caused while it was alive (50 percent at Level 1 to 125 percent at Level 300). Maintaining a summoned enemy drains the caster's Mana. You may not maintain two summoning spells simultaneously.

CORPSE BOMB

Branch Level: 25

Mana Cost: 20

This spell turns all corpses within a radius of several feet (10 feet at Level 1 to 20 feet at Level 276) into bombs that cause Acid Damage to nearby creatures (5 at Level 1 to 20 at Level 276). The Acid Damage decreases gradually out to a radius of 20 feet. At Level 65, the bomb emits a choking gas cloud with a radius of 8 feet that inflicts 6 Poison Damage to all enemies in the area of effect over a period of 30 seconds.

RAISE UNDEAD

Branch Level: 50

Mana Cost: 40

This spell summons, to fight for the caster, an undead creature with a percentage of its normal Hit Points and damage (Zombie: 50 percent at Level 1 to 100 percent at Level 30; Greater Skeleton: 76 percent at Level 50 to 100 percent at Level 70; Soul Reaver: 92 percent at Level 100 to 150 percent at Level 251). At higher levels, the undead creature gains a damage bonus (+1 at Level 10 to +6 at Level 251). At still higher levels, the spell summons other types of undead (Zombie at Level 1, Greater Skeleton at Level 50, and Soul Reaver at Level 100). Maintaining a summoned undead warrior drains the caster's Mana. You may not maintain two summoning spells simultaneously.

UNDEAD ENERGY

Branch Level: 75

Mana Cost: 80

Raised creatures gain Hit Points (+10 at Level 1 to +60 at Level 226) and a damage bonus (+1 at Level 1 to +10 at Level 226). At higher levels, the raised creature's Acid, Electrical, and Fire Damage Resistance also increase (+30 at Level 50 to +75 at Level 226).

Vampire

Branch Level: 110
Mana Cost: 160

The caster's successful hits from melee weapons take health away from the enemy and give a percentage back to the caster (10 percent at Level 1 to 20 percent at Level 191) for a limited time (60 seconds at Level 1 to 120 seconds at Level 191).

Nature's Fury Branch

Nature is red in tooth and claw, a maxim reflected by this branch of spells.

Feral Lash

Branch Level: 1
Mana Cost: 10

This spell increases the amount of damage a targeted creature takes from physical attacks (10 percent at Level 1 to 35 percent at Level 300) for a limited time (30 seconds at Level 1 to 72 seconds at Level 300).

Shamans Eye

Branch Level: 25
Mana Cost: 20

With this spell, the caster summons a spiritual eye to the targeted location to look around the area without risk of detection for 20 seconds. In addition, this spell increases the caster's Find Traps/Secret Doors Skill (+5 at Level 1 to +50 at Level 276). The eye has a limited sight radius (20 feet at Level 1 to 40 feet at Level 276) and cannot detect secret areas or traps.

Balance of Nature

Branch Level: 50
Mana Cost: 40

This spell deflects a percentage of physical damage (20 percent at Level 1 to 35 percent at Level 251) from the caster back at the attacker for a limited time (30 seconds at Level 1 to 72 seconds at Level 251).

Monster Summoning

Branch Level: 75
Mana Cost: 80

This spell summons a random monster with a percentage of its normal Health Points (70 percent at Level 1 to 250 percent at Level 226), which fights for the caster for 3 minutes, doing a percentage of its normal damage (75 percent of Level 1 to 250 percent at Level 226). At Level 75, this spell summons two monsters. Maintaining a summoned creature drains the caster's Mana. You may not maintain two summoning spells simultaneously.

Insect Plague

Branch Level: 110
Mana Cost: 160

This spell summons a plague of insects, which cause Acid and Disease Damage (5–7 each at Level 1 to 8–11 each at Level 191) to all enemies within a radius of 13 feet every 2 seconds for a limited time (12 seconds at Level 1 to 30 seconds at Level 191). At Level 40, the creature also has a 10 percent chance of taking 1–4 Poison Damage every 2 seconds for 4–10 seconds.

Protective Branch

These spells enable the caster to be as quick and cagey as a fox or tough and resilient as a rhino.

Absorb Spirit

Branch Level: 1
Mana Cost: 10

This spell takes Hit Points (3–10 at Level 1 to 15–30 at Level 300) from the target corpse and gives them to the caster.

SHROUD OF DARKNESS
Branch Level: 25
Mana Cost: 20

The caster is surrounded by a supernatural darkness, making the target harder to see. The caster's Armor Class (+5 at Level 1 to +20 at Level 276) and Sneak Skill (+5 at Level 1 to +40 at Level 276) are increased for a limited time (45 seconds at Level 1 to 100 seconds at Level 276).

ARMOR OF BONES
Branch Level: 50
Mana Cost: 40

This spell blocks a percentage of Crushing and Slashing Damage (10 percent at Level 1 to 30 percent at Level 251) and a percentage of Cold, Electrical, and Fire Damage (10 percent at Level 1 to 25 percent at Level 251) for a limited time (45 seconds at Level 1 to 90 seconds at Level 251).

ANIMAL GRACE
Branch Level: 75
Mana Cost: 80

The caster's Agility increases (+1 at Level 1 to +2 at Level 226) for a limited time (45 seconds at Level 1 to 90 seconds at Level 226). At higher levels, the caster's Lockpick Skill also increases (+5 at Level 5 to +50 at Level 226) and Luck (+1 at Level 25).

MANA SHIELD
Branch Level: 110
Mana Cost: 160

Damage taken by the caster is split up between the player's Mana Pool and Hit Points for a limited time (50 seconds at Level 1 to 193 seconds at Level 191). A percentage of the damage (20 percent at Level 1 to 40 percent at Level 191) is taken from the caster's Mana Pool and the remaining damage is taken from Hit Points.

THOUGHT MAGIC

Power is gained in this Magic Discipline from learning to channel the arcane magical spells and abilities that leaked through from the Disjunction. This magical type is the most directly aggressive.

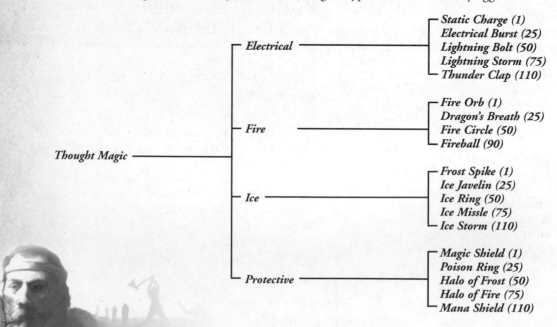

Electrical Branch

These spells channel the wild energies of electrical storms into explosive torrents of magical power.

STATIC CHARGE

Branch Level: 1

Mana Cost: 10

An electrostatic sphere is fired at the targeted creature, causing Electrical Damage (2–7 at Level 1 to 15–20 at Level 300). At higher levels, the sphere also has a chance of stunning its target (10 percent at Level 25 to 35 percent at Level 300) for a limited time (2 seconds at Level 25 to 4 seconds at Level 300).

ELECTRICAL BURST

Branch Level: 25

Mana Cost: 20

This spell projects a quick flash of electrical charge to all enemies in a radius around the caster (8 feet at Level 1 to 18 feet at Level 276), causing Electrical Damage (4–7 at Level 1 to 18–25 at Level 276) to enemies within the field of effect.

LIGHTNING BOLT

Branch Level: 50

Mana Cost: 40

This spell summons a bolt of lightning from the air, causing Electrical Damage (10–18 at Level 1 to 45–70 at Level 251) to the targeted creature.

LIGHTNING STORM

Branch Level: 75

Mana Cost: 80

Lightning bolts rain down within a radius of the targeted area (6 feet at Level 1 to 10 feet at Level 226) for a limited time (8 seconds at Level 1 to 16 seconds at Level 226). All enemies in the area of effect suffer Electrical Damage (5–9 at Level 1 to 12–20 at Level 226) every 2 seconds.

THUNDER CLAP

Branch Level: 110

Mana Cost: 160

All enemies within a radius of the caster (8 feet at Level 1 to 12 feet at Level 191) take Electrical Damage (15–30 at Level 1 to 30–45 at Level 191), and have a 50 percent chance of being knocked down for a moment (3 seconds at Level 1 to 10 seconds at Level 191).

Fire Branch

Fire spells char the caster's foes, quickly reducing them to ash and smoke.

FIRE ORB

Branch Level: 1

Mana Cost: 10

The targeted creature takes Fire Damage (2–8 at Level 1 to 25–30 at Level 300). After a delay of 2 seconds, the creature takes another hit of Fire Damage (1 at Level 1 to 1–10 at Level 300).

DRAGON'S BREATH

Branch Level: 25

Mana Cost: 20

This spell projects a fire stream 20 feet in a chosen direction from the caster. Those in the fire stream take points of Fire Damage (4–8 at Level 1 to 25–35 at Level 276).

FIRE CIRCLE

Branch Level: 50

Mana Cost: 40

This spell creates a circle of fire with a radius of 8 feet at the targeted area for a limited time (8 seconds at Level 1 to 20 seconds at Level 251). All enemies in the area of effect suffer Fire Damage (4–8 at Level 1 to 12–18 at Level 251) every 2 seconds until the circle dissipates (8 seconds at Level 1 to 20 seconds at Level 251).

FIREBALL

Branch Level: 90
Mana Cost: 80

A ball of fire hits the targeted area, dealing Fire Damage to all enemies within a radius of the caster (10 feet at Level 1 to 20 feet at Level 211). Enemies at the center of the area of effect take the most damage (25 at Level 1 to 45 at Level 211); enemies farther away take proportionally less damage, depending on their distance from the targeted area. A targeted enemy also takes additional Fire Damage (1 at Level 1 to 1–10 at Level 211) 2 seconds after the initial explosion. At higher levels, there is a chance (50 percent at Level 50 to 90 percent at Level 211) the targeted enemy is knocked down.

Ice Branch

The caster can focus the terrible power of deepest winter into physical projectiles that chill and rend their foes.

FROST SPIKE

Branch Level: 1
Mana Cost: 10

The targeted creature suffers Cold Damage (2–6 at Level 1 to 25–30 at Level 300) upon impact. The creature is also slowed by 5 percent for each hit.

ICE JAVELIN

Branch Level: 25
Mana Cost: 20

The targeted creature takes Cold Damage (5–10 at Level 1 to 40–50 at Level 276) upon impact and its Armor Class is reduced (-5 at Level 1 to -50 at Level 276) for 60 seconds.

ICE RING

Branch Level: 50
Mana Cost: 40

Projects missiles of ice in 8 directions, causing Cold Damage (8–10 at Level 1 to 35–45 at Level 251) to creatures in the missiles' path. There is also a chance (25 percent at Level 1 to 60 percent at Level 251) that the damaged creatures will be slowed to 75 percent of their movement speed for 60 seconds.

ICE MISSILE

Branch Level: 75
Mana Cost: 80

The targeted creature takes Cold Damage (12–18 at Level 1 to 25–40 at Level 226) upon impact. In addition, creatures near the target take Splash Damage. Creatures closest to the target take the most damage (10 at Level 1 to 35 at Level 226), and that amount decreases out to the spell's radius (6 feet at Level 1 to 14 feet at Level 226). There is also a chance (25 percent at Level 1 to 60 percent at Level 226) that the targeted creature will be slowed to 75 percent of its movement rate for 60 seconds.

ICE STORM

Branch Level: 110
Mana Cost: 160

Large chunks of ice rain down, causing Cold Damage (10–14 at Level 1 to 18–26 at Level 191) every 2 seconds for a limited time (12 seconds at Level 1 to 16 seconds at Level 191) to all enemies within a radius of the targeted area (6 feet at Level 1 to 20 feet at Level 191). There is also a 10 percent chance of slowing damaged creatures to 70 percent of their base movement speed for 10 seconds.

Protective Branch

The clever thought mage is careful to protect his or her physical form with these spells while engaged in burning or freezing enemies.

MAGICAL SHIELD

Branch Level: 1

Mana Cost: 10

The caster's Armor Class is increased (+5 at Level 1 to +25 at Level 300) for a limited time (25 seconds at Level 1 to 150 seconds at Level 300). At higher levels, the caster's Crushing, Piercing, and Slashing Damage Resistances (+2 at Level 30 to +30 at Level 300) and Thresholds (+1 at Level 30) are increased.

POISON RING

Branch Level: 25

Mana Cost: 20

Projects poison spikes in 8 directions around the caster, causing Poison Damage (1–4 at Level 1 to 17–22 at Level 276) to creatures in the spikes' path and an additional amount of Poison Damage (1–4 at Level 1 to 17–22 at Level 276) after 2 seconds.

HALO OF FROST

Branch Level: 50

Mana Cost: 40

A moving ring of cold with a radius of 15 feet is created around the caster, causing Cold Damage (1–3 at Level 1 to 6–12 at Level 251) every 2 seconds to all enemies within the area of effect for a limited time (25 seconds at Level 1 to 125 seconds at Level 251). At Level 40, there is also a chance (10 percent at Level 40 to 60 percent at Level 251) of slowing affected creatures to 70 percent of their base for 10 seconds.

HALO OF FIRE

Branch Level: 75

Mana Cost: 80

A moving ring of fire with a radius of 15 feet is created around the caster, causing Fire Damage (2–4 at Level 1 to 7–12 at Level 226) every 2 seconds to all enemies within the area of effect for a limited time (45 seconds at Level 1 to 125 seconds at Level 226). At Level 40, affected creatures also suffer an additional 30 percent residual Fire Damage 2 seconds after being hit.

MANA SHIELD

Branch Level: 110

Mana Cost: 160

Damage taken by the caster is split between the player's Mana Pool and Hit Points for a limited time (50 seconds at Level 1 to 193 seconds at Level 191). A percentage (20 percent at Level 1 to 10 percent at Level 191) of the damage is taken from the caster's Mana Pool and the remaining damage is taken from Hit Points.

PERKS

CHARACTER PERKS

As a character gains levels, skills move slowly from unfocused to more concentrated, and a select group of skills becomes the core of a character's power. Every third level, the character gains a Perk, which is similar to a Racial Trait except that Perks have no negative side. Players can thus focus a character's development toward a particular skill set.

Not all Perks are available to every character. Everything from base stats, skills, level, and race determine which Perks can be chosen. The following is a list of the game's available Perks and their requirements. Use this section to plan your character's development.

Adrenaline Rush

Requirement:

Character level must be equal to or greater than Level 5.

With this Perk, when the situation is dire and the fight seems to be lost, you're just getting warmed up. If your Hit Points drop below half of their maximum, you gain +1 in Agility and Strength. If your Hit Points drop below a quarter of their maximum, you gain an additional +1 in Agility and Strength.

Ancestral Armor

Requirements:

Defensive must be equal to or greater than 30, but less than 300.
Character level must be equal to or greater than Level 5.

The spirits of your ancestors have an interest in defending your earthly body. Add 15 points to your Tribal Magic Protective Branch.

Backstab

Requirements:

Agility must be equal to or greater than 7.
Sneak must be equal to or greater than 50.

You do a lot more damage to unsuspecting opponents with melee weapons. When you attack an enemy from behind in Sneak mode, you do +50 percent damage if your attack scores a successful hit. Each rank increases your extra damage by an additional 50 percent.

Bonus Hand-to-Hand Damage

Requirements:

Agility must be equal to or greater than 6.
Strength must be equal to or greater than 6.
Must have Pugilist Perk.
Character level must be equal to or higher than Level 5.
Unarmed Skill must be equal to or higher than 50.

Experience in Unarmed combat gives you the edge in dealing damage. You deal +1 point of damage in Unarmed combat for each level of this Perk. This Perk may be selected twice.

228

Bonus Ranged Damage

Requirements:

Perception must be equal to or greater than 6.
Agility must be equal to or greater than 6.
Character level must be equal to or greater than Level 5.

Your training with bows and other ranged weapons has made you more deadly in ranged combat. You do +3 damage with ranged weapons when you select this Perk.

Bonus Rate of Fire

Requirements:

Ranged Weapon Skill must be equal to or greater than 50.
Agility must be equal to or greater than 7.
Intelligence must be equal to or greater than 6.
Character level must be equal to or greater than Level 14.

Because of your diligent practice, you can draw the string and fire a bow or crossbow quickly without sacrificing accuracy. This Perk allows you to more quickly load and fire bows.

Brutish Hulk

Requirements:

Strength must be equal to or greater than 7.
Endurance must be equal to or greater than 5.
Character level must be equal to or greater than Level 17.
Must have Lifegiver Perk.
Must be of Feralkin race.

Your great strength and fortitude allows you to shrug off blows that would kill lesser people. You gain double the Hit Points each time you gain a level.

Cold Soul

Requirements:

Ice Skill must be equal to or greater than 40.
May not have Mark of Fire Perk

You wandered into the woods as a child and an odd being made of ice and frost rescued you. Most of your memories about the event were erased…until now. Images too numerous and peculiar to categorize flit at the edge of your consciousness, but it is certain that you have a bond with the cold. Use this Perk to enhance any items or spells that deal cold-based damage. All cold-based spells and items do +15 percent damage.

Damage Resistance

Requirements:

Endurance must be equal to or greater than 6.
Luck must be equal to or greater than 6.
Character level must be equal to or greater than Level 5.
May not have Hide of Scars Perk.
May not have Tough Hide Perk.

Sticks and stones may break your bones…but not often. Each level of this Perk adds +8 percent to your Crushing, Piercing and Slashing Damage Resistance.

Dark Majesty

Requirements:

Perception must be less than 7.
Intelligence must be less than 7.
Character level must be equal to or greater than Level 11.
May not be of Sylvant race.

Last night you had the strangest dream. A shadowy being approached you with an offer that sounded too good to be true. For signing a blank piece of paper, he makes you a warrior of unparalleled puissance. You get +3 skill points in your melee skills, +10 percent to Poison Resistance, +1 skill points per level, and a house in a warm climate for your old age. What a deal! Sylvants cannot select this Perk.

Deadly Accuracy

Requirements:

Agility must be equal to or greater than 5.
Character level must be equal to or greater than Level 2.
Ranged Skill must be equal to or greater than 40, but less than 300.

You immediately gain 15 points to your Ranged Weapon Skill.

Die Hard

Requirements:

Endurance must be equal to or greater than 6.
Character level must be equal to or greater than Level 2.

You don't easily give up. When your Hit Points get below 20 percent, all your resistances increase by 20 percent and your Armor Class increases by 5.

Disease Ward

Requirements:

Endurance must be equal to or greater than 5.
Character level must be equal to or greater than Level 11.
May not have Venom Ward Perk.

You eat the plague for breakfast and vacation in leper colonies. Your body converts a percentage of any Disease Damage dealt you into Hit Points. You cannot also have the Venom Ward Perk.

Displacement

Requirements:

Must have Die Hard Perk.
Character level must be equal to or greater than Level 11.

When seriously injured, you partly connect with the spiritual world, slipping your body out of phase with reality. When your Hit Points fall below 20 percent of their maximum, you partly fade out, granting +10 to your Armor Class and +1 Agility. While in this state, your Mana regeneration doubles.

Divine Privilege

Requirements:

Divine Favor must be equal to or greater than 30, but less than 300.
Character level must be equal to or greater than Level 5.

Whatever power source you tap into has shown you deference. Add 15 points to your Divine Magic Divine Favor Branch.

Divine Protector

Requirements:

Defensive must be equal to or greater than 30.
Defensive must be less than 300.
Character level must be equal to or greater than Level 5.

Help from beyond has allowed you to fortify your defenses. Add 15 points to your Divine Magic Protective Branch.

Dodger

Requirements:

Agility must be equal to or greater than 6.
Character level must be equal to or greater than Level 5.

You are less likely to be hit in combat if you have this Perk. Every level adds +5 to your Armor Class, in addition to the AC bonus from any worn armor. It also adds 3 skill points to your Evasion Skill.

Earthen Contact

Requirements:

Charisma must be equal to or greater than 6.
Perception must be equal to or greater than 6.

Tribal Defensive and Offensive Skills must be equal to or greater than 100.

Your connection with nature has been cultivated and borne fruit. This Perk attunes you to Earth's ways, decreasing the casting cost of Tribal Magic spells by 15 percent.

Educated

Requirements:

Intelligence must be equal to or greater than 6.
Character level must be equal to or greater than Level 5.

You've become educated in the ways of the world and have learned to see things and draw conclusions that once eluded you. Every time you gain a level you receive 2 additional skill points. This Perk is best purchased at low levels.

Eloquence

Requirements:

Speech must be equal to or greater than 30, but less than 300.
Character level must be equal to or greater than Level 2.

Continued study of your fellow people and some light reading has shown you how to display your thoughts and ideas to others in new and profound ways, adding 15 points to your Diplomacy Skill.

Enlightenment

Requirements:

Magic Divine Defensive and Offensive Skills must be equal to or greater than 100.
Charisma must be equal to or greater than 6.
Perception must be equal to or greater than 6.

Your spiritual devotion has brought you closer to the divine. Selecting this Perk reduces the casting costs of Divine Magic spells by 15 percent.

Fire Evasion

Requirements:

Agility must be equal to or greater than 6.
May not have Pyromaniac Perk.

You know when to duck and roll. Add 2 to your Armor Class. Also, fire-based attacks do 15 percent less damage to you because of your unusual evasion ability.

Fortune Finder

Requirements:

Luck must be equal to or greater than 8.
Character level must be equal to or greater than Level 2.

You have a talent for finding money. Selecting this Perk allows you to find coins on the bodies of your foes that they didn't even know they had.

Gain Agility

Requirements:

Character level must be equal to or greater than Level 11.
Agility must be less than 10.

This Perk increases your Agility by 1.

Gain Charisma

Requirements:

Character level must be equal to or greater than Level 11.
Charisma must be less than 10.

This Perk increases your Charisma by 1.

Gain Endurance

Requirements:

Character level must be equal to or greater than Level 11.
Endurance must be 10 or less.

This Perk increases your Endurance by 1.

Gain Intelligence

Requirements:

Character level must be equal to or greater than Level 11.
Intelligence must be 10 or less.

This Perk increases your Intelligence by 1.

Gain Luck

Requirements:

Character level must be equal to or greater than Level 11.
Luck must be 10 or less.

This Perk increases your Luck by 1.

Gain Perception

Requirements:

Character level must be equal to or greater than Level 11.
Perception must be 10 or less.

This Perk increases your Perception by 1.

Gain Strength

Requirements:

Character level must be equal to or greater than Level 11.
Strength must be 10 or less.

This Perk permanently increases your Strength by 1.

Ghost

Requirements:

Sneak must be equal to or greater than 50, but less than 300.
Character level must be equal to or greater than Level 5.

You move like a ghost with this Perk, slipping in and out of shadows with ease. Your Sneak Skill is enhanced +20.

Grace Under Fire

Requirements:

Perception must be less than 10.
Character level must be equal to or greater than Level 11.

You've learned to do your best work under pressure. When things look grim, your hands grow steady and your eyes sharp. If your Hit Points drop below 40 percent of maximum, you gain 1 Perception and add 15 points to your Ranged Weapon Skill.

Here and Now

Requirement:

Character level must be equal to or greater than 8.

You realize what you've been doing wrong. Gain one level.

Hide of Scars

Requirements:

Endurance must be equal to or greater than 6.
Character level must be equal to or greater than Level 11.
May not have Damage Resistance Perk.
May not have Tough Hide Perk.

Battle has scarred nearly every inch of your hide, making it tough. Add 6 percent to all resistances except fire because of your toughened skin.

Inherited Resistance

Requirements:

Endurance must be equal to or greater than 5.
Character level must be equal to or greater than Level 2.

Neither your mother nor your father had a sick day in their lives, and as their child you have an uncanny ability to shrug off diseases and poisons. Add 10 percent to Poison and Disease Resistance. Also, your Disease and Poison Damage Thresholds increase by 1.

Lifegiver

Requirements:

Endurance must be equal to or greater than 4.
Character level must be equal to or greater than Level 5.

Your daily regimen of pushups and eating nails has paid off. Every time this Perk is selected, you gain 6 Hit Points.

Lightning Rod

Requirement:

Electrical must be equal to or greater than 40.

You have a bond with electricity that you can use in your casting. This Perk allows electrical-based spells to do +15 percent damage.

Mark of Fire

Requirements:

Fire must be equal to or greater than 40.
May not have Cold Soul Perk.

You have a bond with fire that you can use in your casting and beyond. This Perk allows Fire Damage spells or items to do +15 percent more damage.

Master of Arms

Requirements:

Strength must be equal to or greater than 7.
Character level must be greater than 26.
One-Handed and Two-Handed Melee Skills must be equal to or greater than 200.
Unarmed Skill must be less than 100.

You know where to aim your weapon to cause the most pain. With this Perk, all Slashing and Crushing Damage is increased by 25 percent.

Master of Domination

Requirements:

Domination must be equal to or greater than 30 but less than 300.
Character level must be equal to or greater than Level 5.

Bending the minds of others to your will has never been easier! Add 15 points to your Tribal Magic Domination Branch.

Master Thief

Requirements:

Lockpick Skill must be equal to or greater than 50 but less than 300.
Find Traps/Secret Doors Skill must be equal to or greater than 50 but less than 300.
Sneak Skill must be equal to or greater than 50 but less than 300.
Character level must be equal to or greater than Level 11.

Rob from the rich, and give to yourself. Add 20 points to your Find Traps/Secret Doors, Lockpick, and Sneak Skills.

Master Trader

Requirements:

Charisma must be equal to or greater than 7.
Barter must be equal to or greater than 60.
Character level must be equal to or greater than Level 8.
Must have Salesman Perk.

You have mastered the ability to pester merchants into offering you their wares at a discount. With this Perk, give yourself a 15 percent discount when purchasing items from a store or trader, and add 15 points to your Diplomacy Skill.

Master Necromancer

Requirements:

Summoning must be equal to or greater than 30 but less than 300.
Character level must be equal to or greater than Level 5.

The task of connecting with the spirit world and calling forth minions to do your bidding has been made easier. Add 15 points to your Necromancy Branch.

Mastery of Fortitude

Requirements:

> Fortitude must be equal to or greater than 30, but less than 300.
> Character level must be equal to or greater than Level 5.

Healing thyself is your thing. Add 15 points to your Divine Magic Fortitude Branch.

Mastery of Fury

Requirements:

> Wounding must be equal to or greater than 30, but less than 300.
> Character level must be equal to or greater than Level 5.

Your ancestors hate your enemies almost as much as you do. Add 15 points to your Tribal Magic Nature's Fury Branch.

Mastery of Smiting

Requirements:

> Smite must be equal to or greater than 30, but less than 300.
> Character level must be equal to or greater than Level 5.

You are the heavy hand of the heavens. Add 15 points to your Divine Magic Smite Branch.

Mental Focus

Requirements:

> Magic Thought Defensive and Offensive Skills must be equal to or greater than 100.
> Charisma must be equal to or greater than 6.
> Perception must be equal to or greater than 6.

The interrelationships between magic and the world around you are becoming clear. This Perk allows you to decrease the casting costs for all Thought Magic spells by 15 percent.

More Criticals

Requirements:

> Luck must be equal to or greater than 6.
> Character level must be equal to or greater than Level 5.

You have learned where on your foes the insertion of a sharp object or the application of blunt trauma does the most harm. Each time you select this Perk, you add 5 percent to your chance to cause a critical hit.

Necrosage

Requirements:

> Intelligence must be equal to or greater than 5.
> Character level must be equal to or greater than Level 8.

Your morbid fascination with the countless corpses you've left in your wake has led to a deeper understanding of their peculiarities. When fighting undead, you do +2 points of damage per melee attack. Any undead you summon does +1 damage when it attacks.

Observant

Requirements:

> Perception must be equal to or greater than 5.
> Find Traps/Secret Doors must be equal to or greater than 30, but less than 300.
> Lockpick must be less than 300.

You notice when things are out of place. You are always checking for traps in the vicinity. Give yourself +25 points to your Find Traps/Secret Doors Skill and +5 points to your Lockpick Skill.

One-Handed Weapon Finesse

Requirements:

One-Handed Melee must be greater than 55, but less than 300.

May not have Heavy-Handed Skill.

Practice makes perfect, or at least better. This Perk increases your One-Handed Melee Skill by 10 points.

One-Handed Weapon Specialization

Requirements:

One-Handed Melee Skill must be greater than 100.

Must have One-Handed Weapon Finesse Perk.

You have mastered the art of fighting with one-handed weapons. This Perk gives you +3 damage with one-handed weapons, and +5 to your One-Handed Melee Skill.

Power from Beyond

Requirements:

Intelligence must be equal to or greater than 5.

Character level must be equal to or greater than Level 5.

Only Sylvants and Demokin races may have this Perk.

Your spirit has given you access to a pool of magical energy. This power source gives you a +1 Healing Rate bonus and 1 extra skill point per level.

Pugilist

Requirements:

Unarmed Skill must be greater than 25.

Character level must be equal to or greater than Level 5.

When the fists fly, you're willing to punch, kick, and gouge your way to victory…and you do it pretty effectively. Taking this Perk grants an additional 1 or 2 points of damage to your Unarmed attacks. Pugilist is a prerequisite for the Bonus Hand-to-Hand Damage Perk.

Pyromaniac

Requirements:

Intelligence must be equal to or greater than 5.

Character level must be equal to or greater than Level 8.

May not have Fire Evasion Perk.

You have an affinity for fire and a knack for setting things ablaze—especially other people. You do an extra 10 percent damage with fire-based weapons or spells.

Rejuvenation

Requirement:

Endurance must be equal to or greater than 5.

When you were a child, your mother dipped you in a magical pool, and your wounds have always healed faster than those of others. This Perk adds 1 to your Healing Rate.

Retribution

Requirement:

Character level must be equal to or greater than Level 8.

A mysterious power has taken an interest in killing your foes. Whatever its reason, it's good for you! Your Crushing and Slashing Damage are increased by 10 percent.

Salesman

Requirements:

Thieving/Barter Skill must be equal to or greater than 50, but less than 300.
Character level must be equal to or greater than Level 5.

Long practice has made you an adept salesman. This Perk adds 10 points to your Diplomacy Skill and gives you a 10 percent discount when purchasing items from a store or trader.

Sharpshooter

Requirements:

Perception must be equal to or greater than 7.
Intelligence must be equal to or greater than 6.
Character level must be equal to or greater than Level 8.

You've become good at killing your enemies at long range. This Perk increases your Perception by 1 when you are using a bow or crossbow.

Slayer

Requirements:

Agility must be equal to or greater than 8.
Strength must be equal to or greater than 8.
Unarmed Skill must be equal to or greater than 200.
Character level must be equal to or greater than Level 33.

The Slayer walks the earth! In hand-to-hand combat, all your hits are upgraded to critical hits with a successful Luck roll.

Snake Eater

Requirements:

Endurance must be equal to or greater than 3.
Character level must be equal to or greater than Level 5.
May not have the Venom Ward Perk.

You have gained a slight immunity to poison, adding 30 percent to your Poison Resistance.

Sniper

Requirements:

Agility must be equal to or greater than 8.
Perception must be equal to or greater than 8.
Ranged Weapon Skill must be equal to or greater than 200.
Character level must be equal to or greater than Level 33.

You have mastered the bow or crossbow as a source of pain. With this Perk, any successful hit in combat with a ranged weapon will be upgraded to a critical hit if you also make a Luck roll.

Spirit Guide

Requirements:

Character level must be equal to or greater than Level 2.
Charisma must be equal to or greater than 7.
Perception must be equal to or greater than 7.

You have an unearthly talent for obtaining extra Mana from the spirits you find and absorb. You receive an additional 10 percent Mana from absorbing spirits.

Strong Back

Requirements:

Strength must be equal to or greater than 6.
Endurance must be equal to or greater than 6.
Character level must be equal to or greater than Level 2.

This Perk is also known as "mule." You can carry an additional 50 pounds of equipment for each level of this Perk.

Superior Senses

Requirements:

Perception must be equal to or greater than 5, but less than 10.
Character level must be equal to or greater than Level 14.

Your tribal ancestors have gifted you with superior senses. This Perk gives you a +1 bonus to Perception and adds 15 points to your Find Traps/Secret Doors Skill.

Swift Learner

Requirements:

Intelligence must be equal to or greater than 4.
Character level must be equal to or greater than Level 2.

There's a lesson in everything, and you rarely miss it. This Perk grants a 5 percent bonus whenever you earn experience points.

Thief

Requirements:

Character level must be equal to or greater than Level 2.
Sneak and Lockpick/Disarm Traps Skills must be less than 300.

Thief is an unflattering term, but you're good at finding things other people don't want found. This Perk grants a one-time bonus of 10 points to your Lockpick, Find Traps/Secret Doors, and Sneak Skills.

Thought as Armor

Requirements:

Defensive must be equal to or greater than 30, but less than 300.
Character level must be equal to or greater than Level 5.

You have gained the ability to focus your mind in the greater defenses of self. Add 15 points to your Thought Magic Protective Branch.

Tough Hide

Requirements:

Endurance must be less than 8.
Character level must be equal to or greater than Level 11.
Only Sylvant and Feralkin races may have this Perk.
May not have Hide of Scars Perk.
May not have Damage Resistance Perk.

Exposure to extreme conditions has hardened you against the elements. You gain 5 to Armor Class and 5 percent to resistances. Only Feralkins and Sylvants can pick this Perk, and they must have Endurance of 7 or less.

Trapper

Requirement:

Agility must be equal to or greater than 4.

Stripping animals of their hides has become second nature to you. You are able to strip a wolf or bear of its hide every time you kill one. These hides are more valuable because of your great skill.

Two-Handed Weapon Finesse

Requirements:

Two-Handed Melee must be greater than 55, but less than 300.
May not have Heavy-Handed Trait.

This Perk increases your Two-Handed Melee Skill by 10 points.

Two-Handed Weapon Specialization

Requirements:

Two-Handed Melee Skill must be greater than 100.
Must have Two-Handed Weapon Finesse Perk.

You have mastered the art of fighting with two-handed weapons. This Perk gives you +3 damage with two-handed weapons, and +5 points to your Two-Handed Melee Skill.

Undead Glory

Requirements:

Raise Undead must be equal to or greater than 50.
Intelligence must be equal to or greater than 6.

A vision during meditation has given you wondrous insight into the machinations of life after death. This Perk grants skeletons or zombies whom you raise 15 percent more Hit Points and an increased chance to hit.

Venom Ward

Requirements:

Endurance must be equal to or greater than 5.
Character level must be equal to or greater than Level 11.
May not have Disease Ward or Snake Eater Perks.

The spirit inside you has learned to convert poisons into healing energy, allowing you to walk fearlessly through the dens of vipers. Rather than harming you, a percentage of the damage dealt by poison is added to your Hit Points. You cannot also have the Disease Ward Perk or the Snake Eater Perk.

Weapon Handling

Requirements:

Agility must be equal to or greater than 5, but less than 10.
Character level must be equal to or greater than Level 14.

Your long familiarity with weapons has made you adept at their employment. This Perk adds 1 to your Agility and 3 points to One-Handed and Two-Handed Melee Skills.

NPC AND EVENT PERKS

The following are Perks granted as a result of an action performed within the game. They often require speaking with a certain NPC and performing a service for him or her.

Brambles' Patience

Requirement:

You must kill Relican in the southeast corner of the Slave Pit Exterior. Relican drops a cure for Brambles.

Brambles shared a sense of inner calm learned from his years of living as a tree. Because of his teachings, you see things in more perspective and gain a greater sense of strength from your earthly surroundings. You gain +6 Hit Points, +5 skill points to both Sneak and Lockpick, and +1 to your critical chance from your enhanced Perception.

Dervish of the Crescent

Requirement:

You must complete the fighting tasks of the Dream Djinn Kabool. You may not have Scholar of the Crescent to earn this Perk.

By besting the champions of the Dream Djinn Kabool, you have displayed courage and strength. You have become a Favored One of the Knights of Saladin and earned the title of Dervish of the Crescent. All your skills in the Fighting Discipline are raised by 5.

Drunken Boxing

Requirement:

Buy the drunk in the Serpent's Bile three drinks and he teaches you a new technique.

A moment's kindness to a drunken bar patron impresses upon you the benefits of unorthodox fighting styles. The drunken bar patron teaches you a new style of fighting based on drunken boxing. Your Unarmed Skill increases by 3.

Debt of Brimstone

Requirement:

You must lure Faust from his cell to the demon in the Inquisition Dungeon.

Releasing the demon from the Inquisition's clutches caused a geas to be placed on his dark soul. In an attempt to free himself from this debt, the demon has cast a dire enchantment that adds +1 to critical chance and 5 skill points to the Tribal Spell Branch of Necromancy. The negative energy associated with this boon may cause other characters to react negatively toward you.

Galileo's Magical Battery

Requirement:

Free Galileo's friend Faust from his cell in the Inquisition Chambers.

Galileo has shown you a new approach to drawing upon and storing Mana. This increases your Mana capacity by 50. This is a one-time bonus.

Scholar of the Crescent

Requirement:

Successfully answer the Dream Djinn's riddles. You may not have the Dervish of the Crescent to have this Perk.

By besting the Dream Djinn Kabool in a contest of wits, you have become a Favored One and earned the title of Scholar of the Crescent. Images of the desert now drift at the edges of your consciousness, beckoning your mind to expand its horizons. Tales of Arabia that seemed like idle ramblings when you were a child now give you insight into the ways of the world. Your Intelligence increases by 1 and your Speech by 10.

Stargazer

Requirement:

Look into the telescope in Galileo's Observatory located in the Barcelona Temple District's center.

Your horizons have been expanded from looking into the telescope in Galileo's Observatory. The experience has broadened your awareness of the world and the universe as you perceive it. Your Perception increases by 1.

Weng Choi's Shaolin Secret

Requirement:

Return eight books to Weng Choi for his collection to receive this Perk.

Weng Choi has taught you the forbidden martial arts of the East. You have gained supernatural quickness in battle, gaining +20 Evasion and +20 Unarmed.

TITLE PERKS

Title Perks are granted when a specific action is performed. They have no effect on a character's stats and skills, but do affect the way NPCs view the character.

Beggar Comrade

You have performed a great service for the beggars of Barcelona.

Dark Lord of Calle Perdida

You have mastered the Dark Arts under the tutelage of Relican and delivered La Calle Perdida to the cruel whims of your mentor.

Hero of the Inquisition

Your brave and decisive action has rooted out La Calle Perdida, exposing the greatest collection of heretics within Barcelona.

Goblin Champion

You have slain Raylark and Fenclaw and recovered the Everlasting.

Goblin Slayer

You have slain a great number of goblins. Your brave actions have kept their population in check and contributed to the defense of Barcelona.

Merchant Slayer

The underground has noticed that you like to kill merchants.

Necromancer

You have mastered the Dark Arts under the tutelage of Relican and delivered La Calle Perdida to the cruel whims of your mentor.

Thief Comrade

You have performed a great service for the thieves of Barcelona.

BESTIARY

Throughout your journey, you must defeat creatures through the power of your mind or the strength of your sword. Many of the monsters you encounter have the ability of Speech, which suggests you may reason with them. More often than not, however, you have to combat these enemies.

What follows is a regional breakdown the enemies you encounter, listed by their first appearance. You engage many of these creatures in several areas. Get to know their strengths and weaknesses before engaging them in battle.

THE TABLES

The tables provide a variety of information on the creatures you combat in the game. For many creatures there are varying degrees of difficulty. The numbers under the "Normal," "Tough," and "Super" headings indicate the stats for each of these degrees.

AC (Armor Class)

AC refers to each creature's Armor Class, which represents its toughness.

HP (Health Points)

HP stands for Health Points. As you inflict damage, your target's Health Points diminish until it is dead.

Skill

Skill denotes whether the enemy has any special skills, such as One-Handed or Two-Handed Melee, or a ranged skill, which can be associated with bowman-type enemies. This also suggests how the enemy attacks.

DMG (Damage)

Damage tells you the range of damage the creature can inflict with each successful attack.

XP (Experience)

If you are successful in slaying the creature, you are rewarded experience points for the kill. XP shows how many experience points you receive for each enemy destroyed.

If you used Sneak to get past an enemy, you also gain experience. But if you then decide to kill the creature, the difference between the experience you earned for the Sneak and the experience you earn when the creature is dead cannot exceed the total experience for that specific creature. The amount of experience you receive from slaying a monster varies depending on the monster and your level.

BARCELONA AREA AND THE SEWERS

Your quest begins in Barcelona, home to many prominent and powerful people. But under the city's brick-lined streets, enemies live in the slime-covered Sewers. These beginning creatures are easy, but don't underestimate them. They may be easy to defeat alone, but they rarely travel solo. Be prepared for simultaneous attacks by multiple enemies.

Regions

Sewer Entrance
Thieves Congregation
Hall of Beggars

Sewer Creatures

Creatures included in the Barcelona/Sewer category:

Alpha Wererat	*Huge Lava Troll*	*Thief Swordsman*
Brigand	*Large Decayed Ghoul*	*Vodyanoi*
Brittle Skeleton	*Large Ghoul*	*Vodyanoi Feral*
Decayed Ghoul	*Lava Troll*	*Weak Screaming Terror*
Decayed Zombie	*Lesser Brimstone Reaver*	
Frail Ghoulish Hag	*Prime Wererat*	*Weak Terror*
Gate District Goblins	*Thief*	*Wererat*
Greater Skeleton	*Thief Archer*	*Wererat Pup*
Guard Dog	*Thief Bowmaster*	*Zombie*
Huge Brittle Skeleton	*Thief Captain*	

Stats

ALPHA WERERAT

Stat	Normal	Tough	Super	Notes
AC	150	172	190	125 Immune to Disease
HP	56	69	85	100 Poison Resistance
Skill	16	22	29	Slashing
DMG	4–11	—	—	2–5 Strong Disease
XP	121	—	—	—

BRIGAND

Stat	Normal	Tough	Super	Notes
AC	120	135	155	—
HP	28	33	39	—
Skill	10	15	21	—
DMG	3–11	—	—	—
XP	68	—	—	—

BRITTLE SKELETON

Stat	Normal	Tough	Super	Notes
AC	90	110	125	35/25/20 Piercing/ Cold/Slashing
HP	15	25	30	—
Skill	0	5	10	—
DMG	—	—	—	—
XP	48	—	—	—

DECAYED GHOUL

Stat	Normal	Tough	Super	Notes
AC	100	120	135	25/10 Cold/Piercing
HP	23	32	43	—
Skill	4	9	15	—
DMG	—	—	—	—
XP	91	—	—	—

DECAYED ZOMBIE

Stat	Normal	Tough	Super	Notes
AC	85	100	120	25/20 Cold/Piercing
HP	20	28	39	—
Skill	3	8	13	—
DMG	—	—	—	—
XP	53	—	—	—

FRAIL GHOULISH HAG

Stat	Normal	Tough	Super	Notes
AC	100	120	135	25/10 Cold/Piercing
HP	23	32	43	—
Skill	4	9	15	—
DMG	—	—	—	—
XP	91	—	—	—

GATE DISTRICT GOBLINS

Stat	Normal	Tough	Super	Notes
AC	75	—	—	—
HP	12	—	—	—
Skill	0	—	—	—
DMG	—	—	—	—
XP	43	—	—	—

GUARD DOG

Stat	Normal	Tough	Super	Notes
AC	—	—	—	—
HP	—	—	—	—
Skill	—	—	—	—
DMG	1–3	—	—	—
XP	36	—	—	—

HUGE BRITTLE SKELETON

Stat	Normal	Tough	Super	Notes
AC	125	145	165	35/25/20 Piercing/ Cold/Slashing
HP	55	80	105	—
Skill	10	15	23	—
DMG	—	—	—	—
XP	86	—	—	—

Huge Lava Troll

Stat	Normal	Tough	Super	Notes
AC	170	185	200	100% Fire/Disease/Poison
HP	83	97	111	50% Acid/Slashing/Piercing
Skill	16	22	29	-15% Damage Bonus with Cold
DMG	6–16	—	—	—
XP	219	—	—	—

Large Decayed Ghoul

Stat	Normal	Tough	Super	Notes
AC	120	135	155	35/20 Cold/Piercing
HP	66	82	101	—
Skill	13	18	26	—
DMG	—	—	—	—
XP	285	—	—	—

Lava Troll

Stat	Normal	Tough	Super	Notes
AC	150	165	190	100% Fire/Disease/Poison
HP	46	62	79	35% Acid/Slashing/Piercing
Skill	12	18	25	-15% Damage bonus with cold
DMG	5–12	—	—	—
XP	127	—	—	—

Lesser Brimstone Reaver

Stat	Normal	Tough	Super	Notes
AC	125	140	159	25/25/10 Cold/Fire/Piercing
HP	65	78	94	—
Skill	12	18	24	—
DMG	—	—	—	—
XP	136	—	—	—

Prime Wererat

Stat	Normal	Tough	Super	Notes
AC	185	205	220	200 Disease
HP	215	253	296	150 Poison
Skill	30	40	50	—
DMG	6–12	—	—	Strong Disease Resistance
XP	1,000	—	—	—

Thief

Stat	Normal	Tough	Super	Notes
AC	120	135	155	—
HP	26	33	39	—
Skill	7	11	18	—
DMG	2–7	—	—	—
XP	51	—	—	—

Thief Archer

Stat	Normal	Tough	Super	Notes
AC	120	135	155	—
HP	21	26	33	—
Skill	7	11	18	—
DMG	1–6	—	—	—
XP	52	—	—	—

Thief Bowmaster

Stat	Normal	Tough	Super	Notes
AC	130	144	163	—
HP	35	47	61	—
Skill	9	14	20	—
DMG	2–8	—	—	—
XP	72	—	—	—

THIEF CAPTAIN

Stat	Normal	Tough	Super	Notes
AC	165	187	205	—
HP	54	66	79	—
Skill	16	22	29	—
DMG	4–16	—	—	—
XP	99	—	—	—

THIEF SWORDSMAN

Stat	Normal	Tough	Super	Notes
AC	135	149	169	—
HP	38	54	68	—
Skill	9	14	20	—
DMG	3–9	—	—	—
XP	71	—	—	—

VODYANOI

Stat	Normal	Tough	Super	Notes
AC	00	100	1)0	100% Poison/Disease Resistant
HP	25	36	48	Ranged Piercing Damage
Skill	0	5	10	—
DMG	1–5	2–8	2–10	—
XP	42	42	42	—

VODYANOI (AGILE)

Stat	Normal	Tough	Super	Notes
AC	100	120	150	100% Poison/Disease Resistant
HP	12	18	25	Deals Slashing Damage
Skill	0	3	7	—
DMG	1–6	1–8	1–10	—
XP	37	37	37	—

VODYANOI FERAL

Stat	Normal	Tough	Super	Notes
AC	100	120	150	100% Poison/Disease Resistant
HP	18	21	25	Weak Poison
Skill	0	5	10	Ranged Piercing Damage
DMG	1–4	1–6	1–8	—
XP	49	49	49	—

WEAK SCREAMING TERROR

Stat	Normal	Tough	Super	Notes
AC	135	150	170	50/50/200/10 Cold/Fire/Electrical/Piercing
HP	30	42	65	—
Skill	1	10	20	—
DMG	—	—	—	—
XP	76	—	—	—

WEAK TERROR

Stat	Normal	Tough	Super	Notes
AC	135	150	170	50/50/50/10 Cold/Fire/Electrical/Piercing
HP	35	50	70	—
Skill	18	22	26	—
DMG	—	—	—	—
XP	74	—	—	—

WERERAT

Stat	Normal	Tough	Super	Notes
AC	120	135	155	100 Disease Resistant
HP	36	48	61	50 Poison Resistant
Skill	8	13	19	—
DMG	1–6	—	—	+2–3 Disease
XP	67	—	—	—

WERERAT PUP

Stat	Normal	Tough	Super	Notes
AC	115	128	147	100 Disease
HP	31	42	57	50 Poison
Skill	8	13	19	—
DMG	1–4	—	—	+1–2 Disease
XP	48	—	—	—

THE WILDERNESS

Just outside Barcelona's gates lies the Wilderness. Home to many hostile creatures, the Wilderness provides a challenge in defeating enemies. Wander through the Wilderness, earning valuable experience and money by collecting and selling the items dropped by slain enemies.

Regions

Barcelona Coast
Bounty Hunter
Camp
Darkwood Cave
El Bosque
Goblin Camp
Goblin Warrens
Lago Del Rio Ebro
Ravine Cave East

Ravine Cave West
Rio Ebro
Scar Ravine
Slave Pit Exterior
Slave Pits
The Crossroads
Waterfall Passage
Wererat Cave

Wilderness Creatures

Creatures included in the Wilderness category:

Bear
Black Wolf
Brown Wolf
Brittle Skeleton
Cursed Wasp
Decayed Zombie
Decayed Ghoul

Frail Ghoulish Hag
Ghoul
Ghoulish Hag
Goblin
Goblin Archer
Goblin Swordsman
Goblin Village

Archer
Goblin Village
Swordsman
Greater Skeleton
Grey Wolf
Hat Goblin
Huge Brittle
Skeleton
Large Decayed
Ghoul
Large Ghoul
Lesser Brimstone
Reaver

Tainted Wasp
Thug Bowman
Thug Swordsman
Vodyanoi
Wasp
Weak Screaming
Terror
Weak Terror
Wererat
Zombie

Stats

BEAR

Stat	Normal	Tough	Super	Notes
AC	50	80	100–130	Deals Slashing Damage
HP	17	39	46–53	—
Skill	3	0	5–10	—
DMG	6–12	6–12	6–16	—
XP	41	41	41	—

BLACK WOLF

Stat	Normal	Tough	Super	Notes
AC	110	125	150	Deals Piercing Damage
HP	22	26	33	—
Skill	5	10	15	—
DMG	3–6	4–7	4–8	—
XP	52	52	52	—

BROWN WOLF

Stat	Normal	Tough	Super	Notes
AC	85	95	110	Deals Piercing Damage
HP	21	25	30	—
Skill	0	5	10	—
DMG	2–6	2–7	3–8	—
XP	44	44	44	—

CURSED WASP

Stat	Normal	Tough	Super	Notes
AC	110	125	150	20/40/50% Crushing, Slashing, Fire Resistance
HP	25	32	40	1/2/3 Piercing Threshold
Skill	10	15	20	Medium Disease
DMG	3–7	3–9	4–11	Deals Piercing Damage
XP	266	266	266	—

GOBLIN

Stat	Normal	Tough	Super	Notes
AC	100	125	150	—
HP	28	36	44	—
Skill	7	12	17	—
DMG	3–6	—	—	—
XP	49	—	—	—

GOBLIN ARCHER

Stat	Normal	Tough	Super	Notes
AC	90	115	135	—
HP	25	30	37	—
Skill	5	10	15	—
DMG	2–8	—	—	—
XP	66	—	—	—

GOBLIN VILLAGE ARCHER

Stat	Normal	Tough	Super	Notes
AC	115	—	—	—
HP	30	—	—	—
Skill	10	—	—	—
DMG	2–8	—	—	—
XP	69	—	—	—

GOBLIN VILLAGE SWORDSMAN

Stat	Normal	Tough	Super	Notes
AC	125	—	—	—
HP	36	—	—	—
Skill	12	—	—	—
DMG	3–8	—	—	—
XP	58	—	—	—

GREY WOLF

Stat	Normal	Tough	Super	Notes
AC	80	90	105	Deals Piercing Damage
HP	18	21	25	—
Skill	0	3	7	—
DMG	2–5	2–6	3–6	—
XP	39	39	39	—

HAT GOBLIN

Stat	Normal	Tough	Super	Notes
AC	125	150	200	The Khan is a "Super."
HP	60	80	110	—
Skill	10	15	25	—
DMG	5–9	—	5–13	—
XP	94	94	186	—

TAINTED WASP

Stat	Normal	Tough	Super	Notes
AC	90	100	120	20/40/50% Crushing Resistance
HP	11	14	18	Weak Disease
Skill	0	5	10	Deals Piercing Damage
DMG	1–6	1–8	1–10	—
XP	37	37	37	—

THUG BOWMAN

Stat	Normal	Tough	Super	Notes
AC	45	—	—	Deals Piercing Damage
HP	20	—	—	—
Skill	20	—	—	—
DMG	1–4	—	—	—
XP	40	—	—	—

THUG SWORDSMAN

Stat	Normal	Tough	Super	Notes
AC	50	—	—	Deals Slashing Damage
HP	25	—	—	—
Skill	20	—	—	—
DMG	2–6	—	—	—
XP	44	—	—	—

WASP

Stat	Normal	Tough	Super	Notes
AC	90	100	120	20/40/50% Crushing Resistance
HP	11	14	18	Weak Poison
Skill	0	5	10	Deals Piercing Damage
DMG	2–4	2–6	2–8	—
XP	29	29	29	—

MONTSERRAT

Listen for the Snakebreed's rattle as you travel through Montserrat Grove to reach the abbey. You can sometimes hear the rattle of the Snakebreed tail before you feel the sting of its venomous bite. These creatures are resistant to any poison attacks, but they can be defeated by magic. Have a supply of antidotes in your inventory before venturing into Montserrat.

Regions

Montserrat Grove
Montserrat Abbey

SNAKEBREED CREATURES

Creatures included in the Snakebreed category:

Snakebreed
Snakebreed Crusher
Snakebreed Viper

Stats

SNAKEBREED

Stat	Normal	Tough	Super	Notes
AC	150	175	220	100% Poison Resistance
HP	75	90	120	—
Skill	15	20	25	—
DMG	3–10	3–12	3–14	Slashing
XP	111	—	—	—

SNAKEBREED CRUSHER

Stat	Normal	Tough	Super	Notes
AC	175	200	250	100% Poison Resistance
HP	125	175	250	—
Skill	18	23	30	—
DMG	3–10	3–12	3–14	Slashing + Strong Poison
XP	199	—	—	—

SNAKEBREED VIPER

Stat	Normal	Tough	Super	Notes
AC	160	185	235	100% Poison Resistance
HP	50	60	80	—
Skill	13	18	25	—
DMG	1–6	1–8	1–10	Ranged: Piercing + Medium Poison
XP	152	—	—	—

MOUNTAINS

You may encounter the powerful Titans around the Pyrenees Mountains, but their current camp of choice is the once-populated village of Toulouse. The Titans are intelligent creatures, with the ability to reason and be reasoned with. If you must battle them, try to encounter them as singles. Their attacks are slower than many of the monsters you encounter, but the amount of damage they cause makes up for their lack of speed. Because Titans are made of stone, they are naturally resistant to poisons and acids. Use a weapon with the capability of causing the most physical damage.

Region

Toulouse

Titan Creatures

Creatures included in the Titan category:

Rock Titan
Rock Titan (Elder)

Stats

ROCK TITAN

Stat	Normal	Tough	Super	Notes
AC	230	255	280	100% Poison/Acid Resistance
HP	125	155	185	25% Slashing/Piercing Resistance
Skill	25	33	40	—
DMG	4–20	6–22	8–24	—
XP	266	—	—	—

ROCK TITAN (ELDER)

Stat	Normal	Tough	Super	Notes
AC	225	250	275	30% Piercing/Slashing Resistance
HP	250	325	450	Piercing/Slashing Threshold = 5
Skill	30	35	40	100% Poison/Acid Resistance
DMG	10–20	12–24	14–28	—
XP	326	—	—	—

PYRENEES MOUNTAINS

The brutish Ogres can be found roaming the mountainous regions around Toulouse and the Pyrenees Mountains. The Ogres are not impervious to magic, so use your strongest spells against them to defeat them quickly.

Region

Pyrenees Mountains

Ogre Creatures

Creatures included in the Ogre category:

Brutish Ogre
Ogre
Ogre Hurler

Stats

BRUTISH OGRE

Stat	Normal	Tough	Super	Notes
AC	215	242	270	—
HP	83	101	129	—
Skill	28	34	43	—
DMG	3–15	3–17	3–19	—
XP	211	—	—	—

OGRE

Stat	Normal	Tough	Super	Notes
AC	200	224	256	—
HP	128	154	181	—
Skill	25	32	39	—
DMG	3–15	3–17	3–19	—
XP	225	—	—	—

OGRE HURLER

Stat	Normal	Tough	Super	Notes
AC	185	206	233	—
HP	47	59	74	—
Skill	27	34	41	—
DMG	3–10	3–12	3–14	—
XP	196	—	—	—

NOSTRADAMUS CAVERNS

The Hujark are adept with the sword and shield, and they are equally as cunning with magic. All Hujark are resistant to fire magic. Use Electrical and Cold spells against these creatures, which roam the caverns of Nostradamus.

Regions

Heart of Fire Entrance
Clan of the Hand
Clan of the Skull
Tourniquet of Pain

Hujark Creatures

Creatures included in the Hujark category:

Shaman (Greater)
Shaman (Lesser)
Swordsman
Swordsman (Shield)
Swordsman (Shield/Helmet)
Swordsman (Dual)

Stats

HUJARK SWORDSMAN

Stat	Normal	Tough	Super	Notes
AC	175	200	235	25% Fire Resistance
HP	45	55	70	5 Fire Threshold
Skill	35	45	55	—
DMG	3–9/1–3	4–10/1–4	5–12/2–5	—
XP	223	—	—	—

HUJARK SWORDSMAN (SHIELD)

Stat	Normal	Tough	Super	Notes
AC	200	225	260	25% Fire Resistance
HP	45	55	70	5 Fire Threshold
Skill	40	50	60	—
DMG	3–8/1–4	3–9/2–5	4–10/2–6	—
XP	268	—	—	—

HUJARK SWORDSMAN (SHIELD/HELMET)

Stat	Normal	Tough	Super	Notes
AC	210	235	275	25% Fire Resistance
HP	45	55	70	5 Fire Threshold
Skill	40	50	60	—
DMG	3–8/1–4	3–9/2–5	4–10/2–6	—
XP	299	—	—	—

HUJARK SWORDSMAN (DUAL)

Stat	Normal	Tough	Super	Notes
AC	180	210	245	25% Fire Resistance
HP	50	60	75	5 Fire Threshold
Skill	45	55	65	—
DMG	3–9/1–3	4–10/1–4	5–12/2–5	—
XP	286	—	—	—

Hujark Shaman (Lesser)

Stat	Normal	Tough	Super	Notes
AC	200	225	260	25% Fire Resistance
HP	35	45	60	5 Fire Threshold
Skill	35	45	55	Fire Orb
DMG	—	—	—	—
XP	399	—	—	—

Hujark Shaman (Greater)

Stat	Normal	Tough	Super	Notes
AC	250	275	310	25% Fire Resistance
HP	60	70	80	5 Fire Threshold
Skill	25	30	40	Fireball
DMG	—	—	—	—
XP	582	—	—	—

CRYPT

Waves of the undead inhabit the Crypt's halls. Have a variety of spells at the ready as these undead creatures have varying resistances. Antidotes must be a staple in your inventory, even if your Poison Resistance is high. You battle against Zombies in almost every hall of the Crypt. All undead are immune to poison and disease and are also immune to fear, charm, and sleep spells. All undead have damage resistances of at least 50 percent to Piercing and 75 percent to Cold. Be prepared.

Regions

Retreat of Souls	*Crypte De Trois*
Mausoleum of Clovis	*Merovingian Crypt*
Defiled Vault of	*Burial Chambers*
Remiquis	*Crypt of the Lance*
Doomed Plateau	

The Undead Creatures

Creatures included in the undead category:

Arctic Succubus	*Greater Skeleton*
Brimstone Soul	*Huge Ghoul*
Reaver	*Lesser Soul Reaver*
Brittle Skeleton	*Mana Reaver*
Charred Terror	*Revenant*
Disemboweled	*Screaming Terror*
Gangler	*Second Guardian*
Ethereal Succubus	*Skeleton*
Festering Ghast	*Soul Reaver*
Frozen Terror	*Terror*
Ghoul	*Zombie*
Ghoulish Hag	

Stats

Brimstone Soul Reaver

Stat	Normal	Tough	Super	Notes
AC	200	250	300	25/25/10 Cold/Fire/Piercing
HP	100	125	175	—
Skill	15	20	25	—
DMG	—	—	—	—
XP	238	—	—	—

Charred Terror

Stat	Normal	Tough	Super	Notes
AC	225	260	325	50/50/50/10 Cold/Fire/Lightning/Piercing
HP	45	60	80	—
Skill	15	20	25	—
DMG	—	—	—	—
XP	136	—	—	—

FROZEN TERROR

Stat	Normal	Tough	Super	Notes
AC	63	—	—	2–6 Piercing, 6–10 Disease
HP	40	—	—	50% Resist Electricity
Skill	—	—	—	Each successful hit has 10% chance of causing sleep in target
DMG	—	—	—	—
XP	186	—	—	—

GREATER SKELETON

Stat	Normal	Tough	Super	Notes
AC	140	180	220	35/25/20 Piercing/Cold/Slashing
HP	100	150	225	—
Skill	15	20	25	—
DMG	—	—	—	—
XP	187	—	—	—

MANA REAVER

Stat	Normal	Tough	Super	Notes
AC	200	250	300	25/25/10 Cold/Fire/Piercing
HP	75	100	150	Drain Mana
Skill	15	20	25	—
DMG	—	—	—	—
XP	293	—	—	—

REVENANT

Stat	Normal	Tough	Super	Notes
AC	180	220	260	—
HP	150	200	250	—
Skill	18	23	30	—
DMG	—	—	—	—
XP	499	—	—	—

SCREAMING TERROR

Stat	Normal	Tough	Super	Notes
AC	200	230	275	50/50/50/10 Cold/Fire/Lightning/Piercing
HP	35	50	70	—
Skill	20	30	50	Static Charge
DMG	—	—	—	—
XP	177	—	—	—

SOUL REAVER

Stat	Normal	Tough	Super	Notes
AC	175	225	275	25/25/10 Cold/Fire/Piercing
HP	125	150	175	—
Skill	15	20	25	—
DMG	—	—	—	—
XP	191	—	—	—

TERROR

Stat	Normal	Tough	Super	Notes
AC	200	230	275	50/50/50/10 Cold/Fire/Lightning/Piercing
HP	45	60	80	—
Skill	19	24	30	—
DMG	—	—	—	—
XP	144	—	—	—

ZOMBIE

Stat	Normal	Tough	Super	Notes
AC	50	70	100	25/20 Cold/Piercing
HP	20	25	35	—
Skill	10	15	20	—
DMG	—	—	—	—
XP	82	—	—	—

THE ENGLISH INVASION

You won't face these enemies until you are in the second half of the game. All are formidable, but with the exception of the WarGolems are not immune to magic. Increase your Armor Class to provide protection against the English's Piercing and Crushing abilities. Use Cold magic against a Fire WarGolem, and Fire magic against an Ice WarGolem.

Regions

Crossroads to
England
Druid Shrine
Temple of the
Initiate
Stone Chamber of
Wyrmkind

Meditation
Chamber
Antechamber of Lore
Chamber of the
Crystal
Inner Sanctum
Exalted Chambers

The English Creatures

Creatures included in the English category:

Druid
English Bowman
English Bowmaster
English Captain
English Guardsman
English Lieutenant

English Sergeant
English Soldier
Fire WarGolem
Ice WarGolem
Lightning WarGolem
Royal Guardsman

Stats

DRUID PRIEST

Stat	Normal	Tough	Super	Notes
AC	250	270	300	—
HP	80	110	150	—
Skill	90	120	150	Fire orb
DMG	15	17	22	+Magical shield 150/200/250
XP	746	—	—	+Spike 90/120/150

ENGLISH BOWMAN

Stat	Normal	Tough	Super	Notes
AC	255	280	305	—
HP	65	85	110	—
Skill	55	65	77	—
DMG	2–8	2–10	2–12	Piercing
XP	358	—	—	—

ENGLISH BOWMASTER

Stat	Normal	Tough	Super	Notes
AC	275	297	323	—
HP	115	137	168	—
Skill	60	72	87	—
DMG	2–10	2–12	2–14	Piercing
XP	417	—	—	—

ENGLISH CAPTAIN

Stat	Normal	Tough	Super	Notes
AC	300	315	340	—
HP	100	123	148	—
Skill	57	68	81	—
DMG	3–12	3–14	3–16	—
XP	398	—	—	—

ENGLISH GUARDSMAN

Stat	Normal	Tough	Super	Notes
AC	285	305	340	—
HP	115	137	168	—
Skill	55	65	77	—
DMG	3–12	3–14	3–16	—
XP	378	—	—	—

ENGLISH LIEUTENANT

Stat	Normal	Tough	Super	Notes
AC	295	315	345	—
HP	147	117	206	—
Skill	57	68	87	—
DMG	3–12	3–14	3–16	Crushing
XP	427	—	—	—

ENGLISH SERGEANT

Stat	Normal	Tough	Super	Notes
AC	285	305	340	—
HP	115	137	168	—
Skill	55	65	77	—
DMG	3–12	3–14	3–16	—
XP	378	—	—	—

ENGLISH SOLDIER

Stat	Normal	Tough	Super	Notes
AC	270	295	325	—
HP	75	110	145	—
Skill	50	60	70	—
DMG	3–12	3–14	3–16	—
XP	348	—	—	—

FIRE WARGOLEM

Stat	Normal	Tough	Super	Notes
AC	297	324	339	200/50 Fire/ Piercing Resistance
HP	177	216	242	—
Skill	75	110	150	Fire orb
DMG	14	17	22	—
XP	1,399	—	—	—

ICE WARGOLEM

Stat	Normal	Tough	Super	Notes
AC	297	324	339	200/50 Cold/ Piercing Resistance
HP	177	216	242	-50% Crushing Resistance
Skill	1	35	75	Ice Missile
DMG	15	18	20	—
XP	1,399	—	—	—

LIGHTNING WARGOLEM

Stat	Normal	Tough	Super	Notes
AC	297	324	339	200/50 Electrical/ Piercing Resistance
HP	177	216	242	-20% Crushing Resistance
Skill	1	25	60	Lightning Bolt
DMG	14	18	24	—
XP	1,399	—	—	—

ROYAL GUARDSMAN

Stat	Normal	Tough	Super	Notes
AC	295	315	345	—
HP	147	173	206	—
Skill	57	68	87	—
DMG	3–12	3–14	3–16	—
XP	427	—	—	—

ALAMUT

Your final destination is Alamut. All your questing and fighting lead here, to the Old Man of the Mountain. Before you face that which has haunted you these many months, you must defeat the creatures resident to this area. Most enemies in this category are resistant to most attacks. Take your time and face off against each enemy individually; you'll emerge victorious.

Regions

Chaos Dragon
England to Alamut
Desert Sprawl
Shifting Dunes
Lair of Azi Dahaka

Maw of the Assassin
Acid Wash
Chamber of Torment
Dark Temple
Final Encounter

Alamut Creatures

Creatures included in the Alamut category:

Assassin
Assassin Master
Assassin Zealot
Desert Scorpion
Egyptian Sand Spirit

Egyptian Sand Spirit Elder
Guard Dog
Monstrous Scorpion
Sand Dragon (Azi Dahaka)

Stats

ASSASSIN

Stat	Normal	Tough	Super	Notes
AC	310	340	380	—
HP	150	200	300	—
Skill	65	70	80	—
DMG	4–20	6–24	8–28	—
XP	775	—	—	—

ASSASSIN (BOW)

Stat	Normal	Tough	Super	Notes
AC	310	340	380	—
HP	150	200	300	—
Skill	60	65	75	—
DMG	4–20	—	—	—
XP	775	—	—	—

ASSASSIN MASTER

Stat	Normal	Tough	Super	Notes
AC	335	375	430	—
HP	400	500	650	—
Skill	70	75	90	—
DMG	6–24	—	—	—
XP	1202	—	—	—

ASSASSIN ZEALOT

Stat	Normal	Tough	Super	Notes
AC	325	360	430	—
HP	300	350	425	—
Skill	65	70	85	—
DMG	9–26	—	—	—
XP	1,075	—	—	—

CHAOS DRAGON

Stat	Normal	Tough	Super	Notes
AC	300	310	320	Resistance to Cold 35%–40%, Immune to Sleep, Charm, and Fear
HP	1,200	1,350	1,500	50%–65% All Damage Resistance
Skill	250	260	270	90% Fire Resistance
DMG	—	—	—	Fire Breath
XP	25,000	—	—	—

DESERT SCORPION

Stat	Normal	Tough	Super	Notes
AC	195	220	255	30% Fire Resistance
HP	300	350	450	25% Piercing/ Slashing Resistance
Skill	60	65	80	—
DMG	10–18	12–20	14–22	—
XP	455	—	—	—

EGYPTIAN SAND SPIRIT

Stat	Normal	Tough	Super	Notes
AC	300	325	375	50% Slashing Resistance
HP	150	200	300	75% Crushing Resistance
Skill	65	70	80	80% Piercing Resistance
DMG	8–12	10–16	12–20	—
XP	848	—	—	—

EGYPTIAN SAND SPIRIT ELDER

Stat	Normal	Tough	Super	Notes
AC	300	325	375	50% Slashing Resistance
HP	150	200	300	75% Crushing Resistance
Skill	65	70	80	80% Piercing Resistance
DMG	8–12	10–16	12–20	—
XP	848	—	—	—

MONSTROUS SCORPION

Stat	Normal	Tough	Super	Notes
AC	285	310	375	30% Fire Resistance
HP	400	500	650	25% Piercing/Slashing Resistance
Skill	70	75	90	—
DMG	12–24	14–28	16–32	—
XP	685	—	—	—

SAND DRAGON (AZI DAHAKA)

Stat	Normal	Tough	Super	Notes
AC	230	245	260	Resistances 30%–55%, Immune to Sleep, Charm, and Fear
HP	900	1,050	1,200	Cold Resistance 20%–55%
Skill	170	180	190	70% Fire Resistance
DMG	—	—	—	Fire Breath
XP	11,000	—	—	—

ITEMS, WEAPONS, AND ARMOR

The following is a list of the items in Lionheart. Most items are randomly generated according to your character's level. You create a magical item by taking a basic item, such as a sword, and adding as many as three enchantments to it. For instance, you might find a "Short Sword, Carnage, Enduring, Fleshseeking." This uses the basic stats for the Short Sword but adds three weapon enchantments, making the sword a magical item.

> **NOTE** *The values on most items are variable and thus are expressed as a range, such as 5–25. This means that the item would have a set value between these two numbers. In some instances, the item has a variable range such as (1–4 min)–(3–20 max). This means that the item's attributes are variable. The minimum value is a set value between the first two numbers, inclusive, and the maximum value falls between the second two numbers, inclusive. Such an item may have a value of 2–8 or 3–15 when you find it, but no less than 1–3 and no more than 4–20.*

Description: The description of an item. (Shown on screen when you select the item.)

Slot: Part of the body where you wear or use the item.

Hands Needed: Number of hands required to hold the object (one, two, or none).

Weight: Item's encumbrance.

Constant Value: Item's base value in gold. (Altered by each character's Charisma and Thieving/Barter Skill.)

BASIC ARMOR

AMULET

Description: Ornament you wear on the neck, worthless unless enchanted.

Slot: Neck

Hands Needed: None

Weight: 0

Constant Value: 25g

BELT

Description: Ordinary cinch you wear around the waist, worthless unless enchanted.

Slot: Waist

Hands Needed: None

Weight: 1

Constant Value: 2g

BOOTS

Description: An ordinary pair of boots, worthless unless enchanted.

Slot: Foot

Hands Needed: None

Weight: 2

Constant Value: 2g

BRACERS

Description: +1 AC.

Slot: Arm

Hands Needed: None

Weight: 2

Constant Value: 3g

CHAIN MAIL ARMOR

Description: +20 AC, +5 Piercing Resistance, -6 Sneak Skill.

Slot: Body

Hands Needed: None

Weight: 17

Constant Value: 75g

FULL PLATE ARMOR

Description: +40 AC, +10 Crushing and Slashing Resistance, +2 Crushing and Slashing Threshold, +15 Piercing Resistance, -15 Electrical Resistance, -25 Sneak Skill, -15% Walking Speed, -15 to Evasion Skill.

Slot: Body

Hands Needed: None

Weight: 45

Constant Value: 750g

GAUNTLETS

Description: +2 AC, +1 Unarmed Damage.

Slot: Arm

Hands Needed: None

Weight: 2

Constant Value: 8g

HARD LEATHER ARMOR

Description: +15 AC, +5 Fire and Cold Resistance.

Slot: Body

Hands Needed: None

Weight: 7

Constant Value: 35g

HAUBERK MAIL ARMOR

Description: +25 AC, +5 Crushing, Piercing, and Slashing Resistance, -10 Sneak Skill, -5% Walking speed, -5 Evasion Skill.

Slot: Body

Hands Needed: None

Weight: 20

Constant Value: 100g

HELMET

Description: +3 AC, reduces sight distance.

Slot: Head

Hands Needed: None

Weight: 2

Constant Value: 6g

LARGE SHIELD

Description: +7 AC, +10% Crushing Resistance, +15% Piercing Resistance, +10% Slashing Resistance, -8% Attack Speed, -15 Unarmed Skill.

Slot: Hand

Hands Needed: One

Weight: 10

Constant Value: 25g

LEATHER ARMOR

Description: +10 AC, +3 Fire and Cold Resistance.

Slot: Body

Hands Needed: None

Weight: 5

Constant Value: 15g

MEDIUM SHIELD

Description: +4 AC, +5% Crushing Resistance, +5% Piercing Resistance, +5% Slashing Resistance, -3% Attack Speed, -10 Unarmed Skill.

Slot: Hand

Hands Needed: One

Weight: 5

Constant Value: 20g

NECKLACE

Description: Ornament you wear on the neck, worthless unless enchanted.

Slot: Neck

Hands Needed: None

Weight: 0

Constant Value: 15g

PLATE MAIL ARMOR

Description: +30 AC, +8 Crushing and Slashing Resistance, +1 Crushing and Slashing Threshold, +10 Piercing Resistance, -10 Electrical Resistance, -15 Sneak Skill, Walking speed -10%, -10 to Evasion Skill.

Slot: Body

Hands Needed: None

Weight: 30

Constant Value: 350g

RING

Description: Ornament you wear on the hand, worthless unless enchanted.

Slot: Finger

Hands Needed: None

Weight: 0

Constant Value: 15g

SMALL SHIELD

Description: +2 AC, +3% Crushing Resistance, +3% Piercing Resistance, +3% Slashing Resistance, -5 Unarmed Skill.

Slot: Hand

Hands Needed: One

Weight: 3

Constant Value: 10g

Armor Enchantments (Amulets)

COLD RESISTANCE

This ornate amulet feels warm. Its wearer is comfortable on even the coldest nights and is provided protection from even magical frost. +5–15 Cold Resistance while equipped (uncommon).

THE DEAD OF NIGHT

A favorite among thieves, amulets such as this add 15 points to its wearer's Sneak Skill and 10 to Lockpick, and increase Poison Resistance by 20 percent (very rare).

ELEMENTAL ATTUNEMENT

This amulet increases its wearer's Perception 1 point. Further, if its owner is bound to an elemental spirit, it also adds 2 skill points to the Divine spells Healing and Aid, and the Tribal spell Balance of Nature (very rare).

EXORCISM

This amulet adds 12 skill points to its wearer's Exorcism Skill (rare).

FIRE RESISTANCE

While worn, this amulet increases Fire Resistance 5–15 percent (uncommon).

THE NIGHT

Adds 6 points to the wearer's Sneak Skill, 5 to Lockpick and increases Poison Resistance by 5 percent (uncommon).

POISON RESISTANCE

Commonly worn by kings, bishops, and other potentates who might fear assassination, amulets such as this increase the wearer's Poison Resistance by 5–15 percent (rare).

PROTECTION

This useful medallion increases its wearer's Armor Class by 1–8 (common).

Armor Enchantments (Belts)

BRAWLING

This coveted belt makes its wearer a nigh-unstoppable force in unarmed combat, adding 10 points to Unarmed Skill and 4 points to Armor Class, and increasing Unarmed Damage by 10 percent (unique).

COLD RESISTANCE

This belt increases its wearer's Cold Resistance by 5–15 percent (uncommon).

ENDURANCE

This belt increases its wearer's Endurance by 2 (unique).

FERAL POWER

Rare belts such as this increase its wearer's Strength by 1 point and Unarmed Skill by 4 points. If the wearer is a Feralkin, it also provides 6 Two-Handed Melee Skill points and adds 3 to Armor Class (very rare).

FIRE RESISTANCE

This belt increases its wearer's Fire Resistance by 5–15 percent (uncommon).

POISON RESISTANCE

Endowed with unicorn hair, adders' tongues, and other potent antidotes, this belt increases its wearer's Poison Resistance 5–15 percent (uncommon).

PROTECTION

Enchantments laid on this belt add 1–5 to its wearer's Armor Class (rare).

THE THIEF

Charms woven into this belt give its wearer 10–20 skill points to Find Traps/Secret Doors and Lockpick (rare).

TITAN STRENGTH

Increases the wearer's Strength by 2 (unique).

VOODOO

While worn, this belt enhances all Tribal spell skills by 1 point. When it is worn with the Necklace of Voodoo, the wearer gets one more skill point to spend per level up (very rare).

Armor Enchantments (Body)

ACID RESISTANCE

The materials used to make this armor are resistant to acids, conferring +5–20 Acid Resistance on the wearer (very rare).

THE ARCHER

This suit of armor adds 10–25 points to its wearer's Ranged Weapon Skill (rare).

ARCHERY

The mounted archers of the Asian steppes originally created these magical suits of armor. They increase their wearer's Ranged Weapon Skill 15 points (rare).

BRAWLING

This armor grants +1–3 Agility and 5–20 Unarmed Skill points to its wearer (unique).

CARRYING

This magical armor allows its wearer to carry an additional 50 pounds of loot and gear (uncommon).

CRIPPLING

The wearer of this armor delivers critical hits 5–20 percent more often (unique).

DEEPEST WINTER

A magical aura of frost eManates from this armor, periodically dealing (1–2 min)–(2–7 max) damage points to enemies around its wearer (very rare).

DISEASE DEFIANCE

This armor grants +1 Endurance and +10 Disease Resistance to its wearer (very rare).

DISEASE RESISTANCE

Similar to suits first crafted for the Conquistadors' trips into the tropics, this enchanted suit of armor confers +5–25 Disease Resistance to its wearer (rare).

DRAGONSCALES

This suit of armor adds 5–15 percent to its wearer's Fire Resistance. Foes foolish enough to strike a warrior clad in dragonscale armor take 10 percent of that damage (very rare).

ELEMENTAL AMPLIFICATION

This armor amplifies the power of Electrical, Fire, and Cold attacks dealt by the wearer by 5 percent (very rare).

ELECTRICAL RESISTANCE

This suit of armor offers 5–20 percent Electrical Resistance to its wearer (rare).

FIRE RESISTANCE

This armor increases its wearer's Fire Resistance by 5–20 (uncommon).

FORTITUDE

This armor increases its wearer's Fortitude attribute by 10–25 points (rare).

GIANT STRENGTH

The spirit of a slain giant caged in this suit of armor, granting its wearer +1 Strength (very rare).

GOBLIN STITCHING

This armor is made of human leather and stitched with human hair, but gives a magical +5 to AC. It exudes a sickly sweet smell that makes you want to gag and lowers your Speech Skill by 2 (rare).

THE HUJARK

This helmet's hardy construction offers excellent protection, adding 4 to its wearer's Armor Class (rare).

THE MAGE

This armor confers 5–20 percent Acid, Cold, Fire and Electrical Resistance to the wearer; and adds +1 skill point to each of the magical skill branches (unique).

MAGERY

This armor increases the rate at which its wearer regains Mana (very rare).

MASTERY

This armor's wearer gains an additional skill point upon leveling up (very rare).

NECROMANCY

Constructed of material better left unidentified, this armor oozes blood and ichor, staining everything it touches. Necromantic armor adds 10–25 points to its wearer's Necromancy Skill (rare).

ORATION

The words this armor's wearer speak carry unusual weight. While worn, this suit adds 10–25 points to its wearer's Speech Skill (rare).

POISON RESISTANCE

This armor increases its wearer's Poison Resistance by 5–25 percent (uncommon).

POLYELEMENTAL REFLECTION

This armor type reflects 10–20 percent of the Fire, Cold, or Electrical Damage received by its wearer to the attacker (very rare).

PROTECTION

Protective runes on this suit of armor grant an additional +1–20 to its wearer's Armor Class (common).

SPIRIT ENHANCEMENT

This armor focuses and enhances magical energy, increasing magical damage dealt by its wearer by 5 percent (rare).

STEALTH

This suit of armor adds 16–30 points to its wearer's Sneak Skill and 10 to Lockpick (rare).

THIEF EYES

This armor increases its wearer's Find Traps/Secret Doors skill by 10–25 points and adds 10 to Lockpick (rare).

TITAN BONES

Infused with a slain Titan's spirit, this armor grants its wearer +1–2 Strength (unique).

WEAPON MASTERY

Frequently commissioned by noblemen desirous of martial prowess without the inconvenience of years of practice, a suit such as this grant 5–20 points to its wearer's One-Handed and Two-Handed Melee Skills (rare).

WOUND CONSTRICTION

This armor is enchanted to mend damage to its wearer, healing 1–(2–8 max) points a few seconds after the damage occurs (rare).

Armor Enchantments (Boots)

THE ADDER

Stitched from the skin of a magical serpent, these boots enable their wearer to resist 20 percent of Poison Damage and add 10 to their wearer's Poison Ring spell (very rare).

LOAD BEARING

These boots enable their wearer to carry an additional 50 pounds without slowing (uncommon).

SPEED

Sometimes called Mercury's Shoes, boots such as these make their wearer move more quickly (rare).

SPIRIT REGENERATION

Forging a connection between Earth and some type of ethereal plane, these boots increase their wearer's Mana regeneration rate (very rare).

WALKING DEAD

These boots are knit of a material better left unexamined. They emit both a palpable taint and a fetid reek, reducing their owner's Charisma by 1. They do, however, provide +3 to their wearer's Armor Class and 8 points to the Tribal spell Raise Undead and the Divine spell Exorcism (unique).

Armor Enchantments (Bracers)

ARCHERY

These bracers add 5–10 skill points to their wearer's Ranged Weapon Skill (rare).

BLESSED ARCHERY

Divine enchantments laid upon these bracers add 20–45 points to their wearer's Ranged Weapon Skill (rare).

COLD RESISTANCE

These bracers add 5–15 percent to their wearer's Cold Resistance (rare).

DEFENSE

A favorite of wielders of two-handed weapons, bracers such as these add an additional 1–5 to their wearer's Armor Class (very rare).

FIRE RESISTANCE

These bracers increase their wearer's Fire Resistance by 5–15 percent (rare).

POISON RESISTANCE

These bracers increase their wearer's Poison Resistance 5–15 (rare).

Armor Enchantments (Gauntlets)

ARCHERY

These gloves add 5–10 points to their wearer's Ranged Weapons skill (rare).

BLESSED ARCHERY

These ensorcelled gloves add 20–45 points to their wearer's Ranged Weapons skill (very rare).

DEFENSE

These gauntlets increase their wearer's Armor Class by an additional 4–15 points (very rare).

DOUBLE BALANCE

These gauntlets add 7–40 skill points to the wearer's Two-Handed Melee Skill (rare).

THE GLADIATOR

These potent gauntlets increase their wearer's Strength by 1, Slashing Damage by 5 percent, and Two-Handed Melee Skill by 10 (unique).

HEROIC STRENGTH

The wearer's Strength is increased by 1 (very rare).

THIEVERY

These gloves add 6–30 points to their wearer's Lockpick and Find Traps/Secret Doors Skills (rare).

Armor Enchantments (Helmets)

COLD RESISTANCE

This helm increases its wearer's Cold Resistance by 5–15 percent (uncommon).

THE EAGLE

Gives the wearer an additional 8 points in Ranged Weapons skill, 5 in Lockpick and 7 in Find Traps/Secret Doors (rare).

THE FALCON

Adds 8 points to the wearer's One-Handed Melee Skill, 5 points to Lockpick and 4 to Sneak (rare).

FIRE RESISTANCE

Runes etched into this helm increase its wearer's Fire Resistance by 5–15 percent (uncommon).

FOCUSED LOGIC

Gives the wearer 1 point of Intelligence (unique).

HARD BARGAINING

Despite being outlawed in much of Christendom, hats and helms such as this remain popular with savvy businessmen. While worn, this helm increases the wearer's Thieving/Barter Skill by 20 points and grants 1 point of Charisma (unique).

POISON RESISTANCE

This helm is enchanted to increase its wearer's Poison Resistance 5–15 percent (uncommon).

PROTECTION

Spells laid on this helm increase its wearer's Armor Class by +1–5 (uncommon).

SPIRIT REGENERATION

Forging a connection between Earth and some type of ethereal plane, this helm increases the Mana regeneration rate of its wearer (unique).

THE SYLVANT

Rare helms such as this grant the wearer 4 points in One-Handed and Two-Handed Melee Skills, and an additional 1 point in Armor Class. If the wearer is a Sylvant, it adds 4 skill points to Unarmed Skill and 3 points to Armor Class (unique).

Armor Enchantments (Necklaces)

COLD CARNAGE

This bejeweled necklace enhances Cold Damage caused by the wearer 10 percent (rare).

CRUSHING CARNAGE

All Crushing Damage caused by this necklace's wearer is enhanced 10 percent (very rare).

ELECTRICAL CARNAGE

All Electrical Damage dealt by this necklace's wearer is enhanced 10 percent (rare).

FIRE CARNAGE

All Fire Damage dealt by this necklace's wearer is enhanced 10 percent (rare).

NECROMANCY

This strange necklace is icy and sticky, making it uncomfortable to wear. While worn, it increases its owner's Necromancy Skill 10 points (rare).

PIERCING CARNAGE

All Piercing Damage the wearer causes is enhanced 10 percent (very rare).

SLASHING CARNAGE

Slashing Damage this necklace's wearer causes is enhanced 10 percent (very rare).

VOODOO

The wearer's Tribal spell branches are granted 1 skill point. If this necklace is worn with the Belt of Voodoo, its owner is granted one more skill point to spend per level up (very rare).

Armor Enchantments (Rings)

ARROW DAMPENING

The wearer of this ring takes 5–15 percent less damage from arrows and bolts (very rare).

THE BRAWLER

During combat, the wearer of this ring strikes with his or her bare hands as if he or she were wearing brass knuckles, adding 3 points to his or her Unarmed Skill and 5 percent to all Unarmed Damage (uncommon).

COLD RESISTANCE

This ring increases its wearer's Cold Resistance by 5–15 percent (uncommon).

CRUSHING RESISTANCE

This ring's magic reduces the Crushing Damage its wearer takes by 5–15 percent (very rare).

DIVINE ATTUNEMENT

This ring grants its wearer an additional 2 skill points to Divine spell branches (rare).

FIERY DEATH

This ornate ring pulses and glows with an inner fire. While worn, it enhances any Fire Damage its wearer deals by 20 percent (unique).

FIRE RESISTANCE

This band increases its wearer's Fire Resistance 5–15 percent (uncommon).

LACERATION

While worn, this ring enhances the wearer's ability to do damage with blades. Not only is Slashing Damage increased by 5–15 percent, but both One-Handed and Two-Handed Skills also are increased by 5–15 points (unique).

MAGICAL DEVOTION

All Cold, Electrical, and Fire Damage this ring's wearer deals is enhanced by 5 percent (unique).

THE METAL FIST

While worn, this ring gives the hand that wears it the characteristics of steel. Its wearer's Unarmed Skill is enhanced 5–15 points. and when fighting Unarmed, the wearer deals 5–15 percent more Unarmed Melee Damage. However, the hand that wears this ring is too twisted and stiff to wield weapons effectively, and weapon skills are decreased by 2–9 (unique).

ONE-HANDED COMBAT

This powerful band of metal increases your One-Handed Weapon Skill by 5–30, Critical Chance by 1–5 percent, and Lockpick skill by 10–20 (unique).

POISON RESISTANCE

While you wear this ring, your Poison Resistance increases 5–15 percent (uncommon).

PROTECTION

The runes etched across the inner face of this ring increase its wearer's Armor Class by 4–15 (common).

THE SNAKE

The magic in this ring increases its wearer's Poison Resistance by 10 percent and Sneak Skill by 5 points (rare).

TWO-HANDED COMBAT

This powerful metal band increases your Two-Handed Melee Skill by 5–30, Chance to Hit by 1–5 percent, and Lockpick skill by 10–20 (unique).

THE UNDEAD

Vibrating with an unearthly pulse, this ring increases its wearer's Raise Undead spell by 20 points (very rare).

Armor Enchantments (Other)

ACID TOUCH

Inflicts 1–3 points of Acid damage to any enemy within the character's melee range (unique).

EVASION

This item adds 15 skill points to the player's Evasion Skill (unique).

ICY FURY

Inflicts 1–3 points of Cold Damage to any enemy within melee range of the character (unique).

LAVA BURN

Inflicts 1–3 points of Fire Damage to any enemy within the character's melee range (unique).

LUCK

This item increases a player's Luck attribute by +1 and Lockpick skill by 10 (unique).

Armor Enchantments (Small Shields)

ARROW DEFLECTION

This shield offers exceptional protection against arrows, increasing its bearer's Piercing Damage threshold by +1–3 (very rare).

CHARISMA

This glittering shield grants +2 Charisma to its bearer (unique).

CRUSHING DEFIANCE

This magical shield's bearer gains a +1–3 bonus to Crushing Damage (very rare).

ELECTRICAL RESISTANCE

This shield confers +5–20 Electrical Resistance to its bearer (rare).

FIRE RESISTANCE

This shield confers +5–20 Fire Resistance to its bearer (uncommon).

THE FIREDRAKE

This shield grants 5–20 percent Fire Resistance, increases its bearer's One-Handed Melee Skill by 5–20 points, and strengthens its bearer's fire attacks by 5–20 percent (very rare).

THE FROSTWYRM

This shield confers +5–20 percent Cold Resistance and grants a +5–20 percent Cold Damage bonus to its bearer (very rare).

IRON CUNNING

This shield grants its bearer +10–20 Fire and Cold Resistance and 5–10 One-Handed Melee Skill points (unique).

POISON RESISTANCE

This shield confers +5–20 Poison Resistance to its bearer (uncommon).

PROTECTION

This shield grants an additional +1–10 AC bonus to its bearer (uncommon).

SLASHING DEFIANCE

This shield empowers its bearer's slashing attacks, granting a +1–3 Slashing Damage bonus (very rare).

SPIRIT ENHANCEMENT

This shield increases the Mana capacity of its bearer by +50 (very rare).

Armor Enchantment (Medium Shield)

ARROW DEFLECTION

This shield offers exceptional protection against arrows, increasing its bearer's Piercing Damage threshold by +1–3 (very rare).

CHARISMA

This glittering shield grants +2 Charisma to its bearer (unique).

CRUSHING DEFIANCE

The bearer of this magical shield gains a +1–3 bonus to Crushing Damage (very rare).

ELECTRICAL RESISTANCE

This shield confers +5–20 Electrical Resistance to its bearer (rare).

FIRE RESISTANCE

This shield confers +5–20 Fire Resistance to its bearer (uncommon).

THE FIREDRAKE

This shield grants 5–20 percent Fire Resistance, increases its bearer's One-Handed Melee Skill by 5–20 points and strengthens its bearer's fire attacks by 5–20 percent (very rare).

THE FROSTWYRM

This shield confers +5–20 percent Cold Resistance and grants a +5–20 percent Cold Damage bonus to its bearer (very rare).

IRON CUNNING

This shield grants its bearer +10–20 Fire and Cold Resistance and 5–10 One-Handed Melee Skill points (unique).

POISON RESISTANCE

This shield confers +5–20 Poison Resistance to its bearer (uncommon).

PROTECTION

This shield grants an additional +1–10 AC bonus to its bearer (uncommon).

SLASHING DEFIANCE

This shield empowers its bearer's slashing attacks, granting a +1–3 Slashing Damage bonus (very rare).

SPIRIT ENHANCEMENT

This shield increases its bearer's Mana capacity by +50 (very rare).

Armor Enchantments (Large Shields)

ARROW DEFLECTION

This shield offers exceptional protection against arrows, increasing its bearer's Piercing Damage Threshold by +1–3 (very rare).

CHARISMA

This glittering shield grants +2 Charisma to its bearer (very rare).

CRUSHING DEFIANCE

This magical shield's bearer gains a +1–3 bonus to Crushing Damage (very rare).

ELECTRICAL RESISTANCE

This shield confers +5–20 Electrical Resistance to its bearer (rare).

FIRE RESISTANCE

This shield confers +5–20 Fire Resistance to its bearer (uncommon).

THE FIREDRAKE

This shield grants 5–20 percent Fire Resistance, increases its bearer's One-Handed Melee Skill by 5–20 points and strengthens its bearer's fire attacks by 5–20 percent (very rare).

THE FROSTWYRM

This shield confers +5–20 percent Cold Resistance and grants a +5–20 percent Cold Damage bonus to its bearer (very rare).

IRON CUNNING

This shield grants its bearer +10–20 Fire and Cold Resistance and 5–10 One-Handed Melee Skill points (unique).

POISON RESISTANCE

This shield confers +5–20 Poison Resistance to its bearer (uncommon).

PROTECTION

This shield grants an additional +1–10 AC bonus to its bearer (rare).

SLASHING DEFIANCE

This shield empowers its bearer's slashing attacks, granting a +1–3 Slashing Damage bonus (very rare).

SPIRIT ENHANCEMENT

This shield increases the Mana capacity of its bearer by +50 (very rare).

BASIC WEAPONS

BASTARD SWORD

Description: (One-Handed) Slashing Damage 1–10. You need a One-Handed Melee Skill of 50 to equip this item.

Slot: Weapon

Hands Needed: One

Weight: 10

Constant Value: 40g

BATTLE AXE

Description: (Two-Handed) Slashing Damage 2–12.

Slot: Weapon

Hands Needed: Two

Weight: 9

Constant Value: 10g

CLUB

Description: (One-Handed) Crushing Damage 1–6.

Slot: Weapon

Hands Needed: One

Weight: 4

Constant Value: 5g

COMPOSITE LONG BOW

Description: (Two-Handed) Does 15% more piercing damage than a regular bow, and this can increase as your Ranged Weapons skill increases. You need a Ranged Weapons skill of 50 to equip this item.

Slot: Weapon

Hands Needed: Two

Weight: 7

Constant Value: 700g

CROSSBOW

Description: (Two-Handed) Though the crossbow is slower than a longbow by 10%, its bolts deal more damage.

Slot: Weapon

Hands Needed: Two

Weight: 5

Constant Value: 100g

GREAT BATTLE AXE

Description: (Two-Handed) Slashing Damage 4–14. You need a Two-Handed Melee Skill of 50 to equip this item.

Slot: Weapon

Hands Needed: Two

Weight: 12

Constant Value: 100g

GREAT MACE

Description: (Two-Handed) Crushing damage 3–10.

Slot: Weapon

Hands Needed: Two

Weight: 11

Constant Value: 150g

LONG BOW

Description: (Two-Handed) Basic bow.

Slot: Weapon

Hands Needed: Two

Weight: 5

Constant Value: 50g

LONG SWORD

Description: (One-Handed) Slashing damage 1–8.

Slot: Weapon

Hands Needed: One

Weight: 6

Constant Value: 20g

MACE

Description: (One-Handed) Crushing damage 2–7.

Slot: Weapon

Hands Needed: One

Weight: 6

Constant Value: 15g

MORNING STAR

Description: (One-Handed) Crushing damage 2–7.

Slot: Weapon

Hands Needed: One

Weight: 7

Constant Value: 20g

SCIMITAR

Description: (One-Handed) Slashing damage 1–6.

Slot: Weapon

Hands Needed: One

Weight: 6

Constant Value: 20g

SHORT SWORD

Description: (One-Handed) Slashing damage 1–5.

Slot: Weapon

Hands Needed: One

Weight: 4

Constant Value: 10g

TWO-HANDED SWORD

Description: (Two-Handed) Slashing damage 2–12.

Slot: Weapon

Hands Needed: Two

Weight: 10

Constant Value: 40g

War Hammer

Description: (Two-Handed) Crushing damage 2–12.

Slot: Weapon

Hands Needed: Two

Weight: 9

Constant Value: 50g

Melee Weapon Enchantments

Acid

This weapon does an extra (1–2 min)–(2–12 max) Acid Damage every time it strikes an enemy (rare).

Agility

This well-balanced and enchanted weapon grants its wielder +1–3 Agility when wielded (very rare).

Carnage

Does +1–15 Acid damage per successful attack (common)

Cold Biting

This weapon does an extra (1–2 min)–(2–12 max) Cold Damage on strikes (rare).

Demonic Bile

On a strike, this potent weapon has a 5 percent chance of doing an extra 40–105 points of Fire Damage (very rare).

Double Biting

A hit causes an additional (1–3 min)–(2–7 max) points of Acid damage to the target every 5 seconds for 15 seconds (rare).

Enduring

This weapon's wielder gains +1–3 Endurance while it is equipped (very rare).

Exorcism

This sanctified weapon deals an extra (1–4 min)–(4–15 max) points of damage to the undead (rare).

Firestorms

With each successful strike, there is a 10 percent chance that a firestorm will engulf the target, dealing an additional (1–6 min)–(4–15 max) points of fire damage (very rare).

Flame

This weapon deals (1–2 min)–(2–12 max) Fire Damage points every time it strikes an enemy (rare).

Fleshseeking

This weapon has a +1–25 chance to hit (common).

Goblin Slaying

The bane of Goblinkind, weapons such as this deal an extra 3–10 points of damage to Goblins (very rare).

Haste

This weapon strikes quickly, allowing its wielder to attack 15 percent faster (very rare).

Heartseeking

This weapon deals +1–4 Acid damage with every hit and also has a 15–25 percent chance of causing a further 1–4 points of Acid damage to its target (very rare).

Hunting

This weapon does an extra (1–3 min)–(2–15 max) points of damage to simple animals (very rare).

Lethargy

On each successful attack, there is a 15–40 percent chance that the target's attacks and movements will be slowed to 75 percent of normal (uncommon).

Lightning

Each successful hit has a 5 percent chance to shock the target for (3–10 min)–(12–22 max) points of damage (very rare).

Luck

This weapon grants +1–3 Luck to its wielder while equipped (unique).

NUMBING

Each hit with this weapon has a 20 percent chance of freezing its target for 4 seconds (unique).

PESTILENCE

Does an additional (1–2 min)–(3–14 max) points of Disease Damage per successful attack (rare).

REVEALING

Enchantments laid upon this weapon add 20–60 points to its wielder's Find Traps/Secret Doors skill, and 10 to Lockpick (uncommon).

RIPPING

The savage wounds this weapon inflicts cause its target to take an additional (1–4 min)–(3–20 max) points of slashing damage 4 seconds after each successful attack (rare).

SHOCKING

Deals (1–2 min)–(3–12 max) Electrical Damage on a successful attack (rare).

SKILL

While equipped, this item increases its user's One-Handed Melee and Two-Handed Melee Skills by 5–20 and grants +10 percent to Slashing and Crushing Damage (rare).

SNAKEBITING

The poison this weapon secrets causes an extra 1–6 points of damage every 5 seconds for 20 seconds (rare).

STRENGTH

This weapon's wielder gains +1–3 Strength (very rare).

STRIKING

This weapon has a +5–25 chance of inflicting critical hits (very rare).

VAMPIRISM

Every strike with this weapon heals its wielder at least one hit point and has a further 25 percent chance of transferring (1–3 min)–(2–8 max) Hit Points from its target to its wielder (rare).

VENOM

5–50 percent of the time, a hit with this poisonous weapon causes an extra 1–6 points of damage to the target every 5 seconds for 10 seconds (rare).

Ranged Weapon Enchantments

ACCURACY

This crossbow grants a +3–12 percent Chance to Hit (common).

AGILITY

Powerful incantations and a Wind Demon's soul provide +1–3 to Agility to this crossbow's holder (unique).

CARNAGE

Missiles fired from this crossbow do an extra 1–10 points of Acid Damage (common).

EVASION

This enchanted crossbow increases its wielder's Evasion Skill by 10–35 points (uncommon).

FIRE

Missiles fired from this crossbow do an extra (1–2 min)–(2–7 max) Fire Damage to their target (rare).

FORTITUDE

A blessing on this crossbow provides 7–35 points to its wielder's Divine Fortitude spell branch (very rare).

LUCK

Powerful enchantments and a Brimstone Devil's forked tongue provide +1–3 to Luck to this crossbow's bearer (unique).

MASTERY

This weapon increases the skill of the person wielding it, allowing +10 percent more piercing damage. In addition, this crossbow increases the wielder's ranged attack speed (very rare).

NECROMANCY

Dark energy fills this crossbow, increasing its wielder's Necromancy spell branch by 7–35 points (rare).

SPEED

This crossbow increases its wielder's fire rate by 10 percent (very rare).

STEALTH

This enchanted crossbow increases its wielder's Sneak Skill by 10–35 points (very rare).

THIEVERY

Dark enchantments on this crossbow increase both its wielder's Find Traps/Secret Doors skill and Lockpick skill by 10–35 points (rare).

AMMUNITION

ARROWS

Description: Piercing Damage 1–8.

Slot: Arrow

Hands Needed: None

Weight: 0

Constant Value: 1g

BOLTS

Description: Piercing damage 2–10.

Slot: Bolt

Hands Needed: None

Weight: 0

Constant Value: 1g

Ammunition Enchantments

BITING

Deal +(1–2 min)–(2–9 max) Acid damage per hit (very rare).

CARNAGE

These missiles deal +1–7 damage (common).

FIRE

These missiles deal +(1–2 min)–(2–9 max) Fire Damage per hit (rare).

FLESHSEEKING

These missiles have a +1–12 Chance to Hit (common).

FREEZING

Deal +(1–2 min)–(2–9 max) Cold Damage per hit (very rare).

GOBLIN SLAYING

These missiles grant a +5 to hit and kill any Goblin they strike (unique).

INFINITY

These bolts/arrows never run out (unique).

POISON

These missiles deal +1–4 points of Poison damage to their target every 5 seconds for 20 seconds (rare).

SHOCKING

These missiles deal +(1–2 min)–(2–9 max) Electrical Damage per hit (unique).

Keys

HALL OF BEGGARS KEY

Key used to open doors in the Hall of Beggars.

INQUISITION KEY

Key used to open jail cells in the Inquisition Chambers.

KEY (TEMPLE DISTRICT KEY FROM JUANITA SUAREZ)

This key opens the house of a Spanish noble in the Temple District.

KEY TO BROTHER MICHEL'S HOUSE

This otherwise nondescript key has the name Michel etched into it.

SHYLOCK KEY

Key used to open a chest in Shylock's home.

STONE KEY

This strange key is made of stone.

Miscellaneous Items

ALE

Description: Consumption of alcohol increases the Strength and Endurance of the imbiber, but also dramatically reduces Intelligence and Perception.

Slot: Hotkey

Hands Needed: None

Weight: 1

Constant Value: 3g

BEAR SKIN

Description: Stripped from a dead bear.

Slot: None

Hands Needed: None

Weight: 3

Constant Value: 10g

BEAR SKIN, HIGH QUALITY

Description: Stripped from a dead bear.

Slot: None

Hands Needed: None

Weight: 3

Constant Value: 25g

EYE OF THE DRAGON

Description: The gem is of extraordinary value and hums with a hushed resonance. A soft blue light flickers across the facets.

Slot: None

Hands Needed: None

Weight: 1

Constant Value: 3,000g

FIREPOWDER KEG

Description: This small keg contains a combustible powder that, when dropped, creates a tremendous explosion. The powder comes from the Far East trade routes, where the secrets of its creation are shrouded in mystery. The substances inside are rare in Europe, and many believe it to be the work of the devil—which is not altogether incorrect. Weng Choi has trapped a fire demon within the keg to detonate it after a count to three.

Slot: Hotkey

Weight: 5

Constant Value: 40g

GEM

Description: Valuable stone that a master craftsman shaped.

Slot: None

Hands Needed: None

Weight: 0

Constant Value: 25g

POTION

Description: Potions can do anything from restoring Hit Points to temporarily increasing a character's skills. In this case, the potion lacks enchantment and is little more than water.

Slot: Hotkey

Hands Needed: None

Weight: 1

Constant Value: 5g

SCROLL

Description: Scrolls are much like potions and have a variety of effects when enchanted. In this case, the scroll lacks enchantment and is little more than a black piece of paper.

Slot: Hotkey

Hands Needed: None

Weight: 1

Constant Value: 5g

SERPENT'S BILE

Description: There is no stronger drink than the Serpent's Bile. This brew makes you feel like you have the strength of two, but might leave you with half the reason and wit.

Slot: Hotkey

Hands Needed: None

Weight: 1

Constant Value: 5g

TEAR OF KWAN YIN

Description: Legend says that the tears of Kwan Yin, the eastern goddess of mercy and healing, form precious stones when they touch the ground.

Slot: None

Hands Needed: None

Weight: 0

Constant Value: 2,000g

WASP STINGER

Description: Pulled from a dead wasp.

Slot: None

Hands Needed: None

Weight: 2

Constant Value: 10g

WINE

Description: Consumption of alcohol increases the imbiber's Strength and Endurance, but also reduces Intelligence and Perception.

Slot: Hotkey

Hands Needed: None

Weight: 1

Constant Value: 3g

WOLF PELT

Description: Stripped from a dead wolf.

Slot: None

Hands Needed: None

Weight: 3

Constant Value: 10g

WOLF PELT, HIGH QUALITY

Description: Stripped from a dead wolf.

Slot: None

Hands Needed: None

Weight: 3

Constant Value: 25g

Potion Enchantments

ANTIDOTE

This draught increases Poison Resistance by 50 percent for 2 minutes (common).

ARROW DEFLECTION

Downing this potion protects its drinker from half of the damage done by arrows for 2 minutes (very rare).

CURE-ALL

This disgusting brew tastes terrible but increases Disease Resistance by 50 percent for 2 minutes (common).

DEFENSE

This thick brew fortifies its drinker's skin, adding 20 percent to Armor Class for 2 minutes (unique).

EXTRA HEALING

When consumed, this potent draft heals severe wounds. It also cures critical hit effects (uncommon).

FIRE PROTECTION

Drinking this ice-cold concoction increases Fire Resistance 40 percent for 1 minute (rare).

HEALING

When consumed, this potent draft heals wounds (common).

MASS HEALING

When consumed, this potion heals the wounds of its user and nearby allies (uncommon).

MASTER THIEVERY

Consuming this potion increases the drinker's Find Traps/Secret Doors skill by 70 points and Lockpick skill by 25 points for 2 minutes (uncommon).

SPEED

This spicy brew increases its drinker's movement rate and attack speed for 2 minutes. These effects are non-cumulative with other speed effects, including other potions (very rare).

SPIRIT ELIXIR

Drinking this potion provides magical energy (rare).

STEALTH

This potion provides 70 points to the Sneak Skill for 2 minutes (uncommon).

STRENGTH

This thick broth grants 2 points of Strength for 2 minutes when consumed. This effect is non-cumulative with other Strength potions (unique).

VAMPIRISM

This disgusting broth works like the Tribal Vampire spell. It grants its drinker the ability to convert 10 percent of physical damage inflicted into Hit Points for 2 minutes (very rare).

Scroll Enchantments

ACID PROTECTION

The charm inscribed on this scroll increases Acid Resistance by 40 percent for 1 minute (very rare).

COLD PROTECTION

The charm inscribed on this scroll increases Cold Resistance by 40 percent for 1 minute (very rare).

ELECTRICAL PROTECTION

The charm inscribed on this scroll increases Electrical Resistance by 40 percent for 1 minute (very rare).

FIRE PROTECTION

The charm inscribed on this scroll increases Fire Resistance by 40 percent for 2 minutes (very rare).

HEALING

The charm inscribed on this scroll heals 12–14 Hit Points when read (common).

MASS HEALING

The charm inscribed on this scroll heals the caster and allies close by when read (uncommon).

STRENGTH

The charm inscribed on this scroll provides +2 Strength for 30 seconds (unique).

UNIQUE ITEMS

Amulet of Dour Tidings

Description: Buried in 1347 at the Battle of Golasis, this amulet was later found by a poor farmhand bent on adventure…or at least on robbing a few tombs. Events did not go well for the young man, and it wasn't long before the necklace was taken from his corpse by the bandit who killed him. It has since passed from hand to hand over the course of many years. While granting +10 points to its wearer's Sneak Skill and increasing Chance to Hit by 5 percent, it also reduces the hidden derived attribute Fortune by 1 and may cause others to react negatively toward its wearer.

Slot: Neck

Hands Needed: None

Weight: 1

Constant Value: 400g

Amulet of the Grand Inquisitor

Description: Given to those divinely favored, this charm has been imbued with powerful magic. Because those in service to the Church must be able to communicate, this amulet adds +10 to the Speech Skill. With service comes risk, so the amulet also provides +2 to Armor Class and +1 to its wearer's healing rate.

Slot: Neck

Hands Needed: None

Weight: 1

Constant Value: 500g

Amulet of the Prophet

Description: The ancient Amulet of the Prophet is a venerated eastern relic. It bestows magical protection to the wearer, adding +3 to Armor Class and +4 to Slashing Resistance. An Arabic inscription on the back reads: "The Light will prevail against the Darkness."

Slot: Neck

Hands Needed: None

Weight: 0

Constant Value: 100g

Amulet of the Trapped Spirit

Description: The abilities of this amulet are a mystery.

Slot: Neck

Hands Needed: None

Weight: 0

Constant Value: 0g

Art of Barter (Book)

Description: Written by Shylock, this greasy tome outlines how to propose your ideas and close deals to your benefit. It's useful in developing bartering abilities.

Slot: Hotkey

Hands Needed: None

Weight: 1

Constant Value: 50g

Axe of the Feral Curse

Description: (Two-Handed) 6–14 Slashing Damage. The gangrenous odor of blood on this axe tells of its dark past. The demonic runes chiseled onto the blade make it vibrate like a live thing, and it serves as a conduit between Earth and some hellish plane. This conduit causes an additional 66 points of damage to any simple animal, such as a Bear or Wolf, and adds 20 skill points to both Sneak and Evasion. This power has a price, however—Charisma is lowered by 1.

Slot: Weapon

Hands Needed: Two

Weight: 15

Constant Value: 1722g

BLADE OF THE BERSERKER

Description: (Two-Handed) 3–12 Slashing Damage. The powerful enchantments bestowed upon this blade cause the wielder to be more powerful and precise in battle, but more foolhardy about the threat of personal injury. Armor Class decreases by 10, but Chance of Hit increases by 10 percent and Strength increases by 1.

Slot: Weapon

Hands Needed: Two

Weight: 6

Constant Value: 5,500g

BLEEDING LANCE (FALSE)

Description: This thin wood shaft resembles descriptions of the Bleeding Lance, but your intuition tells you something isn't quite right.

Slot: None

Hands Needed: None

Weight: 0

Constant Value: 0g

BLEEDING LANCE

Description: Touching this lance fills your mind with images of suffering and penance, erasing doubt that this is the artifact used to spear Christ when he was on the Cross. While the lance has the texture of wood, it has the resonance of steel. Whoever carries it adds 5 to their Armor Class, 5 skill points to their Divine Protective Branch, 1 to their Chance to Hit, and 1 to their Fortune. An unseen force prohibits it from being used as a weapon.

Slot: None

Hands Needed: None

Weight: 1

Constant Value: 0g

BLOOD RING OF RICHARD THE LIONHEARTED

Description: This ring pulses to unseen heartbeat. Minute inscriptions inside the ring's band indicate that the inset gems were bathed in Richard's blood, and the ring's magic works only for one of his bloodline. For you, the ring gives 10 percent more Crushing and Slashing Damage and increases Mana capacity by 30. For others, the ring is worth as much as a jeweled ring, as it does nothing for them.

Slot: Finger

Hands Needed: None

Weight: 0

Constant Value: 70g

BOOK OF DEATH

Description: Written in dragon blood, this tome details the inner machinations of bringing the dead to life. Reading the tome provides 15 skill points to the Tribal Spell Branch of Necromancy.

Slot: Hotkey

Hands Needed: None

Weight: 0

Constant Value: 0g

BOOTS OF ARID D'JINN

Description: These boots once belonged to a great orator of the Persian desert, and became legendary not for who wore them, but for how far they had been worn. They have wandered Europe, touched the shores of the New World, and returned. This historical information is scorched onto the sole of the boot. These boots provide +12 to Speech and Thieving/Barter, but -3 to One-Handed and Two-Handed Melee Skills.

Slot: Foot

Hands Needed: None

Weight: 2

Constant Value: 295g

BOW OF FIERY SMITE

Description: (Two-Handed) Created to fight Frost Dragons in the Fourth Crusade against the Storm Dragons in 1241, this bow increases its wielder's Fire Damage by 25 percent. Arrows fired from this bow also do 40 percent more Piercing Damage than a regular bow. However, a Ranged Weapons Skill of 125 is required to equip this item.

Slot: Weapon

Hands Needed: Two

Weight: 7

Constant Value: 5,600g

BOW OF ICY CARNAGE

Description: (Two-Handed) Created to fight Fire Drakes in the Fourth Crusade against the Storm Dragons in 1241, this bow increases its wielder's Cold Damage by 20 percent. Arrows fired from this bow also do 20 percent more Piercing Damage than a regular bow. However, a Ranged Weapons Skill of 85 is required to equip this item.

Slot: Weapon

Hands Needed: Two

Weight: 7

Constant Value: 8900g

BRACERS OF STEALTHY CUNNING

Description: Crude notches on the metal edges pay testimony to the number of masters these bracers have seen. Wearing these dirty metal hunks adds 20 to your Sneak Skill and 5 to Speech.

Slot: Arms

Hands Needed: None

Weight: 2

Constant Value: 850g

Centuries (BOOK)

Description: Bound by an unearthly material, written in magical inks, and scripted in an alien tongue, Nostradamus's Centuries exudes a preternatural power. Hidden within its dark pages are the fates of kings, emperors, and paupers alike. Only a learned scholar can fathom this tome's pages and translate the mysterious seer's prophecies.

Slot: None

Hands Needed: None

Weight: 1

Constant Value: 2g

CORTES'S ARM

Description: A mechanical arm created for Cortes by Da Vinci.

Slot: None

Hands Needed: None

Weight: 0

Constant Value: 0g

DARKWOOD

Description: Ashen-colored wood, valuable within certain circles.

Slot: None

Hands Needed: None

Weight: 0

Constant Value: 0g

DA VINCI'S CROSSBOW

Description: (Two-Handed) This special crossbow provides the same fire rate as a normal longbow and grants a bonus to its shooter's Chance to Hit and Piercing Damage.

Slot: Weapon

Hands Needed: Two

Weight: 5

Constant Value: 850g

DRYAD RIVER PEARL

Description: Beautiful to behold.

Slot: None

Hands Needed: None

Weight: 1

Constant Value: 700g

ELOQUENT WORKS (BOOK)

Description: Written by Shakespeare, this collection of prose and suggestions of mannerisms is useful in developing Speech abilities.

Slot: Hotkey

Hands Needed: None

Weight: 1

Constant Value: 50g

ENRIQUE'S SHORT SWORD

Description: (One-Handed) 2–6 Slashing Damage. Engraved on the hilt is the name Enrique.

Slot: Weapon

Hands Needed: One

Weight: 0

Constant Value: 0g

THE EVERLASTING

Description: (Two-Handed) 1–15 Crushing Damage. While many of these hammers were created to turn back the Mongol Horde running rampant throughout Europe in 1242, most have been lost or destroyed by Goblins, who detest them. This is with good cause, as the hammer's enchantments deal an additional 25 points of damage against Goblins. In addition, the weapon adds 15 Two-Handed Weapon Skill points and +5 to Armor Class. The stench of Goblin blood fouls the intricate runes carved along the grip.

Slot: Weapon

Hands Needed: Two

Weight: 19

Constant Value: 5,000g

FERALKIN JOURNAL

Description: This well-written manuscript details the life and trials of a Feralkin in the hands of the Inquisition.

Slot: None

Hands Needed: None

Weight: 1

Constant Value: 1g

FROGS

Description: Important in Goblin culture and shamanistic magic.

Slot: None

Hands Needed: None

Weight: 0

Constant Value: 0g

GAUNTLETS OF HELLFIRE

Description: Reeking of sulfur and unpleasantly warm to the touch, these gauntlets possess an unearthly spirit that makes your body quiver with an unseen power. Although uncomfortable, they provide a +25% Fire Damage modifier and a +5 Fire Damage Threshold.

Slot: Arm

Hands Needed: None

Weight: 5

Constant Value: 4,200g

GAUNTLETS OF LA MANCHA

Description: Faint runes on the side indicate they were created out of respect for a legend, in hopes of bringing alive the glory of the past. Regardless, they provide +1 to Luck and 4 skill points in One-Handed Melee, Two-Handed Melee, Ranged Weapon, and Unarmed Skills. They also provide +2 to AC and +1 to Unarmed Damage.

Slot: Arm

Hands Needed: None

Weight: 5

Constant Value: 850g

GEARS

Description: Required by Da Vinci to make Cortes's mechanical arm.

Slot: None

Hands Needed: None

Weight: 0

Constant Value: 0g

GOBLIN BLOOD BRACER

Description: Reeking of animal blood and dung, this armband is also seeped in dark magic. When equipped, it provides +3 to Sneak and +2 to One-Handed Melee Skills, but -1 to Speech. Even Goblins find it offensive when non-Goblins smell like this.

Slot: Arm

Hands Needed: None

Weight: 1

Constant Value: 50g

HAIR OF A SAINT

Description: Lock of hair considered to be holy.

Slot: None

Hands Needed: None

Weight: 0

Value: 0

HANGOVER CURE POTION

Description: Clears the mind and body after excess alcohol consumption.

Slot: None

Hands Needed: None

Weight: 0

Constant Value: 5g

HELM OF THE TEMPLARS

Description: This battle-weary helm shines with the power of the Templars.

Slot: Head

Hands Needed: None

Weight: 2

Constant Value: 100g

HISTORY OF THE CRUSADES (BOOK)

Description: Collection of tales detailing the various English Crusades.

Slot: None

Hands Needed: None

Weight: 1

Constant Value: 1g

HISTORY OF THE DRAGONS (BOOK)

Description: Chronicles detailing the rise and fall of wyrmkind.

Slot: None

Hands Needed: None

Weight: 0

Constant Value: 1g

HISTORY OF THE FELL SPIRITS (BOOK)

Description: All the pages are filled with unreadable runes.

Slot: None

Hands Needed: None

Weight: 1

Constant Value: 1g

HISTORY OF THE INQUISITION (BOOK)

Description: Dark tales of how the Inquisition became so feared.

Slot: None

Hands Needed: None

Weight: 0

Constant Value: 1g

HISTORY OF THE NECROMANCERS (BOOK)

Description: Dark tales surrounding the ascension of the black arts.

Slot: None

Hands Needed: None

Weight: 0

Constant Value: 1g

INQUISITOR'S CHALICE

Description: A gem-encrusted chalice appearing to be very valuable.

Slot: None

Hands Needed: None

Weight: 0

Constant Value: 600g

IVORY MACE OF DIVINITY

Description: (One-Handed) 5–11 Crushing Damage. Many of these weapons were created for the Knights Templar in the Ritual of 1248. This mace, along with others of its kind, has been wielded against the undead scourge in Europe for hundreds of years. Because of its enchantments, any undead struck suffer an additional 3–9 points of Crushing Damage, and 3 percent of the time are destroyed in a divine power display. The mace also gives 1 skill point in each of the Divine Skill Branches.

Slot: Weapon

Hands Needed: One

Weight: 6

Constant Value: 5,900g

JEWELED TOOTH

Description: This large stone tooth is encrusted with jewels and is covered with faint gold leaf inscriptions. The letters are too faded to be understood.

Slot: None

Hands Needed: None

Weight: 0

Constant Value: 0g

JUANITA'S LOCKET

Description: Engraved in small gilded lettering is the name Juanita.

Slot: None

Hands Needed: None

Weight: 0

Constant Value: 10g

LAMP OF JAH'ROOSH

Description: This is an ancient gold lamp that houses the Efreet Joh'roosh. A note, crudely etched onto the side, indicates that while similar to the mythical Genie, an Efreet has a different definition of subservience to the holder of his lamp.

Slot: None

Hands Needed: None

Weight: 1

Constant Value: 100,000g

LAVA TROLL HIDE

Description: Skin stripped from a dead Lava Troll; resistant to fire.

Slot: None

Hands Needed: None

Weight: 7

Constant Value: 25g

LETTER TO AMIR

Description: Hastily written document describing the trials and tribulations of Ali Huban.

Slot: None

Hands Needed: None

Weight: 0

Constant Value: 0g

LEVER

Description: An old switch handle.

Slot: None

Hands Needed: None

Weight: 0

Constant Value: 5g

LION SHIELD

Description: This large emblazoned shield denotes the power of the Templars. +10 AC; +10% Crushing and Slashing Resistance; +15% Piercing Resistance; +1 Crushing, Slashing, and Piercing Damage Thresholds; -7% Attack Speed; -10 Unarmed Skill.

Slot: Hand

Hands Needed: One

Weight: 5

Constant Value: 500g

LIVER PIE

Description: Created from the woodsman's liver; all fresh ingredients.

Slot: None

Hands Needed: None

Weight: 2

Constant Value: 1g

LUCIUS'S MNEME

Description: This mysterious crystal was pulled from the Titan's dead body.

Slot: None

Hands Needed: None

Weight: 0

Constant Value: 100g

LYCANTHROPY CURE POTION

Description: This rare potion can cure the magical affliction of Lycanthropy.

Slot: None

Hands Needed: None

Weight: 0

Constant Value: 100g

MAELSTROM BOW OF THE HORDE

Description: (Two-Handed) The great Batu Khan commissioned many of these bows for the Mongol army that swept across Europe in 1247 A.D. His dark wizards reforged Bows of Icy Carnage, created for the Storm Dragon Crusades, for use against the Knights Templar. This bow increases the Electrical Damage that its wielder does by 25 percent, and Piercing Damage by 20 percent. A Ranged Weapons skill of 105 is required to equip this item.

Slot: Weapon

Hands Needed: Two

Weight: 6

Constant Value: 7,000g

MAGNETIZED SILVER

Description: Valuable silver chunk that has magnetic qualities.

Slot: None

Hands Needed: None

Weight: 0

Constant Value: 20g

MARCO POLO'S BOOTS

Description: These boots contain Marco Polo's spirit. In addition to adding 20 pounds to the wearer's carrying capacity, they also increase Endurance by 1. They are in good shape for being so old.

Slot: Foot

Hands Needed: None

Weight: 2

Constant Value: 350g

MECHANICAL ROD

Description: Required by Da Vinci to make Cortes's mechanical arm.

Slot: None

Hands Needed: None

Weight: 0

Constant Value: 0g

MICHEL'S AMULET

Description: Brother Michel gave you this old, battered amulet. While worn, it increases your Electrical and Crushing Damage resistances by 15 percent.

Slot: Neck

Hands Needed: None

Weight: 1

Constant Value: 1,500g

MYSTERIOUS POTION TO GIVE TO PRISONER

Description: The effects of this potion are unknown. The stopper is sealed too tightly to be opened.

Slot: None

Hands Needed: None

Weight: 0

Constant Value: 0g

POETRY BOOK

Description: Collected by Butu Khan, this poetry book contains many Goblin free verses.

Slot: None

Hands Needed: None

Weight: 0

Constant Value: 1g

POTION OF LUCK

Description: This potion is almost impossible to create, causing many of great skill to throw up their hands in disgust and become monks. Drinking this rare potion causes the character's Luck to permanently increase by 1.

Slot: Hotkey

Hands Needed: None

Weight: 1

Constant Value: 1,000g

POTION OF TRANSFORMATION

Description: Used in undoing a unique transformation spell.

Slot: None

Hands Needed: None

Weight: 0

Constant Value: 5g

RED ORE

Description: Chunk of a red mineral deposit.

Slot: None

Hands Needed: None

Weight: 0

Constant Value: 0g

RELICAN SUMMONING RING

Description: Used to summon Relican from within La Calle Perdida.

Slot: Finger

Hands Nccdcd: Nonc

Weight: 0

Constant Value: 1g

RING OF THE TRAPPED SPIRIT

Description: The abilities of this ring are a mystery.

Slot: Finger

Hands Needed: None

Weight: 0

Constant Value: 0g

ROD OF THE INQUISITOR

Description: This rod is imbued with divine magical power. Carrying the rod confers 1 to Perception, 10 skill points in the Divine Favor Spell Branch, and 1 to Healing Rate. When used as a magical club, it is a one-handed weapon that does 1–6 Crushing Damage.

Slot: Weapon

Hands Needed: One

Weight: 2

Constant Value: 400g

ROTARY GEAR

Description: Odd metal chunk needed by Da Vinci to create one of his elaborate devices.

Slot: None

Hands Needed: None

Weight: 0

Constant Value: 0g

SACRED SCIMITAR

Description: (One-Handed) 2–11 Slashing Damage. This scimitar is finely crafted and embodies the spirits of the Knights of Saladin. It increases Chance to Hit by 5 percent and increases Piercing resistance by 10. This blade's wielder is also quickened; it raises Agility by 1.

Slot: Weapon

Hands Needed: One

Weight: 5

Constant Value: 850g

SCEPTRE OF BONE

Description: Fashioned darkwood that is an empty shell without a spirit to power it.

Slot: None

Hands Needed: None

Weight: 2

Constant Value: 0g

SCEPTRE OF BONE (ENCHANTED)

Description: Enchanted darkwood that contains a bound spirit. Carrying the sceptre confers 2 skill points in the Thought and Tribal Magic Disciplines. Equipping the sceptre may cause others to react negatively toward you. When used as a magical club, it is a one-handed weapon that does 2–8 Crushing Damage.

Slot: Weapon

Hands Needed: One

Weight: 0

Constant Value: 0g

SCEPTER OF THE CHAMBERS

Description: A small inscription down the side reads: "Crafted to renew and destroy the Magic Wells." When used as a club, it is a One-Handed weapon that does 1–2 Crushing Damage.

Slot: Weapon

Hands Needed: One

Weight: 0

Constant Value: 0g

SCORCHING BLADE

Description: (One-Handed) 1–6 Slashing Damage. Small runes on the hilt proclaim the sword to be the property of the Black Devils. Historical markings indicate that the blade was chiseled from volcanic rock and magically welded with iron to produce a fire that could not be quenched. In addition to the Fire and Slashing Damage that it deals, the blade also confers 25 percent Fire Resistance.

Slot: Weapon

Hands Needed: One

Weight: 6

Constant Value: 24,000g

SHAKESPEARE'S MUSE

Description: This fairy is the magical personification of Shakespeare's writing talent.

Slot: None

Hands Needed: None

Weight: 0

Constant Value: 0

SHAKESPEARE'S PROMISE RING

Description: A smitten William Shakespeare has given you a valuable gift, the enchanting Promise Ring. While you wear the Promise Ring, your Charisma raises by +1 and your Speech by +10.

Slot: Finger

Hands Needed: None

Weight: 1

Constant Value: 550g

SHARD OF DREAMS

Description: The Shard of Dreams evokes a sense of awe and wonder. The mysterious crystal glows and pulses like a living thing. Some have gone mad staring at its prismatic lights, seeking whatever power lies within its brilliant facets.

Slot: None

Hands Needed: None

Weight: 0

Constant Value: 0g

SILVER MINE DEED

Description: Legal document proscribing ownership of the silver mine.

Slot: None

Hands Needed: None

Weight: 0

Constant Value: 0g

SMALL GEARS

Description: Needed by Da Vinci to create a special crossbow.

Slot: None

Hands Needed: None

Weight: 0

Constant Value: 0g

SPIRIT TEMPLAR SHIELD

Description: This emblazoned shield denotes the power of the Templars.

Slot: Hand

Hands Needed: None

Weight: 5

Constant Value: 100g

SPIRIT TRANSFER GEM

Description: Mechanical fittings cover the surface.

Slot: None

Hands Needed: None

Weight: 0

Constant Value: 50g

THE STONE HEART OF IAPETUS

Description: This is the stone heart of the Elder Titan Iapetus. It appears to be made of granite but is oddly pliable.

Slot: None

Hands Needed: None

Weight: 0

Constant Value: 100g

THE STONE HEART OF LETHOS

Description: This is the stone heart of the Elder Titan Lethos. It is cold, heavy, and inert.

Slot: None

Hands Needed: None

Weight: 0

Constant Value: 100g

THE STONE HEART OF MENOETIUS

Description: This is the stone heart of the Elder Titan Menoetius, torn from the giant's lifeless body.

Slot: None

Hands Needed: None

Weight: 0

Constant Value: 100g

THE STONE HEART OF RHEA

Description: This is the stone heart of the Elder Titan Rhea.

Slot: None

Hands Needed: None

Weight: 0

Constant Value: 100g

SWORD OF EDUARDO

Description: (One-Handed) 1–6 Slashing Damage. Inscription: "For my son Eduardo."

Slot: Weapon

Hands Needed: One

Weight: 0

Constant Value: 0g

SWORD OF KUBLAI KHAN

Description: (One-Handed) 4–11 Slashing Damage. Grasping this sword gives the wielder a feeling of power and unrivaled domination. The blood of thousands stains this blade and this shadowy weapon gives +1 to Luck and +10 to the wielder's One-Handed Melee Skill. Its dark history and enchantments may also make others react negatively toward its owner.

Slot: Weapon

Hands Needed: One

Weight: 6

Constant Value: 900g

SWORD OF RIGOR MORTIS FROST

Description: (One-Handed) 2–10 Slashing Damage. Slippery to the touch, this sword's blade is translucent in bright light. Wielding the sword makes your hand go numb, but increases your Cold Resistance by 50 percent. Enemies struck by the blade suffer an additional 2–10 points of cold damage and any undead struck by the blade have a 15 percent chance of being frozen in place for 4 seconds.

Slot: Weapon

Hands Needed: One

Weight: 8

Constant Value: 6,800g

TARGETING LENS

Description: Made of glass pieces positioned next to each other, it is of superb workmanship. Pegs on the bottom look as if they connect to a larger object.

Slot: None

Hands Needed: None

Weight: 0

Constant Value: 0g

TITAN CRYSTAL

Description: Large and unwieldy. Smells bad.

Slot: None

Hands Needed: None

Weight: 0

Constant Value: 200g

TITAN MERCURY

Description: Pure elemental mercury.

Slot: None

Hands Needed: None

Weight: 0

Constant Value: 50g

TITAN SPHERE

Description: Spirit gem.

Slot: None

Hands Needed: None

Weight: 0

Constant Value: 200g

TOME OF GEOMANCY

Description: Highly regarded as the epitome of Geomancy knowledge. This is the only copy in existence.

Slot: None

Hands Needed: None

Weight: 0

Constant Value: 200g

TRUE CROSS

Description: Guarded by the Knights Templar for centuries, this holy object vibrates as if alive. It has grafted itself to your flesh, imbuing you with an inner light and vitality. Feelings and thoughts that are not your own course through your mind, giving you a tinge of fear but an overall sense of power. You sense that your Strength and Endurance have increased by 1, and your combat skills and your Divine Fortitude Branch have increased by 10.

Slot: None

Hands Needed: None

Weight: 0

Constant Value: 0g

VODYANOI SKULL

Description: Skull taken from a dead Vodyanoi.

Slot: None

Hands Needed: None

Weight: 2

Constant Value: 0g

WAND OF SPIRITS

Description: Fashioned darkwood that is an empty shell without a spirit to power it. When used as a club, it is a one-handed weapon that does 1–3 Crushing Damage.

Slot: Weapon

Hands Needed: One

Weight: 2

Constant Value: 0g

WAND OF SPIRITS (ENCHANTED)

Description: Enchanted darkwood that contains a bound spirit. Carrying the rod confers 2 skill points in the Divine and Thought Magic Disciplines, as well as 25 to Mana Capacity. When used as a magical club, it is a one-handed weapon that does 2–8 Crushing Damage.

Slot: Weapon

Hands Needed: One

Weight: 0

Constant Value: 0g

WERERAT FUR

Description: Fur swath taken from the Prime Wererat.

Slot: None

Hands Needed: None

Weight: 0

Constant Value: 0g

WIELDER'S CHARM

Description: A powerful magic item that Quinn the Herbalist says can unlock the secret locale of La Calle Perdida, it increases the wearer's Mana Capacity by 5.

Slot: Neck

Hands Needed: None

Weight: 0

Constant Value: 75g

WIND SCROLL

Description: The scroll is inscribed with a powerful charm that you can use only to change wind currents in the open sea.

Slot: None

Hands Needed: None

Weight: 0

Constant Value: 0g

WOODSMAN'S EYES

Description: Strikingly pretty despite the bloody tissue hanging from them.

Slot: None

Hands Needed: None

Weight: 0

Constant Value: 0g

WOODSMAN'S LIVER

Description: An internal organ that has been removed from the woodsman.

Slot: None

Hands Needed: None

Weight: 0

Constant Value: 0g